BUSINESS REGULATION AND ECONOMIC PERFORMANCE

BUSINESS REGULATION AND ECONOMIC PERFORMANCE

Norman V. Loayza
Luis Servén

Editors

THE WORLD BANK
WASHINGTON, DC

ISBN: 978-0-8213-7407-8
eISBN: 978-0-8213-8145-8
DOI: 10.1596/978-0-8213-7407-8

Library of Congress Cataloging-in-Publication Data
Business regulation and economic performance / editors, Norman V. Loayza and Luis Servén.
    p. cm.
Includes bibliographical references and index.
ISBN 978-0-8213-7407-8 — ISBN 978-0-8213-8145-8 (electronic)
1. Business enterprises—Case studies. 2. Industrial laws and legislation—Case studies. 3. Trade regulation—Case studies. 4. Economic development—Case studies. I. Loayza, Norman. II. Servén, Luis.
    HF1008.B88 2009
    338.7--dc22

                                                              2009041883

Cover design by Bill Pragluski of Critical Stages.

Cover image: "Spiral Path," © images.com/Corbis.

Contents

Figures

Tables

About the Editors

NORMAN V. LOAYZA is Lead Economist in the research department of the World Bank. He obtained a BA degree from Brigham Young University in economics and sociology and a PhD in economics from Harvard University. Since then, he has worked at the research group of the World Bank, except when he worked as senior economist at the Central Bank of Chile in 1999–2000. Norman has taught post-graduate courses and seminars at the University of the Pacific in Lima, the Catholic University of Chile, and the University of Sao Paulo. Norman has edited five books and published more than thirty articles in professional journals.

LUIS SERVÉN manages the World Bank's research program on macroeconomics and growth. He previously managed the Bank's regional research program for Latin America and the Caribbean. Prior to joining the World Bank, he was a member of the founding team of the Fundación de Estudios de Economía Aplicada (FEDEA), a leading think tank in Spain, and he taught at the Universidad Complutense de Madrid, the Pontificia Universidad Catolica in Rio de Janeiro, and the Massachusetts Institute of Technology (MIT). He has published numerous books and journal articles on economic growth, international finance, exchange rates, fiscal policy, saving and investment, and the microeconomic foundations of macroeconomics. Luis received his PhD in economics from MIT.

About the Contributors

RAPHAEL BERGOEING is Associate Professor of Economics at the Department of Economics, Universidad de Chile. He is also the Chief Economist at Banchile Inversiones (Banco de Chile).

MARCELA ESLAVA is Associate Professor of Economics at Universidad de Los Andes, in Bogotá.

JOHN C. HALTIWANGER is Professor of Economics at the University of Maryland.

ADRIANA KUGLER is Professor of Economics at the University of Houston.

MAURICE KUGLER is the inaugural CIGI Chair in International Public Policy at Wilfrid Laurier University, research economist at the National Bureau of Economic Research, and Growth Lab fellow in the Center for International Development at Harvard University.

ANA MARIA OVIEDO is a Young Professional at the World Bank, currently working in the Social Protection unit of the Latin America and the Caribbean region.

ANDREA REPETTO is Professor of Economics at the School of Government of Universidad Adolfo Ibáñez and Academic Director of the Masters Program in Economics and Public Policy.

FABIO SCHIANTARELLI is Professor of Economics at Boston College, in Massachusetts.

NAOTAKA SUGAWARA is a Consultant in the Office of the Chief Economist, Europe and Central Asia Region, World Bank.

Abbreviations and Acronyms

AFR	Africa region
CEEP	European Centre for Public Enterprises with Public Participation
CEPR	Center for Economic and Policy Research
CPI	consumer price index
DYMIMIC	dynamic multiple indicator multiple cause (method)
EAP	East Asia and Pacific region
FDI	foreign direct investment
GDP	gross domestic product
GMM	Generalized Method of Moments
ICRG	International Country Risk Guide
ICT	information and communication technology
IFS	Institute for Fiscal Studies
ILO	International Labour Organization
IMF	International Monetary Fund
INL	industrialized countries
ISIC	International Standard of Industrial Classification
IV	instrumental variable
LAC	Latin America and the Caribbean region
MNA	Middle East and North Africa region
NBER	National Bureau of Economic Research
OECD	Organisation for Economic Co-operation and Development
OLS	ordinary least squares
PMR	product market regulation
R&D	research and development
SAS	South Asia region
TFP	total factor productivity

1

Overview

Norman V. Loayza and Luis Servén

Introduction

Microeconomic efficiency and firm-level dynamics underlie aggregate economic performance in terms of productivity, growth, and volatility. Growth in aggregate output and employment reflects firms' decisions regarding job creation and capital accumulation. Changes in the allocation of inputs and outputs across producers represent an important source of aggregate productivity change, as shown by a variety of studies focused on different countries and time periods. Gains in aggregate productivity largely reflect entry and expansion of high-efficiency firms and production processes and contraction and exit of low-efficiency ones—the Schumpeterian "creative destruction" process, long viewed as an essential ingredient of a dynamic economy—and firm-level decisions regarding product innovation and technological upgrading. Firms' ability to adjust the deployment and utilization of productive factors in the face of disturbances shapes the response of the overall economy to exogenous shocks and determines their consequences for aggregate instability.

In turn, firms' decisions regarding investment, innovation, and job creation reflect a variety of microeconomic incentives and barriers. Prominent among them is the regulation of goods and factors markets. Regulation is purportedly enacted to pursue social goals. Its rationale is the existence of market failures arising from informational asymmetries, economies of scale in production, incomplete markets, and externalities. Under such circumstances, economic agents may not fully internalize the social costs and benefits of their actions, and adequate market regulation can raise social welfare.

However, this presumes that regulatory policy is guided solely by the public interest. In reality, regulation obeys a more complex political economy process, where legitimate social goals may become entangled with the objectives of particular interest groups concerning the level and distribution of rents. As a result, regulation may be biased in favor of special interests, or may become hostage to "political capture," which distorts regulatory goals to pursue political ends.

Regulation can be thought of as a set of rules that constrain the actions of economic agents in (true or purported) pursuance of social goals. Such goals may range from health and safety to environmental protection, job security, and social equity. The effects of regulation on aggregate economic performance arise from the action of those constraints. Regulation may yield benefits in terms of economic performance if it helps correct externalities, informational asymmetries or coordination failures—for example, by preventing the "free-riding" that hampers the provision of productive public services or by improving information disclosure and thus lessening credit rationing in financial markets.

Regulation also imposes economic costs. The most obvious one is the use of productive resources for regulatory compliance rather than production of goods and services. However, the most important costs of regulation accrue through its effects on economic efficiency. Broadly speaking, regulation may affect the allocation of resources across firms and industries by altering their relative profitability or by introducing barriers to the redeployment of resources among microeconomic units. It may also affect within-firm efficiency by changing firms' exposure to competitive pressures in input and output markets. Finally, regulation can impact on the dynamic of output and productivity by changing the incentives for process and product innovation, capital accumulation and job creation.

The objective of this volume is to document the patterns of business regulation across the world and review their impact on aggregate economic performance. The volume adopts a comparative cross-regional perspective, with particular attention to Latin America. The research reported here focuses on establishing the analytical and empirical links between microeconomic regulatory policies on the one hand, and aggregate productivity, growth, and volatility on the other. Thus, the volume adds to a novel but increasingly influential line of policy-relevant research that seeks to understand macroeconomic phenomena from a microeconomic perspective. Such literature is still fairly scarce in the case of industrial countries, and virtually in its infancy for developing countries.

To achieve this end, the volume combines a variety of methodological approaches—analytical and empirical, micro and macroeconomic, single- and cross-country—to an extent limited mainly by the availability of suitable data. Following this overview, the volume comprises six chapters that address the subject from different but complementary perspectives, providing a comprehensive exploration of the various channels through which business regulation affects growth, stability, and other key macroeconomic dimensions.

This introductory chapter offers a brief nontechnical overview of the analysis developed in the rest of the volume, and summarizes the main conclusions. The chapter is organized as follows. The next section outlines the main characteristics of regulation across the world and their relationship with the aggregate economic performance explored in the study. This is followed by a section that summarizes the evidence collected by this research on the transmission channels between regulation and growth and productivity. Next, a brief summary of the study's work on the microeconomic underpinnings of the regulation-macro link is presented, followed by a section providing some concluding remarks.

Regulation and Macroeconomic Performance

Microeconomic regulations pertain to a broad array of dimensions of firms' economic activity. Much of the existing empirical literature on the effects of regulation and regulatory reform has focused on labor market regulation. In particular, considerable attention has been paid to its role in the differential performance of continental European countries vis-à-vis the United States.

In contrast, product market regulation has received much more limited attention—except for the fairly extensive literature on the effects of barriers to international trade. Product market regulation is a broad concept, typically taken to include regulatory provisions on firm entry and exit, barriers to international trade and investment, and possibly also competition policies, as well as the extent of state control over business enterprises.

Chapter 2, "Product Market Regulation and Macroeconomic Performance: A Review of Cross-Country Evidence," by Fabio Schiantarelli, provides a critical review of the existing theoretical literature and relevant microeconometric evidence, discussing along the way the main data and methodological issues related to empirical work on this topic. In addition, it evaluates the cross-country evidence on the effect of product market regulation on firm dynamics, investment, employment, innovation productivity, and output growth. Thus, the chapter sets the stage for the subsequent analysis, and helps the reader better understand how the new evidence presented in this volume fits in with and expands on previous findings on the macroeconomic dimensions of product market regulation.

Unlike the present volume, the bulk of the existing empirical literature has focused on industrial countries, employing a variety of samples and econometric approaches. On the whole, this literature lends support to the conclusion that regulatory barriers in the product market have a negative effect on firms' entry or turnover and are likely to slow the process of resource reallocation. Likewise, the evidence suggests a positive effect of product market deregulation on investment and employment. This is clear in the service sector but less so in manufacturing. Nevertheless, the finding for investment is particularly important because new production processes are often embodied in new capital goods and find their way into the economy through the accumulation of new capital.

Likewise, most studies find a negative effect of tighter regulation on total factor productivity (TFP) or per capita output growth. The results for TFP growth are particularly strong for the service sector. In this respect, the cross-country evidence is consistent with the microeconometric evidence that finds a positive and significant association between competition and productivity growth.

In contrast, cross-country studies have not found a strong positive effect of less stringent regulation on direct input measures of firms' innovative activities. In this regard, the lack of clear empirical results is consistent with the well-known theoretical ambiguities surrounding the relationship between competition and innovation. To make further progress on this front, future research requires not only better measures of innovation, but also a deeper understanding of how the nature of a country's industrial structure, the distance of a country from the technological frontier, the availability of human capital, and other initial conditions may lead to different results.

Past studies of the effects of regulation on aggregate economic performance make use of a heterogeneous assortment of regulatory indicators, which hampers their mutual comparability. To move forward in this area, the first step is to construct a consistent set of measures of microeconomic regulation more suitable for comparison across countries. This task is undertaken in chapter 3, "Regulation and Macroeconomic Performance," by Norman Loayza, Ana Maria Oviedo, and Luis Servén. Drawing from a variety of sources, the chapter develops synthetic indicators of regulation covering a broad array of dimensions relevant to firms' economic activity: firm entry, labor, taxation, trade, finance, contract enforcement, and bankruptcy. The chapter thoroughly documents the procedure followed and the sources employed for this purpose.

These synthetic regulation indicators allow a depiction of the stylized facts concerning regulation around the world (figure 1.1).[1] Two main findings emerge in this regard. First, the burden of regulation shows considerable variation across countries, but in ways that appear systematically related to countries' level of development. The burden of taxes is heaviest in rich countries, while developing countries show the harshest regulatory environments in all other areas. The first of these two facts basically reflects the larger size of the public sector in industrial economies. Second, casual inspection and formal statistical tests show that the overall regulatory framework can be conveniently summarized by the extent of regulation in three major dimensions: fiscal, labor, and product market, where the latter is taken to encompass the regulation of entry, trade, financial markets, bankruptcy, and contract enforcement. In fact, the extent of regulation across the latter five subcategories tends to vary in unison across countries, so that little is lost by combining them into a single indicator.

This general context allows a comparative assessment of the status of regulation in Latin America (figure 1.2). In most dimensions, the levels of regulation in the region are well above those of industrial countries. The exception is fiscal regulation, which on average is lower in Latin America than in any other world region, reflecting the fact that tax burdens are relatively low in most (but not all) countries in the region. In contrast, Latin American countries stand out for their strict regulation of labor, which is the highest among all developing regions considered.

These stylized facts still stand after controlling for the level of per capita GDP. When this is done, the result is that a majority of Latin American countries exhibit higher degrees of regulation than the world norm, as given by countries of comparable income levels. In particular, Brazil, Argentina, Venezuela, and Ecuador rank among the countries in the world furthest above the norm in terms of product market regulation, and (except for Ecuador) in terms of labor market regulation as well.

Chapter 3 then turns to relating these patterns of regulation across the world with countries' economic performance. Loayza, Oviedo, and Servén do this by providing cross-country empirical evidence on the connection between the summary measures of regulation just described on the one hand, and long-term growth and volatility on the other. Specifically, the analysis focuses on the growth rate of GDP per capita and the volatility of the output gap (figure 1.3).

6 LOAYZA AND SERVÉN

Figure 1.1: Regulation around the World

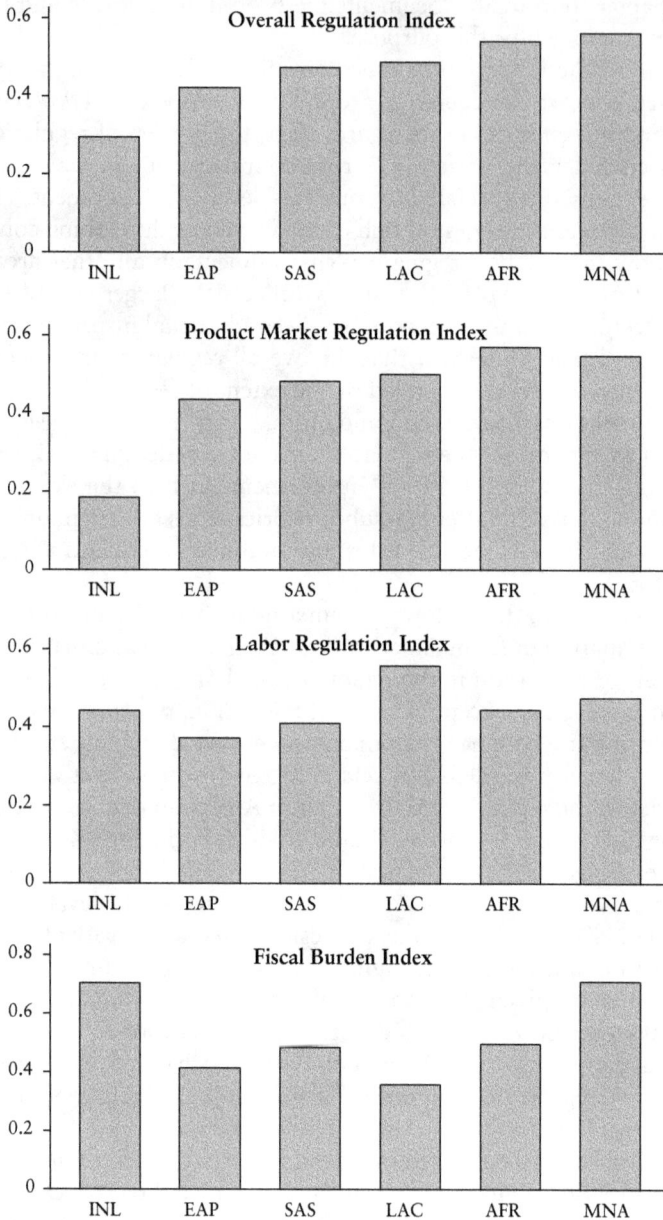

Source: Authors' calculations.
Note: AFR: Africa region; EAP: East Asia and Pacific region; INL: industrial countries; LAC: Latin America and the Caribbean region; MNA: Middle East and North Africa region; SAS: South Asia region. Indices range from 0 to 1.

Figure 1.2: Regulation in Latin America
Overall regulation index, ranging from 0 to 1

Overall Regulation Index

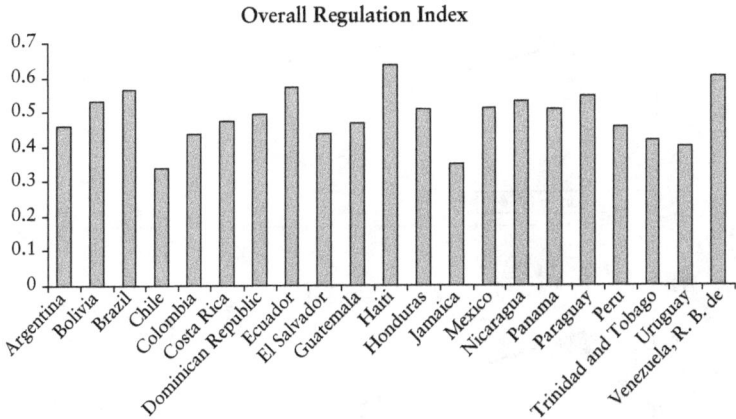

Source: Authors' calculations.

The empirical estimations attempt to take into account two important features of real-world regulation. First, the quality of regulation is likely to vary considerably across countries, reflecting primarily the quality of the countries' overall institutional framework. Second, regulation may be partly endogenous itself, driven by aggregate economic performance. This raises the concern that the observed association between regulation and performance may not reflect the causal effect of the former on the latter—a concern that will also surface in other chapters in this volume (and much of the existing literature). By controlling for this issue in the econometric estimations through the use of instrumental variables, this and the ensuing chapters provide support for the view that their empirical results capture the causal impact of regulation on the macroeconomic variables of interest.

Overall, the estimated results suggest that increasing product market and labor regulations tends to reduce average economic growth (figure 1.4). Conversely, stronger taxation can potentially lead to higher growth, particularly in poor countries. The likely reason is that, in contrast to other regulations, higher taxes permit improving the supply of productive public services, which are badly needed in most developing economies. The results also indicate that better governance tends to dampen and even eliminate the adverse impact of regulations on growth.

Regarding macroeconomic volatility, the empirical results imply that increasing product market and labor regulations tends to induce higher volatility (figure 1.5). However, while better governance can

Figure 1.3: GDP per Capita vs. Regulation Indices

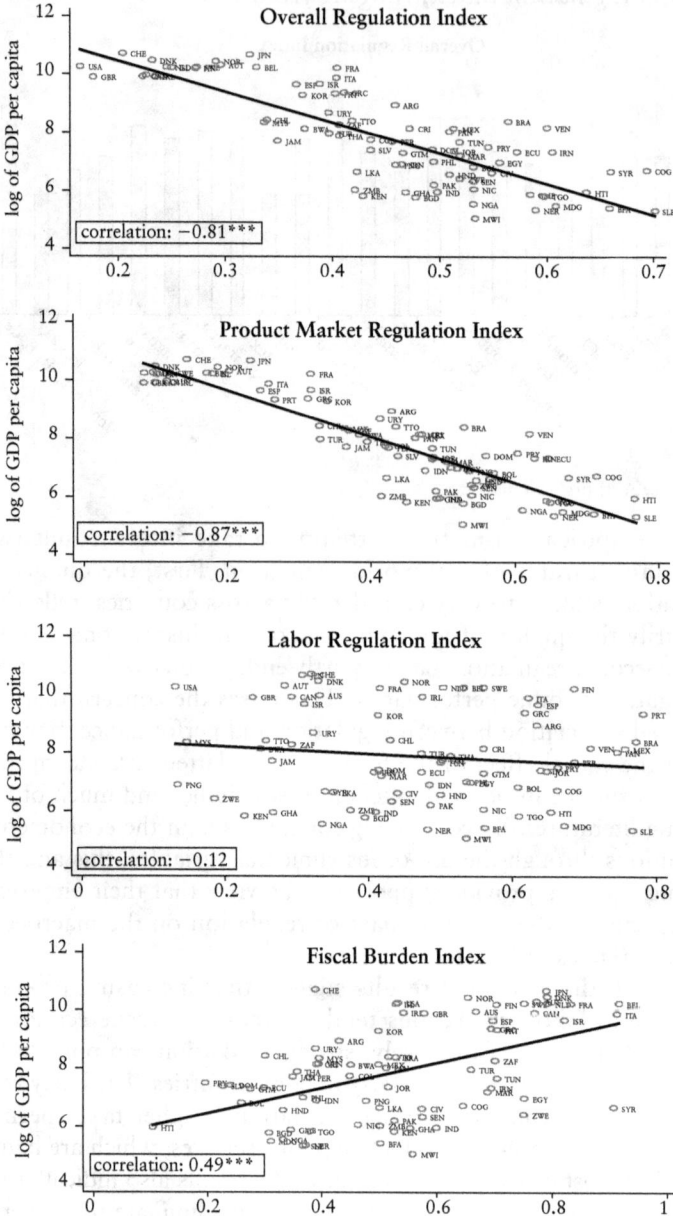

Source: Authors' calculations.
Note: For a list of countries and their 3-letter codes, please see annex 5.1.
    * significant at 10%
    ** significant at 5%
    *** significant at 1%

Figure 1.4: Overall Regulation and Growth

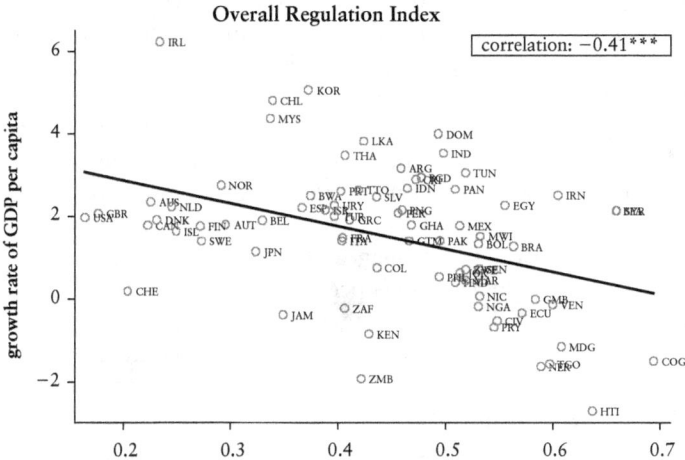

Overall Regulation Index

correlation: −0.41***

Source: Authors' calculations.
Note: For a list of countries and their 3-letter codes, please see annex 5.1.
*** significant at 1%

mitigate the volatility effect of labor regulations, it cannot alleviate the detrimental impact of product market regulations. In turn, fiscal regulations appear not to have a robust detrimental effect on macroeconomic volatility.

Figure 1.5: Overall Regulation and Volatility

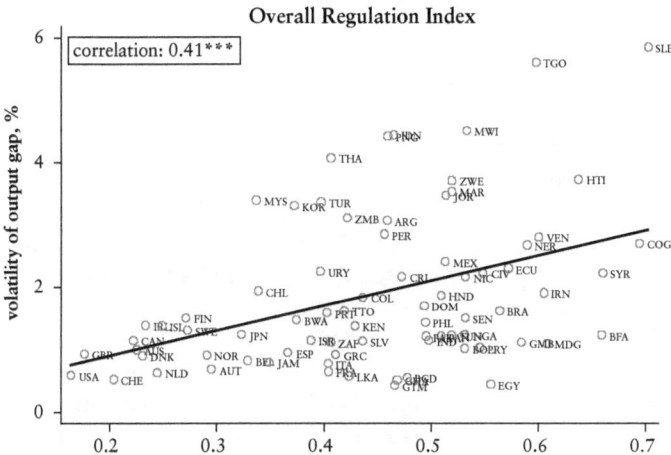

Overall Regulation Index

correlation: 0.41***

Source: Authors' calculations.
Note: For a list of countries and their 3-letter codes, please see annex 5.1.
*** significant at 1%

What do these results mean in practical terms? An illustration can be given by taking the case of Latin America. The empirical findings of chapter 3 imply that the region's relatively high levels of product and labor market regulation, coupled with its relatively weak governance, entail a cost in terms of macroeconomic performance. That cost can be highlighted using our preferred econometric estimates (those that take into account the potential endogeneity of regulation and the effects of governance quality) and the region's pattern of regulation vis-à-vis the rest of the world. In terms of long-run real per capita GDP growth, the empirical results suggest that the average cost to the region is around 0.4 percentage points per annum, a rather significant number. Furthermore, the cost is larger in those countries with stricter regulation and weaker governance. In contrast, countries with relatively milder regulatory frameworks and stronger governance—such as Chile and Costa Rica—actually draw a growth dividend

The Transmission Channels

On the whole, chapters 2 and 3 support the view that regulation has an adverse impact on aggregate growth. But how does such impact arise? There are two broad possibilities. The first one is that reduced growth reflects the efficiency cost of regulatory compliance. One prominent mechanism through which this cost is incurred is the distortionary effect of regulation on the Schumpeterian process of firm renewal. By impeding the reallocation of resources (or orienting it toward inefficient uses), regulation may hamper efficiency-enhancing churning. Through this firm dynamics channel, regulation can have a macroeconomic impact by both worsening recessionary periods and reducing trend growth.

The second option is that reduced growth reflects the efficiency cost of *evading* regulation. This arises from the incentive that regulation may create for firms to work outside the legal framework and become informal. This is a second-best outcome because it entails losing, at least partially, the advantages of legality, such as police and judicial protection, access to formal credit institutions, and participation in international markets. Trying to escape the control of the state forces many informal firms to remain suboptimally small, use irregular procurement and distribution channels, and constantly divert resources to mask their activities or bribe officials. Therefore, as compared with a first-best response, the expansion of the informal sector is typically associated with distorted and insufficient economic growth.

The volume devotes a chapter to explore each of these channels. Chapter 4, "Regulation and Microeconomic Dynamics," by N.

Loayza, A. M. Oviedo, and L. Servén, focuses on the dynamics of firm renewal and resource reallocation as the mechanism through which microeconomic regulations affect economic performance. To develop this analysis, the chapter uses sectoral manufacturing productivity and firm-turnover data drawn from a recently assembled, and still largely unexplored, cross-country firm-level database encompassing both industrial and developing economies.

Specifically, using data for 12 countries (seven OECD and five Latin American) disaggregated at the level of 13 major manufacturing sectors, the chapter studies the relationship between regulatory burden and labor productivity growth. As a preliminary step, the chapter examines the connecting links of this relationship, proposing firm turnover as the mechanism through which the regulatory burden affects firms' productivity growth (figure 1.6). The chapter first observes that in countries where firm turnover is more active, productivity growth is higher. Moreover, it finds that the reallocation-related components of productivity growth (those reflecting entry and exit of firms, as well as reallocation of resources among surviving firms) exhibit the most significant connection with turnover.

Then the chapter turns to the question of whether regulations affect firm turnover. For this purpose, firm turnover rates at the sectoral level are regressed on (country-specific) labor, product market, and taxa-

Figure 1.6: Labor Productivity Growth and Firm Turnover
12 countries and 13 manufacturing sectors

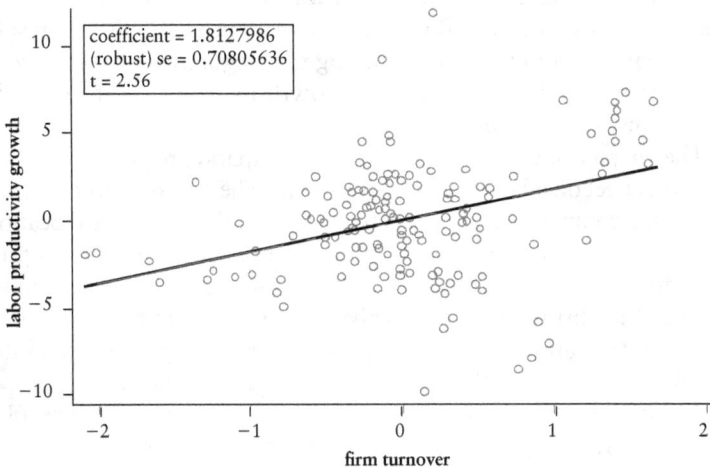

Source: Authors' calculations.
Note: Controlling for initial labor productivity and sector dummies. Errors clustered by country. Robust to outliers.

tion regulation measures and their respective interaction with "normal" turnover (that is, turnover in the United States as the benchmark country). In addition, to help insure against simultaneity bias, the regressions control for the standard deviation of GDP growth and of terms-of-trade growth. These sources of volatility are likely to be correlated with both the country's regulatory stance and its firm turnover rates. The chapter finds that in countries where labor and product market regulations are more burdensome, turnover rates are correspondingly lower on average. Furthermore, this slackening effect appears to be more relevant for sectors characterized by lower normal turnover rates. In contrast with the results on labor and product market regulations, countries with heavier taxation show higher firm turnover. Although at first this may seem a surprising result, it may be explained by the observation that tax-financed public goods and services can indeed facilitate firm renewal.

Having thus highlighted the role of firm dynamics as transmission mechanism (from regulation to turnover, and from turnover to productivity growth), the chapter turns to its basic objective—directly assessing the connection between regulation and productivity growth. It does so by using the same cross-country sectoral database as used in the preliminary exercises but employing a different econometric methodology. This is a variation of the difference-in-difference procedure, designed to eliminate unobserved country-specific and sector-specific effects. Since the regulation measures vary only across countries, their impact on labor productivity growth could not be estimated after removing country-specific effects, unless an additional identification assumption was used. For this purpose, the chapter follows a Rajan-Zingales type of approach, with a twist—identification is obtained by assuming that regulations have a stronger impact on labor productivity growth in sectors that normally require higher turnover.

The chapter finds that labor and product market regulations have a negative effect on labor productivity growth. The adverse effect is stronger on the components of productivity growth that reflect reallocation of resources between firms than on the component that captures productivity growth within firms. Conversely, fiscal taxation appears to be beneficial for firms' labor productivity growth, surely mirroring both the positive relationship between taxation and firm turnover and the beneficial productivity effect of public goods and services.

As noted above, the other broad channel through which regulation may affect aggregate performance is by encouraging firms to become informal in order to evade regulatory constraints. Informality, defined as the collection of firms, workers, and activities that operate outside the legal and regulatory framework, is pervasive in the developing world. It is both a symptom of underdevelopment and a cause of economic retardation. Ultimately, informality reflects a distorted, second-best response from an over-regulated economy. However, regulation is not the only force behind informality—other factors also matter, to an extent that depends on country-specific circumstances.

Chapter 5, "Informality in Latin America and the Caribbean," by Norman Loayza, Luis Servén, and Naotaka Sugawara, explores these issues in the case of Latin America. Proper measurement of informality is a contentious issue, and the chapter presents four alternative measures that show the large degree of heterogeneity across the region. While Bolivia and Haiti rank among the countries having the highest levels of informality in the world, Chile and Costa Rica possess relatively small informal sectors. The typical country in Latin America produces about 40 percent of its GDP and employs 70 percent of its labor force informally (figure 1.7).

The chapter uses the cross-country variation in informality and its covariates to explore the macroeconomic cost of informality and assess its causes, with regulation as one of the candidate explanations. Informality imposes costs because it implies misallocations of resources, as firms remain suboptimally small, divert resources to avoid detection, and congest public infrastructure without contributing to its financing. However, this does not necessarily mean that formalization should result in growth gains. Indeed, informality may deliver better economic performance than a fully-formal but sclerotic economy unable to circumvent its regulation-induced rigidities. In other words, the mechanism of formalization matters. Formalization based on improvements in the regulatory framework and the provision of public services is likely to bring about increased efficiency and growth, but formalization purely based on enforcement may well have the opposite effects. Nevertheless, the empirical analysis of the effects of informality on growth presented in chapter 5 finds a robust negative association between the various indicators of informality and aggregate growth performance. Such association survives when the potential endogeneity of informality is taken into account, and hence it likely captures informality's causal effect on growth. Moreover, the effect is economically significant as well. Similar results obtain regarding the effects of informality on the incidence of poverty across countries.

Informality arises when the costs of belonging to the economy's legal and regulatory framework exceeds the benefits. Thus, informality is more prevalent where the regulatory framework is burdensome, the quality of government services is low, and the state's monitoring and enforcement capacity is weak. However, these

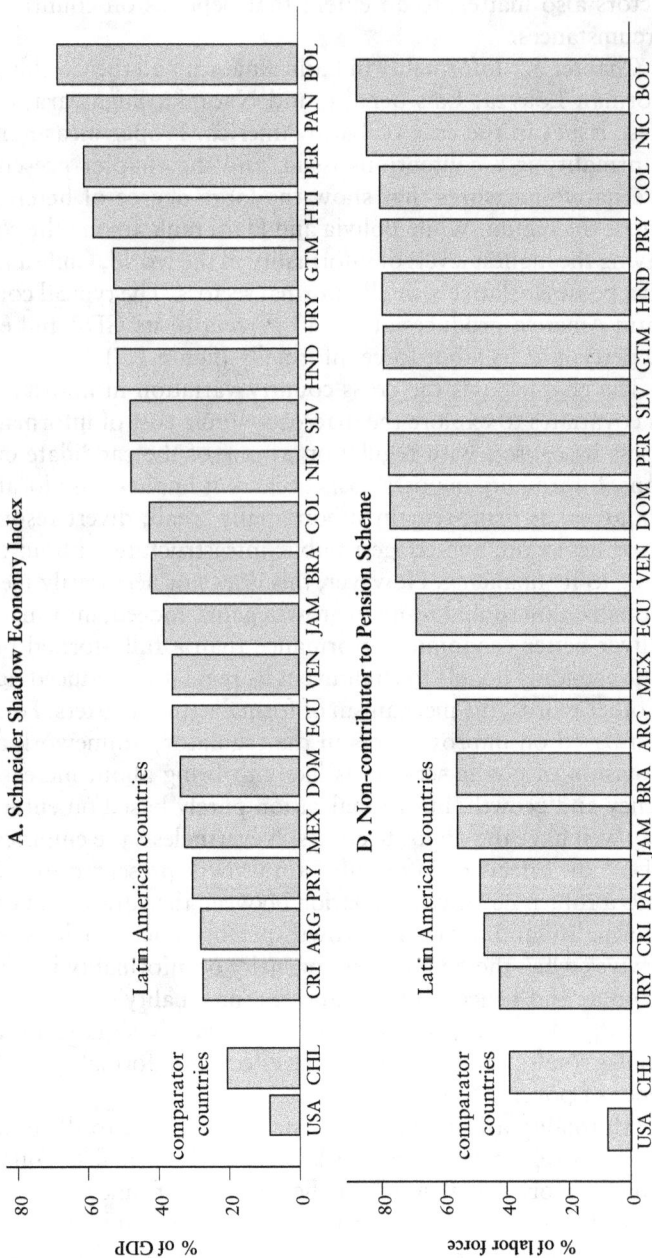

Figure 1.7: Latin America: Size of Informality
Measures of informal production and labor

A. Schneider Shadow Economy Index

% of GDP

comparator countries

Latin American countries

USA CHL CRI ARG PRY MEX DOM ECU VEN JAM BRA COL NIC SLV HND URY GTM HTI PER PAN BOL

D. Non-contributor to Pension Scheme

% of labor force

comparator countries

Latin American countries

USA CHL URY CRI PAN JAM BRA ARG MEX ECU VEN DOM PER SLV GTM HND PRY COL NIC BOL

Source: Authors' calculations.
Note: For a list of countries and their 3-letter codes, please see annex 5.1.

cost-benefit calculations are also affected by key structural characteristics of the economy, such as its productive and demographic
structure and the availability of skilled labor. Chapter 5 argues that
it is important to take into account all of these factors when trying
to ascertain the causes of informality.

This view is confirmed by the chapter's empirical analysis of the
causes of informality. Improvements in law and order, business regulatory freedom, or school achievement all reduce informality (figure 1.8). The same result occurs as the economy's production structure shifts away from agriculture and demographic pressures abate.
In other words, no single determinant is sufficient to explain informality, and the relative role of the various contributing factors varies
across countries. In the case of Latin America, the chapter shows
that informality is primarily the result of a combination of poor
public services and a burdensome regulatory framework. In the
region's lower-income countries, these factors are further exacerbated by the large role of agriculture in the economy and the pressure of a largely young population.

Exploring the Microeconomic Foundations

The analysis described so far—though guided by theoretical considerations and based on microeconomic arguments—has been primarily empirical and aggregate. A necessary complement to this is a
theoretical analysis that, starting from the microeconomic level,
explicitly develops the links between firm dynamics and macroeconomic performance and specifies the mechanisms through which the
regulatory burden affects this relationship. This is the purpose of the
last two chapters of the book.

Chapter 6, "Slow Recoveries," by Raphael Bergoeing, Norman
Loayza, and Andrea Repetto, analyzes how policy-induced rigidities
can impair the economy's ability to absorb and accommodate adverse
shocks, amplifying and prolonging their negative impact (figure 1.9).
The issue is of special relevance to Latin American countries because
most of them suffer high terms of trade volatility, and are also subject to large world financial shocks. Indeed, the region's growth performance during the 1990s was significantly hampered by adverse
world disturbances, and many observers have noted that the effects
of the latter appear to have been more negative and lasting in Latin
America than in other regions.

While this is a macroeconomic issue, its policy and regulatory
roots can be rigorously analyzed only from a microeconomic standpoint. The reason is that policy-induced rigidities affect the dynam-

Figure 1.8: Informality and Its Basic Determinants
Informality measured by the Schneider shadow economy index

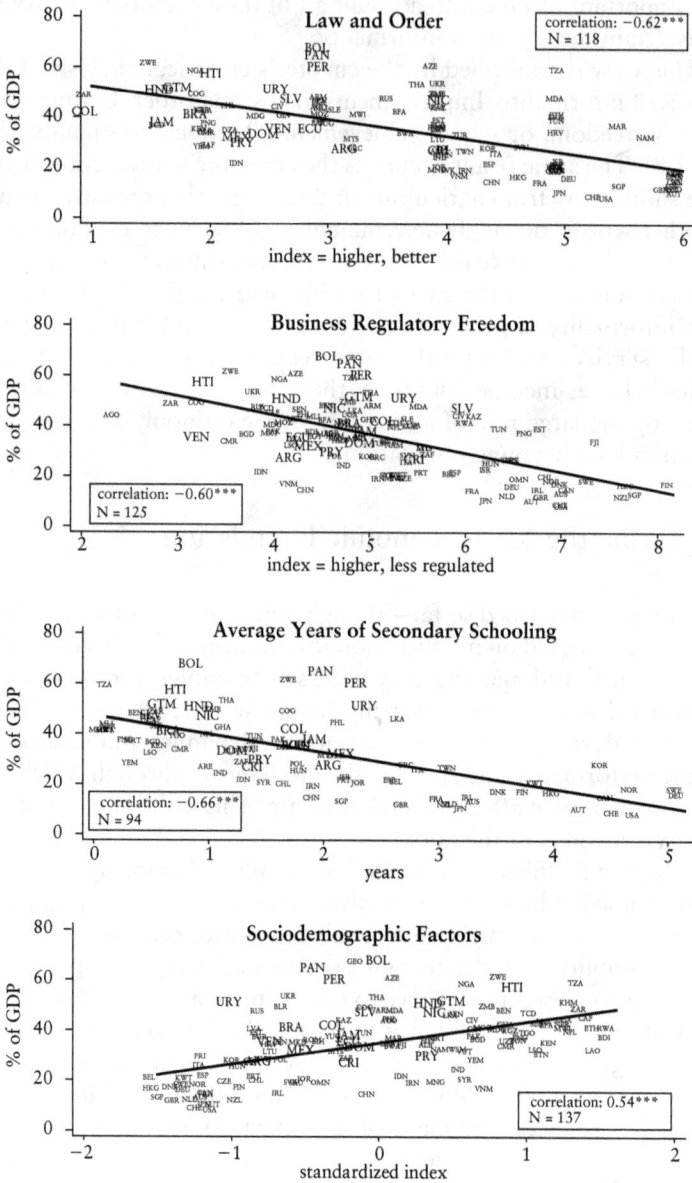

Source: Authors' calculations.
Note: For a list of countries and their 3-letter codes, please see annex 5.1.
*** significant at 1%

ics of creation, growth, and destruction of investment projects and firms in a heterogeneous, idiosyncratic manner, even if the shocks are common. To examine this mechanism, the chapter develops a dynamic general equilibrium model of heterogeneous plants subject to aggregate and idiosyncratic shocks and regulations. These regulations take the form of subsidies and taxes that change the relative cost of firm creation, expansion, and survival, thus altering the natural rate of factor reallocation. The economy's equilibrium path is characterized by an ongoing process of resource reallocation. When an exogenous rigidity is introduced, the natural process of entry and exit is muffled, reducing the amount of efficiency-enhancing firm restructuring. This helps sustain an inefficient allocation of resources and pushes the economy inside its production possibility frontier. This reasoning is consistent with cross-country evidence that suggests that adjustment to adverse shocks is costlier the more pervasive the extent of regulation.

To provide a quantitative illustration of the effects of these microeconomic rigidities on the economy's recovery path following an adverse shock, the chapter simulates two situations representing particular cases of impediments to reallocation. In the first exercise, the authors compare the recovery of two economies that are subject

Figure 1.9: Severity of Recessions and Regulatory Burden: Cross-Country Relationships

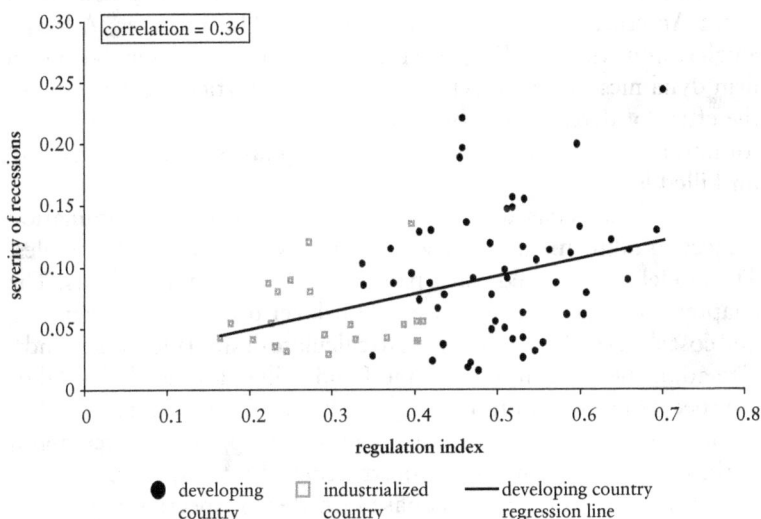

Source: Authors' calculations.
Note: Please see chapter 6, in particular, the text describing figure 6.2, for more information on this graph.

to the same aggregate shock, where one of them is undistorted by taxes or subsidies while the other starts off with a given production subsidy to incumbent firms. Under the benchmark calibration, the undistorted economy that faces a (one-period) transitory aggregate shock equivalent to 5 percent of steady-state per capita GDP loses about 13 percent of its pre-shock output and completes restructuring in a period of one quarter. However, in the presence of a similar shock, an economy that starts off with a 5 percent subsidy to incumbents loses 14.2 percent of initial output with a restructuring period of nine quarters.

In the second exercise, the aggregate shock is the same but this time government intervention—subsidizing incumbents—occurs *after* the shock. This intervention is transitory and phased out gradually, lasting about three quarters in the simulation. In this case, an economy that initially imposes a 6 percent subsidy to incumbents loses about 36 percent of GDP in present value terms with a recovery period that lasts 37 quarters.

The message from these exercises is that policy barriers that hamper flexibility significantly amplify the cost of adverse shocks, even when the barriers aim at smoothing the adjustment process itself. In simpler terms, microeconomic inflexibility entails major macroeconomic costs.

If regulation hampers macroeconomic performance, as the above results imply, what can be expected from deregulation? Chapter 7, "Market Reforms, Factor Reallocation, and Productivity Growth in Latin America," by Marcela Eslava, John Haltiwanger, Adriana Kugler, and Maurice Kugler, studies the effect of deregulation on firm dynamics and productivity growth. In particular, it examines the effect of deregulation on factor adjustment processes, allowing for interrelated adjustments of physical capital as well as skilled and unskilled labor.

The analysis is based on a model of firm-level factor accumulation subject to adjustment costs, which is derived from first principles. The model is calibrated using panel data on Colombian plants. The chapter constructs measures of plant-level productivity, demand, and cost shocks, then it uses them to calculate desired factor demands. The adjustment hazards for capital and skilled and unskilled labor are specified as functions of the gap between desired and actual levels of the respective factor. The model is then applied to seven major Latin American countries by constructing country-specific counterfactual adjustment functions based on their respective regulatory stance. These functions and simulated micro data are used to project the evolution of capital and labor at the microeconomic level for the Latin American countries under consideration. Finally, using these projected series, the chapter estimates the dynamics of aggregate productivity for each country, measuring the potential loss with respect to a hypothetical frictionless environment.

This approach yields valuable insights regarding firm adjustment patterns. First, there is strong evidence of nonlinear adjustments in employment and capital: businesses are much more likely to adjust (or to adjust by a large amount) when the gap between desired and actual levels of production inputs is large. Second, businesses do not tackle input adjustment on an individual-factor basis when faced by cost, productivity, and demand shocks. In fact, there is evidence that employment and capital adjustments reinforce each other, in the sense that capital shortages reduce hiring, and labor shortages reduce investment.

Regarding the reforms undertaken in Latin American countries during the 1990s, the chapter suggests that they significantly improved factor market flexibility and allocative efficiency, especially in radically reforming countries. Along those dimensions, strong reformers edged closer to Chile, whose regulatory stance was already considerably flexible by the 1980s.

An important policy implication from this analysis is that a balanced path to reform is preferable to a piecemeal one emphasizing a single policy or market reform at a time. The reason is that the payoff from removing only one source of friction—e.g., deregulating the market for one production factor—may be significantly lessened by other frictions left in place in still-regulated factor markets. In this regard, the chapter concludes that Latin American countries would experience very large productivity gains if they could remove all the frictions affecting factor adjustment.

Final Remarks

The research summarized here documents the effects of labor and product market regulation on key dimensions of macroeconomic performance, including aggregate productivity, growth, and volatility. Overall, the evidence indicates that the costs of regulation in terms of those key outcomes are significant, not only statistically but, more importantly, economically as well. Further, the evidence also suggests that such adverse effects arise through a variety of channels: impediments to Schumpeterian resource reallocation, obstacles to firms' ability to adjust their use of production factors in the face of disturbances, and enhanced incentives to resort to informality in order to evade microeconomic regulation. However, strong governance helps mitigate—and in some cases even eliminate—the

adverse macroeconomic impact of these forms of business regulation. This is consistent with the view that countries with better institutions tend to create regulatory environments genuinely aimed at
improving business conditions rather than favoring special interests,
and are also more likely to enforce regulation in a transparent and
even-handed manner that reduces the margin for rent-seeking and
corruption.

These findings are a matter of concern for developing countries
in general and Latin America in particular. Many of the region's
economies exhibit levels of labor and product market regulation
well above the international norm, while at the same time suffering
from weak governance. The results reported in this volume imply
that such countries incur substantial costs in terms of aggregate economic performance. From a policy perspective, these results also
stress the interdependence between deregulation and governance
improvement in the reform agenda. Improving governance acquires
a special priority in a highly regulated environment. Equally important, in a framework of weak governance, reducing regulation should
also be at the top of the agenda.

A similar kind of interdependence among reforms also applies to
deregulation itself. The findings of this research—especially those
reported in chapter 7—suggest the need for a balanced approach to
deregulation that advances on several fronts at the same time. Such
an approach is superior to another based on piecemeal reforms that
remove one single regulatory barrier at a time because the payoff
from the latter strategy can be greatly lessened by the continuing
impediments posed by regulations that are left untouched.

Finally, an important qualification regarding the welfare effects of
regulation is in order. The research in this volume finds a negative
effect of regulations on firm renewal, microeconomic flexibility, and
business formality and, consequently, an adverse impact on macroeconomic performance. Does this mean that regulations should be
eliminated altogether? This volume does not intend to assess the
impact of regulation on social goals that could be beyond the sphere
of economic growth—broad goals such as social equity and peace,
or narrow ones such as worker safety, environmental conservation,
and civil security, which typically motivate specific regulations.
Thus, the preceding conclusions on the costs of regulation must necessarily be weighed in a more comprehensive context against its
social benefits before drawing definitive social welfare implications.

At any rate, to the extent that aggregate economic performance
in terms of growth, employment, and stability is itself an important
social goal, the results of this study imply that streamlining regula-

tion and strengthening governance in highly regulated countries—such as most Latin American economies—should have a significant social payoff.

Note

1. All figures presented in this chapter are prepared by the authors, based on data introduced in the rest of the volume.

2

Product Market Regulation and Macroeconomic Performance

A Review of Cross-Country Evidence

Fabio Schiantarelli

Introduction

During the last 15 years, many countries at different levels of development have introduced significant regulatory reforms of their product markets, their factor markets, and their financial sectors. Most of the empirical literature on the effect of product and factor markets regulation (or regulatory reform) has focused on labor markets. Much of it has focused on explaining the different performances of continental European countries vis-à-vis the United States and other OECD countries or the effect of the relaxation of constraints in particular countries. Substantial literature has also developed on the effect of financial reform on a country's real performance for both developed and developing countries.

This research has been supported by the World Bank Latin American Regional Studies Program. I would like to thank F. Giavazzi, R. Griffith, N. Loayza, G. Nicoletti, S. Scarpetta, A. Sembenelli, and L. Servén for useful conversations and comments. The views expressed here are those of the author and do not necessarily represent those of the World Bank, its Board of Directors, or the countries they represent.

One area that has been comparatively under-researched is the effect of product market regulation on macroeconomic outcomes, with the exception of the effect of barriers to trade. Recently, however, a number of contributions have started redressing this imbalance and have shed light on the overall effects of product market regulation. The main purpose of this chapter is to provide a critical overview of the recent empirical contributions that use cross-country data to provide insights on the effect of such product market regulations and reforms on countries' macroeconomic performance.

In this chapter, the evaluation of the cross-country evidence is preceded by a discussion of the main channels through which regulation can affect economic outcomes and by a review of a few seminal micro-level studies that are relevant for the issues under discussion. We then discuss the main characteristics of the available regulatory data, the main stylized facts about regulatory reform, and the methodological challenges that researchers face in assessing the effect of regulation on performance. Finally, we review the salient empirical contributions in these areas. The final outcome measures we focus on are the demand for labor and capital, firms' innovative activity, productivity, and output growth. Intermediate outcome variables are markups and firms' entry, exit, and turnover rates. The chapter closes with a summary of the main conclusions.

The Effect of Product Market Regulation on Macro Performance: Channels and Related Micro Evidence

In this section we start with a discussion of a few theoretical contributions that can help us understand the complex links that exist between product market regulation and economic performance. We then selectively review microeconometric studies for individual countries that either address the relationship between competition and performance or discuss the consequences of specific episodes of regulatory reform.

Theoretical considerations

Product market regulation affects the overall performance of an economy in several ways (see Griffith and Harrison 2004). It has an impact on the allocation of resources among sectors producing different goods and among firms with different productivity within each sector. Moreover, it affects the productivity of existing firms. Finally, it has an impact on the pace of productivity growth by altering the incentives to innovate and by determining the speed with which new products and processes replace old ones.

When regulatory reforms lead to more competitive output markets, the wedge between prices and marginal costs is reduced and the allocation of goods and resources, in the absence of other distortions, will become more efficient in a static sense: more competitive markets will allocate capital and labor more efficiently to the production of those goods that consumers value more.[1] More importantly, a more competitive climate will lead to pressure for the less-efficient firms to exit and, through this channel, market shares will shift from lower- to higher-productivity firms, leading to a more efficient allocation of the factors of production.

Blanchard and Giavazzi (2003) discuss the effect of product and labor market regulation on employment and wages in the context of a model of identical imperfectly competitive firms for whom labor is the only factor of production, and both the product and labor markets are noncompetitive. In that model, product market reform is modeled either as an increase in the degree of substitutability between goods or as a decrease in entry costs.

The effect of product market reform may differ between the short run and the long run. An increase in the degree of substitutability between goods leads in the short run, for a given number of firms, to lower markups, increased employment, and higher real wages. However, there is no effect in the long run, because the reduced markups lead to firms' exits. Product market reforms that lead to a decrease in entry costs have, instead, long-run effects as well. The entry of new firms will be associated with a lower markup and higher employment and real wages. The fact that only policies that affect the cost of entry have long-run effects, and hence are the ones that should receive the greatest attention, is one of the main policy implications of this paper.[2]

Another class of models allows for heterogeneity between firms. Bernard et al. (2003) and Melitz (2003) focus on external barriers affecting the product market, and their models are based on the assumption of heterogeneity in productivity. These papers allow for entry and exit of firms and show that a lowering of trade barriers generates a reallocation of resources in favor of more productive firms. The exit of low-productivity firms and the expansion in the domestic and foreign markets of higher-productivity firms gives rise to aggregate productivity growth.[3]

Bergoeing, Loayza, and Repetto (2004, reprinted in this volume) also allow for idiosyncratic heterogeneity differences in productivity and focus on how the effect of a negative aggregate productivity shock depends upon government-induced rigidities in the reallocation of resources, modeled as a subsidy to existing firms. Simulation exercises show that the existence or the introduction of such subsidies increases the length of the period in which aggregate output is below potential and generates greater cumulated output losses.[4]

Restuccia and Rogerson (2003) and Hsieh and Klenow (2006) develop models in which government-generated distortions result in heterogeneity in returns to capital and labor across firms and in misallocation of resources. This misallocation may result in sizable lower levels of aggregate total factor production (TFP), as shown by Hsieh and Klenow, using plant-level data for India and China.

Product market reforms also have a direct effect on the productive efficiency of existing firms. Greater competition may increase the incentives to reduce X-inefficiencies and organize work more efficiently. The theoretical literature is immense and, while agency models of managerial behavior can rationalize why greater competition tends to reduce slack, this conclusion is by no means unambiguous. The channels of transmissions are manifold (Nickell, Nicolitas, and Dryden 1997). First, in a more competitive environment, it may be easier for owners to monitor managers because there are greater opportunities for comparison, which can lead to better incentives. Second, it is plausible that an increase in competition will increase the probability of bankruptcy and managers will work harder to avoid this outcome. Third, in more competitive markets characterized by higher demand elasticity, a reduction in costs that allows firms to lower prices will lead to a larger increase in demand and, potentially, profits.

Changes in ownership from public to private may also have important effects on the incentives for managers and workers to reduce slack. Whether or not that happens depends crucially upon the market structure after privatization. One must be careful, in general, not to automatically equate privatization or deregulation with an increase in competitive pressure, particularly in sectors where increasing returns create incentives for the emergence of natural monopolies.

Several principal agent models study the effectiveness of incentives and their dependence on the number of players. One of the papers that addresses more directly the link between competition and performance features the model by Hart (1983).[5] In that paper a fraction of firms are run by managers who respond only partially to monetary incentives, in the sense that they care only whether or not their income exceeds a minimum level. The resulting optimal contract consists of paying managers this minimum provided the firms' profits exceed a given floor (that can be interpreted as the bankruptcy level), and zero otherwise. In this situation, any shock that induces profit-maximizing firms to reduce costs will be transmitted, via lower equilibrium prices, to nonprofit-maximizing firms. Their managers will also try to reduce costs in order to avoid bankruptcy and preserve the utility derived from being in control of the firm. This will lead to an increase in the level of productivity in the economy.

However, if we allow managers to respond to monetary incentives, the effect becomes ambiguous. Greater competition increases the threat of bankruptcy, which is a disciplining device but at the same time reduces profits in equilibrium and, with it, the possibility to provide monetary incentives to managers (Scharfstein (1988) and Schmidt (1997)).

Product market reforms may affect not only the level of productivity, but also its growth rate through the effect that greater competition has on the incentives to introduce new products or processes that replace the existing ones. The view by Schumpeter (1942) of growth as a process of creative destruction, in which the introduction of new processes and products is associated with the destruction of old ones, underlies many recent papers, such as the endogenous growth models of Aghion and Howitt (1992) and Grossman and Helpman (1991) and the contributions by Caballero and Hamour (1994, 1996, 1998). Impediments introduced by product or factor market regulations to the reallocation of factors of production away from low-return activities to high-return ones may have adverse effects on an economy's aggregate performance.[6] In endogenous growth models, for instance, product market regulation may be seen as increasing the cost of introducing an innovation.

However, there are contrasting forces at work. In Schumpeter the expectations of monopoly profits provide the crucial incentive for innovative activity. A decrease in monopoly profits following regulatory reform may, therefore, decrease the pace of innovation and hence growth. In addition, the degree of market power also affects the ability to innovate since it allows the accumulation of internal financial resources that can be used to finance innovation. These internally generated funds are crucial in the presence of information asymmetries that may make it difficult or expensive to obtain external funds for innovation activities. Indeed, in the early quality ladder endogenous growth models by Aghion and Howitt (1992) and Grossman and Helpman (1991) and in the product variety model by Romer (1990), a reduction in rents generated by regulatory changes would adversely affect the incentive to innovate and, hence, decrease steady state growth.[7] Both product variety and quality ladder models, moreover, typically exhibit scale effects in the sense that larger economies with more resources that could be devoted to research grow faster in the steady state.[8] In this context, product market reform in the form

of trade liberalization could have ambiguous effects on growth, since
the positive scale effect is counterbalanced by the (negative) effect
generated by the smaller rents that accrue to innovators.

Note that, whereas in the product variety models the decentral-
ized growth rate tends to fall short of the one chosen by the social
planner, in quality ladder models of creative destruction this may or
may not be the case, basically because the benefits of faster technological progress must be traded off against the losses in rents by the
monopoly producers that are displaced. Similar ambiguities in terms
of welfare implications appear in models in which relationships are
characterized by specificity that generates a hold-up problem (Caballero and Hammour 1996, 1998). Regulations that make the reallocation of resources costly can lead to technological sclerosis, in
which low-productivity units are allowed to survive too long. At the
same time, they may also cause the reallocation process to be unbal-
anced, in the sense that the destruction rate is excessive, given the
low creation rate, and generates too high unemployment of the factor that appropriates part of the rent.

In the earlier quality ladder growth models referred to above,
innovations were made by outsiders and not by the incumbents. In
more recent models (Aghion, Harris, Vickers 1997; Aghion et al.
2001; Aghion et al. 2005; Aghion et al. 2006a; Aghion et al. 2006b;
Aghion and Griffith 2005), incumbents are allowed to innovate. In
these models, the incentive to innovate depends upon the difference
between post- and pre-innovation rents. Greater competition reduces
both, but the latter more than the former, fostering innovation. Basically, competition may stimulate innovation because entry and the
threat of entry provide an incentive to innovate in order to escape
competition. This effect should be stronger in industries where competition occurs between "neck-and-neck" firms, i.e., firms with similar production costs. In other terms, competition is more likely to
stimulate innovation and productivity growth in sectors or countries
close to the technological frontier, while the opposite holds for sectors or countries below the frontier.[9]

Finally, there can also be another channel through which increased
competition can have a beneficial effect on innovation and growth.
When principal agent considerations such as those in Hart (1983)
are inserted in an endogenous growth model, greater competitive
pressure can provide an incentive for managers to speed up the
adoption of new technologies in order to avoid bankruptcy and the
loss of benefits from control associated with it (see Aghion, Dewa-
tripont, and Rey 1999).

In summary, there are many ways through which product market
regulation can have an impact on overall economic performance.

Regulatory reform can affect factor demand and the efficiency with which labor and capital are allocated. It also can have an impact on the extent of managerial slack and on X-inefficiency in existing firms. Moreover, it can exert an influence on the process of firm dynamics and on the introduction of new products and processes, and hence on aggregate productivity growth. However, at the theoretical level there are sufficient ambiguities or caveats concerning the direction of the effect of regulatory reform on innovation that empirical research in this area is absolutely essential to come to a convincing conclusion about the overall impact of product market regulation.

Lessons from microeconometric evidence

A seminal microeconometric contribution that has important implications for the issues we are discussing here is the paper by Nickell (1996), who uses firm-level data for the United Kingdom to investigate where changes in competition affect productivity levels and growth rates. Competition is measured in several ways, including industry-level measures of monopoly rents, concentration, import penetration, and number of competitors. By estimating a dynamic production function with the competition variables as additional regressors, and allowing for endogeneity of input choices, Nickell finds that greater competition has a positive effect on both the level and the growth of productivity. Note that, while firm-level variables are instrumented in the context of a dynamic panel Generalized Method of Moments (GMM) approach, competition variables are not. However, if an increase in productivity leads a firm to increase its market share so that the market becomes more concentrated and less competitive, this would impart a downward bias to the estimates of the effect of competition on productivity. In this case, the estimated effect represents a lower bound on the true effect of competition on productivity.

The results in Nickell are confirmed by the more recent contribution by Disney, Haskel, and Heden (2000), using a larger data set for U.K. firms.[10] Klette (1999) extends the approach by Hall (1986, 1988) to estimate market power and concludes, using Norwegian plant-level data, that plants characterized by greater market power tend to be less productive. Bottasso and Sembenelli (2001) apply a similar methodology on Italian firm level-data and conclude that the EU Single Market Program has led to a decrease in the markup and an increase in productivity for those firms that were expected, ex-ante, to be more sensitive to the abolition of external barriers.

Several other microeconometric contributions address the effect of regulatory reform and privatization on productive efficiency or productivity growth. Many of these studies focus on the service sector, since regulatory changes have been particularly important in utilities, communication, and the transport sector. We will not review in detail the evidence here, but the overall conclusion is that in many instances there have been productivity gains due to increased competition. [11]

An important paper on the effect of regulatory reform on the dynamics of productivity is the one by Olley and Pakes (1996) on the evolution of the U.S. telecommunication industry following deregulation. The industry experienced productivity growth that was not reflective of productivity growth in manufacturing. Olley and Pakes decompose aggregate (weighted) productivity levels between unweighted average productivity and a cross term that captures whether more efficient firms have greater market shares. They use their estimate of production function parameters that control for endogeneity and sample selection to show that improved aggregate productivity performance at the industry level is due to a reallocation of output to more productive plants and not to an increase in the unweighted average productivity.

In addition to the static productivity-level decomposition due to Olley and Pakes (1996), Baily, Hulten, and Campbell (1992) have proposed to decompose aggregate productivity growth in different components. Their contribution has been refined by Griliches and Regev (1995) and by Foster, Haltiwanger, and Krizan (2001). The basic idea is to break down aggregate productivity growth in a "within" component (coming from productivity improvement in continuing firms), a "between" component (due to the reallocation of resources between continuing firms), and of components due to entry and exit.[12] The refinements attempt to deal with the overestimate of the contribution of entering and exiting firms inherent in Baily, Hulten, and Campbell by introducing reference productivity values in calculating the contribution of such firms. Results on the relative importance of each component of total productivity growth decompositions differ according to which decomposition is used, whether one focuses on multifactor or labor productivity, whether one uses employment or product weights, whether they are at the beginning of the period or an average between the beginning and the end of the period, and according to the length of the horizon chosen for the calculation.

Many estimates of the within component of labor productivity imply that it tends to be the most important component, although its weight varies across studies. Bartelsman, Haltiwanger, and Scarpetta (2004a, 2004b) find that this is the case both in developed and nontransition emerging countries. Foster et al. (2001) show that the contribution of entry and exit (net entry) to aggregate productivity becomes important (and positive) only at a five-to-ten-year horizon, reflecting the increasing share of entering/exiting firms and learning/ selection effects. Bartelsman et al. also show that entry is more important (and positive) in most transition countries. The entry contribution tends, instead, to be negative in most OECD countries and in the nontransition emerging economies, while the exit effect is always positive. Evidence on the importance of reallocation of market shares from low- to high-productivity continuing firms is also mixed. For instance, Griliches and Regev, and Scarpetta et al. find that it is small, whereas Baily et al. and Foster et al. find that it is important. Recently, Melitz and Polanec (2008) have argued that even the decompositions of Griliches and Regev and Foster et al. underestimate the contribution of surviving firms and overestimate the contribution of entering firms; they propose a new decomposition based on Olley and Pakes that indeed enhances the empirical importance of productivity developments for the set of continuing firms, particularly of the between component.

There is little micro-based evidence on how product market regulation affects different components of productivity growth or of productivity levels. Useful information for India is contained in Srivastava (1996), who analyzes the effect of the first phase of industrial deregulation in India in 1985, which involved a significant degree of delicensing of entry and expansion and liberalization of intermediate and capital imports.[13] Using production function estimates based on firm-level panel data, he shows that the rate of TFP growth for existing firms increased after deregulation. The increase was particularly evident in those sectors with an above-average use of imported materials. More recently, Aghion et al. (2006b), using a panel of industry/ state-level data, provide evidence that deregulating entry in India in 1985 and 1991 has not had an identifiable effect on entry, but has increased the dispersion of output levels across establishments. Moreover, they show that output increases more after product market deregulation if labor market regulation is less restrictive. The interaction between product and labor market reform is an important issue that deserves further investigation.

Let us turn now to the relationship between innovation and the degree of competition, remembering that the latter can be affected by product market regulation. The empirical results are mixed and suggest that there is no simple linear relationship between competition and innovation.[14] Most studies, particularly the earlier ones, were conducted at the industry level and tended to rely on concentration as a measure of competition; this is problematic because the measure of concentration does not capture the competitive pressure coming from potential entrants. The overall results are not supportive of the proposition that concentration exerts an unambiguous positive effect on innovation activities.[15]

More recently, Blundell, Griffith, and Van Reenen (1999), using U.K. firm-level data, found that firms with greater market shares were more innovative, but that more competitive industries produced more innovation. Recent firm-level evidence suggests that the relationship between markups and innovation is nonlinear and has an inverted U shape, as suggested by the most recent growth models. Aghion et al. (2005) use data on listed U.K. firms for which weighted patent measures of innovation are available. The Lerner index is used as a measure of competition and the problem of its endogeneity is addressed by using as instruments reforms linked to the EU single market, reforms imposed on individual sectors as a result of action by the U.K. competition authorities, and measures of privatization. The results are supportive of an inverted U-shape relationship with innovations being adversely affected by a very competitive or very monopolistic environment. Note that a linear specification would yield a positive relationship between innovation and measures of rents, as suggested by Schumpeter. The results concerning the U shape are stronger in "neck-and-neck" industries, as suggested by the theory.

Aghion et al. (2006a) analyze the effect of foreign firm entry on TFP growth and patent counts. Obviously, entry is endogenous and the latter is instrumented with policy and foreign technology variables that are less likely to have a direct effect on the growth of TFP or on patents. Using individual U.K. firm data, entry is found to have a positive, significant and sizable effect on TFP. The effect is greater when IV procedures are used, and it is greater for an industry closer to the technological frontier.

Data and Methodological Issues

In this section, we will review the main data on regulation that are available across countries and that have been used in empirical work. We will also discuss the main stylized facts that can be identified from the data. The available measures of regulation condition the type of econometric evidence that can be produced, and this often presents an important constraint for the researcher. Although there are serious issues in measuring economic outcomes, such as total factor productivity growth or firms' innovative activities, they are arguably not as severe as those affecting the measurement of tightness of regulation.[16]

We also discuss other important methodological issues involved in estimating the effect of regulation on economic activity. The main issue here is to go beyond any observed statistical association between regulation and performance and to draw inferences on the causal effect of regulation on economic outcomes.

Data and stylized facts

Product market regulation varies by countries and time and often is industry-specific. Moreover, the term "product market regulation" encompasses various dimensions that exert different effects on agents' behavior. A very important aspect to capture is how regulation contributes, directly or indirectly, to the size of entry barriers. Regulation also affects conduct by restricting entrepreneurial choices concerning inputs, supply, or pricing.

Many of these regulations are justified as attempts to address market failures due to the existence of natural monopolies, informational frictions, or externalities. Whether this is indeed the case or whether regulation is the product of the interaction between the desire of politicians to be re-elected and the pressure of interest groups in pursuit of their private gains, which results in even greater government failures has been hotly debated. However, this is not the issue we want to address in this chapter. For our purposes, we simply note that product market regulation tends to restrict competition, and this has potentially important economic consequences. Yet, there are conceptual and practical problems in measuring those dimensions of regulation that are relevant in shaping the competitive environment. Moreover, the data are often not available at the industry-country level, but only at the country level, and/or they are available at only one point in time or at widely spaced intervals.

One of the main data sets used in empirical work on the effect of regulation is collected by the Fraser Institute; it contains information (in the interval 1 to 10, decreasing with stringency of regulation) on price controls, time spent with bureaucracy, ease of starting a new business, government transfers and subsidies (as a percentage of GDP), government enterprises and government investment (as a percentage of GDP), nontariff import barriers, and average tariffs. The indicators reflect a mixture of factual information and perception, and they are available up to the year 2000 at five-year intervals. After that, they are available at a yearly frequency. No sectoral disaggregation of the indices is available.

Another useful data set is the OECD database on regulatory reforms containing detailed economy-wide information for 1998 and 2003 on regulations and administrative burdens on existing and new businesses.[17] For a subset of industries (electricity, gas, air passenger transport, rail transport, postal services, and telecommunications) indices of the importance of barriers to entry, vertical integration, market structure, price controls, and the importance of public ownership are available on an annual basis from 1975 to 2003 (the indices range from 0 to 6 and are increasing with the stringency of regulation). For these sectors, the data availability comes as close as possible to what a researcher would want. Sectoral indicators are available for 1998 and 2003 for retail trade and professional services, covering both entry regulations and conduct regulation.[18] For manufacturing, no time-varying data measuring regulation are available at an annual frequency, except for data on tariff and nontariff barriers, public ownership, and restrictions on foreign direct investment (FDI). However, the OECD data set includes measures at the two-digit level of the "knock-on" effect of nonmanufacturing regulation on all sectors. It is calculated using the indicators for nonmanufacturing sectors and the importance of these sectors as suppliers of intermediate inputs to other sectors (including manufacturing), measured from input-output tables.

For European countries, one can also obtain further information on the evolution of state intervention in the economy using the Eurostat data on sectoral and ad hoc state aid (as a percentage of GDP), public procurement (as a percentage of GDP), and openly advertised public procurement (as a percentage of procurement) for the nineties. Another useful source of data is the European Centre for Public Enterprises with Public Participation (CEEP), which provides information on the share of public enterprises in the business sector at four-to-five-year intervals.

As we have seen, there is greater data availability on various aspects of product market regulation for developed countries. An important source of information that covers developing countries and transition economies as well is the World Bank "Doing Business" database. It contains information on the ease of starting a new business, including the number of procedures, their cost, and the time involved. The data set is based in part on, and expands, the design in Djankov et al. (2000). It also provides useful information on other dimensions of the business environment, such as dealing with licenses, hiring and firing workers, closing a business, paying taxes, etc. Unfortunately, these indices are available only for the period 1996–2002 at a biannual frequency, and lack industry details.

The World Bank also produces the Investment Climate Assessment survey containing information for several developing and transition countries on individual firms' perceptions about the investment climate.[19] It includes information about the time spent dealing with government regulation, the time it takes to get a telephone installed, bribes as a percentage of annual sales, and perceptions about property rights and the legal system and about labor market regulation as an obstacle to economic activity.[20] The individual answers can be aggregated at the industry level to obtain a sector-specific measure of regulation. The information for the time being is mostly cross-sectional, although this may change with the completion of further waves of the surveys.

What are the main stylized facts about product market regulation that can be identified from the data sets we have described? First, regulatory burdens vary widely across the world. In particular, regulation tends to be more stringent in poor countries than in richer ones. There is also evidence that it is greater in countries with a French legal origin or with a socialist legal origin. Second, the dispersion of regulatory regimes is greater in developing countries relative to developed countries. Third, there has been a generalized tendency toward the relaxation of regulation concerning entry. This has been accompanied by a decrease over time in tariff and nontariff barriers to trade in manufacturing. Fourth, there has been a substantial movement toward less restrictive regulation in many developing countries, including India and China. Fifth, OECD countries have experienced substantial deregulation in services, in sectors such as telecommunication, utilities, and transport. The timing and extent of regulatory reform has varied considerably, with the United States moving first in the early 1980s. The United Kingdom, Canada, New Zealand, and the Nordic European countries started to reform a little later, in the mid 1980s. In Australia and most other European countries, market reform occurred from the mid-1990s on and has been less decisive in countries such as France, Italy, and Greece. Finally, regulatory reform has often been accompanied by privatization, so that there has been a tendency for the share of output produced by public enterprises to decrease.[21]

Methodological issues

The main methodological issue facing researchers working in this area is to go beyond any observed statistical association between regulation and performance and draw inferences on the effect of regulation on economic outcomes. In doing so, it is important to control for observed and unobserved factors that have an effect on performance, independent of the regulatory environment. Most papers make a serious effort to control for observed factors. The main issue involves unobserved heterogeneity.

If outcomes are measured at the industry level and the type, level, and change in regulation are also industry-specific, the availability of time varying industry-specific indicators allows one to control for time invariant country and industry effects. It can also allow one to control for factors that vary over time and are common across sectors—like technological innovations or knowledge (which are widely accessible by all countries) or common macro shocks. If the time varying information on regulation is only country-specific, but there continues to be time varying industry specificity in regulation, the measurement error problem may bias the coefficient on regulation toward zero and make it more difficult to detect the true effect of regulatory changes. At a minimum, it would be desirable to distinguish between regulation in manufacturing and in service industries. Yet, in the case that common regulatory changes are dominant, time varying indices at the country level are useful in that one can control, at least, for country- and sector-specific time invariant characteristics.

If the time dimension is not available, industry variation in the product market regulation indicators is still helpful, because at least one can control for additive unobserved country- and industry-specific effects (but not for country-specific industry effects). All the identification in this case comes from cross-sectional country/sector variation in the data.

However, often one has available information that varies only by country, with no industry specificity. This makes it very hard to distinguish the effect of product market regulation from other country-specific unobservable effects. In assessing a country's aggregate performance, some mileage can be gained here by using interaction effects with other variables that vary by country and time. For instance, one may believe that the effect of regulation may be different depending upon circumstances such as the distance of a country from the technological frontier, etc. The lack of identification of the main effect of regulation from other country-specific effects remains.

A distinct problem (less relevant in this area of research) occurs when one only has country-specific information on regulation, even if the latter is truly the only one that matters, because there is no industry specificity, yet one uses outcomes at the industry level as a dependent variable. Moulton (1990) points out that standard errors for the coefficient of the variable (regulation) that varies only by country can be seriously underestimated when the error terms are contemporaneously correlated across industries within countries. The severity of the problem and the appropriate solutions are related, among other things, to the number of groups (countries in our context). If the number of groups is large, things are simpler, although one has to allow for the potential contemporaneous correlation in the error term across sectors within a country in calculating the standard errors. Things are more complicated if the number of groups is small (see Wooldridge (2003) for an overview).

Another, more important, issue is the potential endogeneity of regulation itself, even if one controls for country and industry time invariant effects. Regulation is the result of a political decision process that may indeed be influenced by the economic performance of a country or of an industry. It is difficult to say a priori in which direction the bias would work. For instance, negative macro shocks, particularly if prolonged, can enhance the probability of reforms because the unsatisfactory nature of the status quo weakens opposition to reform. However, it may be easier to introduce reforms in good times because their negative impact on particular groups may be smaller and/or there may be more resources to compensate the losers. In the first case, Ordinary Least Squares (OLS) or within estimators may lead to an underestimate of the true effect of reform; in the latter case, such effects will be overestimated. Recent empirical evidence for OECD countries suggests that poor growth experience in a given year (or in the recent past) leads to less regulated output markets.[22] Similar results hold for trade reform, but, interestingly, not for financial or labor market reform.[23] No systematic evidence is available for developing countries, although it is not unreasonable to conjecture that similar patterns may be observed for product market and trade regulation. The result of all this is that there is the risk of underestimating the effect of product market reforms, since the outcome variables one is interested in, including standard measure of productivity, are generally procyclical.

Product Market Regulation and Economic Performance: Review of Cross-Country Evidence

In this section, we will review a set of recent contributions that have a direct bearing on the effect of product market regulation on various aspects of macroeconomic performance. The review will be selective and focus on papers that provide cross-country evidence. In many cases, researchers have adopted a reduced form approach and have entered measures of regulation as an explanatory variable in equations for factor demand, productivity, or innovation. In other cases, the effect of regulation is mediated through its effect on an intermediate variable, such as the markup or firms' entry, exit, and turnover rates. We will start with reviewing the evidence on the effect of regulation on these "intermediate" variables, and we will then discuss the effect of regulation on the ultimate outcome variables, such as investment, employment, innovation, productivity, and output growth.

Transmission mechanism: Effect on markup and firms' entry/ exit/turnover

Griffith and Harrison (2004) provide a good example of the two-step strategy in estimating the effect of product market regulation. In the first step, they begin by estimating the effect of product market reforms on the level of rents, measured by the ratio between value added and the sum of labor and capital costs. The effect of variations in the markup on factor accumulation R&D and productivity is estimated next, using product market reforms as an instrument for the clearly endogenous markup. This approach is legitimate under the assumption that product market reforms affect the economy only through markup variations and not directly. Since this may or may not be the case, it is important to assess through a test of over-identifying restriction whether this assumption is or is not rejected.

Griffith and Harrison only use regulations that vary with time across countries in order to be able to control for cross-sectional unobservable differences that are relatively constant over time. The indicators of product market regulation are the Fraser Institute index of ease of starting a new business, of price controls, of time spent with government bureaucracy, of average tariff rates, and of regulatory trade barriers; the European Center of Enterprises with Public Participation; and the Eurostat Structural indicators on state aid, on public procurement, and on the percentage of it that is publicly advertised. The indicators are interpolated or extrapolated, if not available for each year, and are entered separately in the equations. Both in the markup and factor demand equation they control for country-specific cyclical factors. Their results suggest that many of the indicators measuring tightness of regulation have a significant positive effect on markups, as one would expect. The effect of variations of markups on various economic outcomes will be discussed below.

Several authors extend and modify the two-step approach found in Griffith and Harrison (2004) by choosing a different intermediate variable for their focus. Cincera and Galgau (2005) first estimate the effect of regulation on entry and exit of new firms and then the effect of entry and exit on factor demand and productivity. Loayza, Oviedo, and Servén (2009b) use firm turnover rates (the number of exiting and entering firms divided by the total number of firms) as the intermediate variable and investigate their effect on productivity growth and its components. Scarpetta et al. (2002), Brandt (2004), and Klapper, Laeven, and Rajan (2004) present results on the effect of regulation on entry, but do not investigate the relationship between entry and other economic outcomes.

Data sources for entry and exit rate vary across studies. The entry and exit rate variables in Cincera and Galgau (2005) are taken from the Dun & Bradstreet database on the number of entries and exits for three-digit sectors for nine OECD countries. The data on firm dynamics in Loayza et al. cover five Latin American countries and seven industrial economies and are taken from the harmonized data set on firm dynamics constructed by Bartelsman, Haltiwanger, and Scarpetta (2004a, 2004b). The entry and exit rates in Scarpetta et al. and Brandt are taken, instead, from the OECD firm-level database constructed from business registers or social security databases. Klapper et al. (2004) use the cross-country firm-level Amadeus data set to construct entry rates for Western and Eastern European countries. In most cases the time dimension of the data on entry and exit tends to be rather short.[24]

The results obtained by Cincera and Galgau, using the first principal component of the Fraser Institute and the within estimator, suggest that deregulation tends to be significantly associated with more entry and exit.[25] When the coefficient on regulation is allowed to differ across sectors the results are not tidy, with the sign and significance varying across sectors. Similarly, allowing for country variations suggests heterogeneity of responses that are not easy to rationalize.

Scarpetta et al. (2002) use as an explanatory variable the time invariant OECD indicators, either country- or country/sector-specific. When only country-level indicators are used, one obviously cannot control for country-specific effects. When industry/country-specific indices are used, the authors control for country and industry additive effects. The more convincing results are those in which Scarpetta et al. control for country and sector effects in the specification that also includes employment protection indices. Product and labor market regulations indices are interacted with firm-size dummies. There is evidence that for firms having from 20 to 99 workers product market regulation has a negative and significant effect on entry. For the 100-to-499-workers class, the effect is positive and significant, which is somewhat puzzling.

The results by Brandt (2004) are obtained using country-specific time invariant measures of barriers to entrepreneurship as the explanatory variable in an equation in which the dependent variable is the averaged residual (across sectors and time) of a regression of entry rate on industry, time dummies, and country-specific Information and Communication Technology (ICT) industries dummies. The focus on barriers to entry is prompted by the fact that some of its subcomponents are the only ones to have some explanatory power. This is not true for indicators summarizing state control and

barriers to trade and investment. The barriers-to-entry coefficient is
not significant, but there is some evidence that its subcomponent
representing regulatory and administrative opacity has some explanatory power for entry rates.

Klapper et al. (2004) focus on the interaction effect between regulation and the "normal" rate of entry in an industry, proxied by the
corresponding entry or turnover rate for the United States. The
drawback is that one cannot make a statement about the overall
effect of regulation on entry, but only on relative magnitudes. The
advantage is that this approach should be less affected by reversed
causality problems, whereas in countries with generally low entry
there may be less pressure to eliminate restrictive regulations. The
results suggest that regulation reduces entry relative to the "normal"
industry-specific rate one observes in a country (the United States)
with low barriers to entry. [26]

Loayza et al. (2009b) include in their equations for turnover various (country-specific) measures of regulation and their corresponding interaction with "normal" turnover (in the United States). To
help ensure against simultaneity bias, they control for the standard
deviation of GDP growth and of terms-of-trade growth. These
sources of macroeconomic volatility are likely to be correlated with
both the country's regulatory stance and its sectoral turnover.[27] The
authors find that countries with heavier regulatory burdens have, on
average, lower firm turnover rates. Furthermore, they observe that
this slowing-down effect is stronger in sectors characterized by lower
normal turnover.

Summarizing, there is substantial evidence that product market
regulation leads to higher markups of prices over costs. Considering
all the empirical contributions on the relationship between regulation and firm dynamics together leads to the conclusion that regulatory barriers in the product market have a negative effect on firms'
entry or turnover and are likely to slow the process of reallocation
of resources.

Effect of product market regulation on fixed capital and labor demand

In this subsection we will review the empirical results on the effect of
product market regulation (PMR) first on investment and then on
employment (unemployment). Alesina et al. (2005) use country/sec-
tor time varying information on regulation to assess its effect on
capital accumulation by introducing regulation indicators directly
into the investment equation. Understanding the behavior of investment is very important for many reasons, including the fact that

process innovations are often embodied in new capital goods. The theoretical model that underlies Alesina et al.'s contribution is an extension of Blanchard and Giavazzi (2003) that assumes perfectly competitive labor markets but introduces capital as a factor of production that is costly to adjust. Product market regulation affects the size of the markup by altering, for instance, entry barriers. Moreover, regulation can influence the cost that even existing firms face when expanding their capital stock.[28] Regulatory reform that generates a decrease of the markup or in the cost of adjusting capital is shown to lead to an increased demand for capital. However, there may be contrary forces at work. For instance, regulation may impose a ceiling in certain sectors on the rate of return. If such a ceiling is binding, a removal of the constraint may reduce the demand for capital. Moreover, deregulation has sometimes been accompanied by privatization. The reduced importance of a dominant publicly owned player facing a soft budget constraint is equivalent to a reduction in entry barriers. However, public enterprises may have been heavy investors, either because of a political mandate imposed on them or because of their incentives to overexpand either because they are empire builders or because they want to maximize political support.

In their empirical work, Alesina et al. focus on investment in nonmanufacturing industries (utilities, communications, and transport) in OECD countries that have experienced profound changes, particularly in the 1990s, in their regulatory framework. They use time varying sector-country-specific measures of regulation collected by the OECD for the period 1975–98. In their investment rate equation, they allow for a sector-country-specific fixed effect and, in some specification, for a sector-specific time trend. This is very important because one needs to control for sector-specific technological shocks that were occurring at the time of regulatory reform and to which reform itself may be responding.

The overall results suggest that a reduction in regulation, particularly if it affects barriers to entry, has a significant and sizable positive effect on the investment rate. The results are robust with respect to the inclusion of several country- or sector-specific controls and to estimating the model in difference by GMM, where the regulatory index is also instrumented with lagged values of itself, with population, GDP per capita, cumulative years of left-wing government, and union density (see Djankov et al. (2000) on the determinants of regulation). When the specification also includes measures of public ownership, the effect of a reduction in entry barriers remains significant. The coefficient of indices of public ownership is also significant, and its sign suggests that privatization has a positive effect on investment. Finally, there is evidence of nonlinearities in the sense that more decisive and deeper deregulations have a greater marginal impact on investment. Moreover, the marginal effects of deregulation are greater when one starts from a more deregulated environment. Note that the positive effect of deregulation on investment not only reflects a static reallocation of resources, but may also have growth effects, if new technologies are embodied in new capital goods.

Several contributions analyze the effect of product market regulation on employment or unemployment. Typically researchers control for cyclical factors and for labor market policies and institutions; in some cases, the interaction between product and labor market regulation is considered. This is not the place to provide a review of the copious literature on the effect of labor market regulation on employment (unemployment). Substantial debates exist on how to measure labor market regulation and on its effects.[29] My reading of the literature suggests that the more up-to-date evidence supports a negative effect on employment of union density and of the generosity of the unemployment benefit system. The effect of employment protection legislation is more ambiguous, as is the effect of the degree of coordination/centralization of the bargaining system. Most studies find a negative effect of product market regulation on employment, but there is disagreement on whether product market deregulation is more effective at the margin in highly regulated labor markets.[30] The most recent evidence is contained in Fiori et al. (2007) and is based on estimating a dynamic specification of the employment rate equation for the business sector in OECD countries that includes country-specific constants and trends and controls for the endogeneity of policies. The evidence suggests that gains from reducing barriers to entry in product markets are larger when labor market policies are tight. In addition, using summary measures of labor market policies, they find evidence that domestic product market deregulation generates a decline in the bargaining power of workers by promoting deregulation of labor markets or by affecting union density and coverage. The authors show that these results are largely consistent with an enhanced version of the Blanchard and Giavazzi (2003) model of bargaining, once one allows for a fuller specification of the fallback position of the union.

Evidence on factor demand, using the two-step approach, is provided by Griffith and Harrison (2004), via the markup, and by Cincera and Galgau (2005), via entry. After Griffith and Harrison show that a decrease in regulation leads to a significant decrease in the markup, their results suggest that the markup is negatively and significantly related to employment and investment (see the section on the effect of PMR on productivity and output growth, below, for a discussion of its effect on R&D and productivity). However, in both cases the test of over-identifying restriction strongly rejects the model, meaning that some of the regulation indicators have a direct effect on employment and investment, besides having an effect through the markup. Taking account also of their direct effect leads to the conclusion that the more important effect on labor and investment comes from the average tariff rate (negative), from price controls (negative), and from the CEEP measure of the importance of public enterprises (negative). Re-estimation of the employment and investment model reveals that services are responsible for the conclusion that an increase in competition stimulates factor demand, while this is not (or less) true for manufacturing.

Cincera and Galgau (2005) use firm entry and exit rates as the intermediate variable through which regulation affects various aspects of performance. Obviously, the entry and exit rates are endogenous and need instrumenting.[31] The instruments chosen by Cincera and Galgau are current and lagged values of the first principal component of the Fraser indices and an index of restrictions on FDI investment, which vary only by country and account only for a portion of the industry-level variation of entry. For this reason, current and lagged values of the number of active, entering, and exiting firms are used as additional instruments, which is a more questionable choice. Lack of rejection by the Sargan test of the over-identifying restrictions is not reassuring. If anything, it reminds us of the low power of the test in many circumstances, particularly when many of the instruments have a low explanatory power in the first stage regression. Be that as it may, the results suggest that entry is not a significant determinant of the growth in investment, while exit is associated with a significant decrease in the pace of capital accumulation. For employment growth, the effect is not significant or has a different sign at different lag lengths of entry, but with a net effect close to zero.

Summarizing, the direct evidence in Alesina et al. (2005) and the indirect one, via effects on the markup in Griffith et al. (2004) suggest a positive effect of deregulation on investment and employment in the service sector. For manufacturing, there is no evidence of a positive (or for that matter, negative) effect. The evidence in Fiori et al. (2007) for the business sector also suggests that employment gains from reducing barriers to entry in product markets are larger when labor market policies are tight. Moreover, there is some evidence that product market deregulation promotes deregulation of labor markets. The results in Cincera and Galgau (2005) suggest that entry is not a key channel of transmission of regulatory changes to the reallocation of labor and capital.

Effect of PMR on innovation

Bassanini and Ernst (2002) present direct evidence for 18 manufacturing industries in 18 OECD countries on the effect of product and labor market regulation on R&D intensity (relative to output). R&D is used as an input-based measure of innovative activities by a firm. The advantage of this measure is the fact that it is more easily available than other measures such as patent counts. The drawback is that R&D is not the only input in the innovation process and, even if it were, R&D intensity may not capture changes in its effectiveness. Finally, not all innovative efforts are measured by formal R&D spending. The regulation variables are the OECD country-level time invariant measures of domestic economic regulation (state control, legal barriers to entry, price controls) and administrative regulation (administrative barriers for new firms, permit and licensing systems), in addition to time varying indicators of tariffs and nontariff barriers. A measure of protection of intellectual property rights is also included. Controls include industry and country dummies in addition to the employment share of large firms and import penetration. As a result, the main effect of the time invariant indices of regulation cannot be estimated; only its differential impact across some cut in the data (high-tech versus low-tech industries in this case) is amenable to estimation.

The results suggest that nontariff barriers have a negative effect on R&D intensity. No effect of tariff barriers is detected, although one wonders whether the presence of the import penetration variable as a regressor or the lack of variation of this indicator across EU countries may be responsible for this result. There is no evidence of a differential effect of domestic or administrative barriers comparing low-tech to high-tech firms. In contrast, there is a positive differential effect for employment protection in high-tech industries relative to low-tech in centralized systems of industrial relations. Note however that the high-tech-centralized industrial relation system interaction has a negative coefficient.

Griffith and Harrison (2004) analyze also the effect of (time varying) product market regulation on R&D through changes in the markup. Even allowing for a quadratic term, for virtually all countries the markup has a positive and significant effect on R&D. Also, in this case, the test of over-identifying restrictions suggests that some of the indicators should be included directly in the equation. The results suggest that a lower tariff rate, fewer barriers to starting a business, and lower regulatory trade barriers are associated with lower R&D in the business sector. The results obtained for the manufacturing sector are similar. However, they are very sensitive to the inclusion of Finland in the sample. When Finland is excluded, one obtains a strong inverted U-shaped relationship between R&D spending and the markup, with a few countries such as France, Italy, and the Netherlands mostly on the downward sloping section; this implies that for these countries an increase in competition would spur innovation, while the opposite is true for the rest of the countries. The sensitivity of the results to country sample selection deserves to be investigated further.[32]

Cincera and Galgau (2005) find a negative effect of entry on R&D intensity that is significant at the 10 percent level. Recall that entry is negatively related to the tightness of regulation. The effect on the R&D spending growth rate is significantly positive contemporaneously and negative after one year. The net effect is close to zero.

Summing up, the cross-country studies are not supportive of a strong positive effect of lower regulation on direct input measures of firms' innovative activities. Actually, the evidence suggests that lower markups associated with product market reform lead to lower R&D for most countries. However, this evidence is sensitive in manufacturing to the particular sample of countries selected for estimation. Note that, on the whole, this evidence is less supportive of a positive role for competition in fostering innovation than the micro evidence discussed in the section on lessons for microeconometric evidence, above.

Effect of PMR on productivity and output growth

Several papers address the relationship between product market regulation and productivity or output growth. In an early contribution, Koedijk and Kremers (1996) find a negative cross-sectional relationship between per capita GDP growth or TFP growth and product market regulation in 11 European countries. More recently, using the economic freedom index published by the Fraser Institute and averaging data over five-year periods, Card and Freeman (2004) fail to find a significant effect of regulation on the level of output per capita (or per worker) or on its growth rate, once they control for year and country effects[33].

Nicoletti and Scarpetta (2003) provide the most detailed empirical contribution on this issue. They focus on the effect of regulation on total factor productivity growth, using cross-country data for several industrial sectors and including the regulatory variable directly in the productivity equation. Their approach is inspired by the contribution of Griffith, Redding, and Van Reenen (2003, 2004), who use an endogenous growth model to rationalize both a direct effect of R&D on growth through its effect on innovation creation, and an indirect one through the absorption of new technology. The importance of the indirect one depends positively upon the distance from the world frontier of each industry. The authors substitute R&D with their measure of product market regulation and also allow for a direct and indirect effect.[34]

The productivity measure is calculated for 17 manufacturing and six service industries for 18 OECD countries. Three sets of results are presented. In the first one the authors use the wide coverage, but time invariant country-level measures of liberalization collected by the OECD in 1998 (which is toward the end of their sample period). The regulation variables are not significant on their own in regressions that do not (cannot) include a country effect. They are significant when interacted with the technology gap in an equation that lacks country effect. The latter could have been used instead of the insignificant time invariant indicators, in order to make a more robust statement about the significance of the differential effect of regulation, depending upon the technology gap. The time invariant character of the indicators precludes an assessment of the significance of the total effect that is robust to unobserved country heterogeneity.

The time varying measures of privatization are introduced on their own and they tend to have a positive and significant effect on productivity growth. When a time varying economy-wide measure of liberalization that summarizes information about deregulation in seven service sectors is introduced, the privatization index becomes insignificant, while the time varying measure of regulation is significant and positive. The issue here is whether the regulatory reforms for the service sector can be used for the economy as a whole.

In another set of results, entry barriers and privatization are considered separately for the (aggregate) manufacturing sector and the (aggregate) service sector. The time varying measure of entry liberalization in manufacturing is based only on data on trade liberalization, while the one for the service sector is the summary measure of liberalization in the seven service industries. In that case, basically no significant direct or indirect effect can be detected. Only when liberalization in manufacturing is redefined as the average of trade liberalization and entry liberalization in nonmanufacturing, does one observe a significant direct positive effect of deregulation on TFP growth.

Finally, in the last set of results, the 1998 time invariant sector-specific OECD measures of liberalization are used together with time varying measures of entry liberalization for manufacturing and service industries (the former calculated again as the average of trade liberalization and entry liberalization in nonmanufacturing). The equations contain country, industry, and year dummies. The results suggest that entry liberalization in services has a positive effect on productivity growth. The only significant interaction is the one between entry liberalization in manufacturing and the technology gap. Privatization continues to have a positive direct effect on productivity growth.

Summarizing, there seems to be some evidence of a positive effect of privatization and entry liberalization on TFP growth. There is also evidence that entry barriers in manufacturing may affect the pace of technology absorption, especially for countries that lie away from the world frontier.

Additional evidence on the effect of regulation on per capita GDP growth for industrial countries is contained in chapter III of the IMF *World Economic Outlook* (2004), while the paper by Loayza, Oviedo, and Servén (2009a) is one of the very few that looks at the effect of regulation on the economic performance of a wide set of countries, including developing countries. The IMF study concentrates on 15 developed countries with a maximum of five observations on growth rates calculated over three-year averages. The estimated equation contains standard controls for cross-country growth regressions and a menu of structural policy indicators, including (present and lagged) values of the time varying average product market regulation indicator developed by the OECD for seven nonmanufacturing sectors, and average effective tax rates. The sample size is therefore small and the product market regulation indicator captures only a subset of the economy. The model is estimated by GMM dynamic panel data methods and suggests that both product market reform and trade reform have a positive and significant effect on growth, although it may take time for the full effects to be realized.

The main challenge when dealing with developing countries is the availability of detailed indices of product market regulation that reflect the cross-sectional and time variability of product market regulation, although some of them, such as tariff barriers, are available at annual frequency and the indices of the Fraser Institute at five-year intervals for many countries. The paper by Loayza et al. (2009a) focuses on time invariant indices constructed from information from the World Bank, the Heritage Foundation, and the Fraser Institute, and are meant to capture the fiscal burden and product market regulation, the latter a composite of entry, trade, financial markets, bankruptcy, and contract enforcement indices. An index of labor market regulation is also constructed.

The indices are used as regressors in standard cross-sectional average growth regressions for output per capita over the 1990s,

allowing their effect to depend on an index of the quality of governance. Their effect on output volatility is also considered. The inability to control for country-specific unobserved effects and the time
invariant nature of the indices over a period that witnessed substantial change is the main limit of the exercise. The effort made by the
authors to instrument for regulation itself and the fact that they
allow for an interaction with the quality of governance are two
attractive features, together with the focus on a sample that includes
developing countries. [35]

The results suggest a negative and significant direct effect of product (and labor) market regulation on growth, but the coefficient of
the interaction with governance is significant (except for the fiscal
burden index), and its sign suggests that better governance reduces
the negative effect of regulation. Actually, the size of the coefficients
is such that the overall effect of regulation is sizeable and negative for
most developing countries, while it is zero or even mildly positive for
countries having quality of governance similar to the United States
and the United Kingdom (and presumably other OECD countries).
The results for macroeconomic volatility are similar: regulation
increases volatility, but the effect is attenuated by good governance.

Note that these results on the interaction between regulation and
governance, which imply that only in countries with low levels of
governance there is a large, significant, and negative effect of regulation on productivity, contrast with the results, reviewed previously,
that support a positive effect of product market reform on growth
for industrial countries, that are likely to be characterized by better
governance.

Gorgens, Paldam, and Wurtz (2005) also investigate whether
there are significant nonlinearities in the effect of regulation on the
growth of GDP per capita, depending upon the level of income. They
use a panel of 123 countries for the period 1970–2000, divided in
seven five-year nonoverlapping periods and estimate by system-
GMM of a growth equation specified as a third-order Taylor series
expansion in lagged values of income and of the Fraser Institute
Economic Freedom Index. Results suggest that the effect of regulation is very different depending upon the level of income. For low-
income countries, regulation has no effect on growth. For middle-
income countries, there is a negative effect of regulation for low
values of regulation. For high values of regulation, there is no effect.
For high-income countries, the effect is monotonic: less regulation
generates more growth.

Let us focus now on the results for productivity growth in developed countries obtained by Griffith and Harrison (2004), using their
two-step approach, in which the intermediate link is the markup.

When the level or the growth rate of labor or total factor productivity in the business sector is regressed on the markup (the latter instrumented by the regulatory variables), a *positive* and significant effect of the markup on both the level and growth rate of productivity tend to be found. The conclusion that a higher markup has a mostly positive effect on productivity is not altered by allowing for nonlinear effects of the markup or by the direct inclusion of some regulation indices in the regression. Taken at face value, these results are consistent with the idea that monopoly rents provide the crucial incentive for productivity-enhancing innovative activity. An alternative explanation is that the new jobs created by deregulation are in lower productivity sectors. A third explanation is that the time period available for estimation does not allow one to capture the complexity of the relationship between markup and productivity. For instance, the new firms that enter following a reduction in regulation may be initially less productive than incumbent surviving firms, and it may take time for them to achieve higher levels of productivity. It is interesting to note that the positive relationship comes from the within variation in the data. If one does not include country dummies in the regression, allowing the between variation to play a role as well, the relationship between markup and productivity tends to become negative and significant.

Cincera and Galgau (2005) present results on the effect of entry and exit on output growth and labor productivity growth instrumented with regulation and other variables. Note that the coefficient of entry does not capture only the direct effect of entry on productivity, but also the indirect effect that entry has on the productivity of existing firms. There is some evidence at the 10 percent level that entry has a positive effect on labor productivity growth, while exit has a significant positive effect on it at the 5 percent level.

Loayza et al. (2009b) directly assess the relationship between various types of business regulations and sectoral labor productivity growth, using cross-country sector-level data (12 countries and 13 manufacturing sectors, to be precise). As a preliminary step, they examine the connection between those two variables and firm turnover. As we have already mentioned in the section on the transmission mechanism, they find that countries with more restrictive regulations tend to exhibit lower turnover rates. They also observe that in countries where turnover is larger, labor productivity growth is correspondingly higher, particularly its reallocation ("between" and "net-entry") components. Having provided support for the transmission mechanism (from regulation to turnover, and from turnover to productivity growth), they then assess the connection between regulation and productivity growth directly. They do so using a

Rajan-Zingales type of approach, assuming that regulations have a stronger effect on the productivity of sectors that normally require higher turnover. They find that, indeed, product market regulations have a negative effect on labor productivity growth. The adverse effect is stronger on the components of productivity growth that reflect reallocation of resources between firms than on the component that captures productivity growth within firms.

In general, there is little systematic evidence showing how regulatory changes in the product market affect different components of productivity growth and hence the channels through which regulatory reform may have enhanced aggregate productivity. This is obviously due to the necessity to have access to comprehensive firm-level data to distinguish between within, between, and entry/exit components. There is some evidence, however, on the effect of regulation on the component of aggregate productivity *levels*. Arnold, Nicoletti, and Scarpetta (2008) show for European countries that indices of product market regulation are significantly inversely related with a measure of allocative efficiency based on the relative importance of the cross term in the Olley and Pakes decomposition of the level of TFP, calculated at the country, sector-year level using the firm-level Amadeus data set.[36] This is particularly true for ICT-using sectors.

Moreover, Haltiwanger and Schweiger (2005), using the Investment Climate Assessment data set for developing and transition countries, show that an adverse business climate has a negative effect both on firm-level average firm productivity (TFP) and on allocative efficiency, measured as the cross product between percentage deviation of firm market shares from average market shares in the country and the deviation of firm-level productivity from average firm-level productivity. The composite business climate variable used as a regressor includes firm-level information about the time spent dealing with government regulation, the time it takes to get a telephone installed, bribes as a percentage of annual sales, perceptions about property rights and the legal system, and about labor market regulation as an obstacle to economic activity. The results hold also when the business climate perception variable is instrumented with country, size, and age, and for most of the individual components of the business climate index.[37]

In summary, most of the studies that include measures of regulation directly in the regression (alone or interacted) tend to find a negative effect of tighter regulation on total factor productivity or per capita output growth. These papers provide the more convincing support to the proposition that deregulation has a positive effect on productivity growth. However, studies that use the markup as the channel of transmission find that decreases in the markup associated with deregulation are associated with lower productivity growth (or level).[38] Controlling for the markup, there is no evidence of an additional positive direct effect of deregulation on productivity (in fact, sometimes the opposite is the case). The cross-sectional dimension of the data suggests that countries with higher markups have lower productivity growth rates, but one has to be aware that in this case we are not controlling for country effects other than their competitive environment. On balance, relying on turnover or entry as the variable through which the effect of deregulation is transmitted suggests a positive effect of lowering regulatory burdens on overall productivity growth.

The general conclusion that can be drawn at this point is that most, but not all, of the evidence points toward a positive effect of less stringent regulation on productivity growth. There is also evidence of nonlinearities in the effect of product market regulation on productivity growth, with the effect of deregulation being larger in more developed countries. On the other hand, better governance seems to mitigate the negative effects of regulation. Finally, it would be premature to draw definitive conclusions in this respect. More work is needed in order to understand how the effect of product market regulation on productivity growth is distributed between the within, between, and entry/exit components and how it affects measures of allocative efficiency based on the Olley-Pakes decomposition of aggregate productivity levels.

Summary and Conclusions

What are the overall lessons that can be derived from this review of the available cross-country evidence on the effect of product market regulation? We have certainly learned a lot from the recent econometric work in this area, but ambiguity remains for some of the issues.

There is considerable evidence that product market regulation that raises barriers to entry contributes to higher markups. Moreover, the results support the conclusion that regulatory barriers in the product market have a negative effect either on firm entry or turnover and are likely to slow the process of reallocation of resources.

As far as factor accumulation is concerned, the direct evidence and the indirect evidence via effects on the markup suggest a positive effect of product market deregulation on investment and employment. The result for investment is particularly important because new processes are often embodied in new capital goods and find their way into the economic systems through the investment process. The evidence tends to be stronger for the service sector, while for manufacturing there is no evidence of a positive (or for that matter, negative) effect, although that may be the result of a lack of adequate sector-specific and time varying measures of regulation. Entry does not seem to be a key channel through which changes in regulation affect the demand for labor and capital, although there is clear evidence that entry responds strongly to the regulatory climate. The effect of entry on the reallocation of factors of production requires additional investigation.

The cross-country studies do not support, at this stage, a strong positive effect of less stringent regulation on direct input measures of firms' innovative activities. Actually, the studies that use the markup as the transmission mechanism find that lower markups discourage innovation. However, this result is sensitive to the choice of the sample of countries used in estimation. There is, instead, some evidence that nontariff barriers have a negative effect on R&D. The results based on the markup are at odds with some recent micro-evidence for individual countries on the existence of an inverted U-shaped relationship between the markup and firms' innovative activities. Clearly, more work is needed to resolve the theoretical ambiguities concerning the effect of product market regulation on firms' innovative activity and to come to more definitive conclusions on this issue. Progress in this area depends upon the availability of cross-country data on firm's innovative activities that go beyond R&D spending; these would include patent counts, measures of firms' innovative investment, survey measures on the introduction of innovations, etc. It also requires a deeper understanding of how the nature of a country's industrial structure, the distance of a country from the technological frontier, the availability of human capital, and other initial conditions may lead to different results.

Finally, most of the studies that include measures of regulation directly in the regression (alone or interacted) tend to find a negative effect of tighter regulation on TFP or per capita output growth. This cross-country evidence is consistent with the microeconometric evidence that finds a positive and significant association between competition and productivity growth. These results are not confirmed by studies that use the markup as the channel of transmission, since in these cases a decreases in the markup following deregulation is associated with lower productivity growth (or level). Relying on entry or turnover as the variable through which the effect of deregulation is transmitted suggests a positive effect of lowering regulatory burdens on overall productivity growth, but more work is needed in order to understand exactly how that is distributed among the within, between, and entry/exit components. The general conclusion that can be drawn at this point is that most, although not all, of the evidence points toward a positive effect of less stringent regulation on productivity growth.

This result is very important on its own, but also has an interesting consequence on a macro variable that has not been the focus of our survey—namely, inflation. The faster rate of productivity growth associated with less stringent product market regulation reduces, ceteris paribus, inflationary pressure. In addition, if we consider the evidence that lower regulatory barriers lead to a smaller markup, it follows that regulatory reform may have favorable effects on inflation at short as well as longer horizons. Further systematic evidence on this issue would be very useful.[39]

An area in which further work is needed is the interaction between product market deregulation with the initial income level of income, the level of labor market regulation, the degree of financial development, and the general quality of governance in a country. Product market deregulation has been introduced in countries at different levels of development and with different institutions. Moreover, many countries have introduced reforms that affect not only the output market, but also the labor market and the financial sector. In this paper, we have discussed some evidence of nonlinearities and interesting interactions of product market regulation with labor market regulation and governance. There is evidence that the effect of product market deregulation on productivity growth is larger in more developed countries. On the other hand, there is also some evidence that better governance seems to mitigate the negative effects of regulation. Finally, some studies suggest that the positive employment effect of product market deregulation is stronger in countries with more regulated labor markets, but that product market deregulation may help in deregulating the labor market. However, more work is needed to come to definitive conclusions about how the effect of product market reform depends upon initial conditions and whether there are synergies in reform.

Notes

1. In some situations, for instance in the presence of natural monopolies, simple deregulation, as opposed to regulatory reform, will not necessarily lead to an increase in competition and in the efficiency of resource allocation.

2. The effect of labor market reform, captured by a decrease in workers' bargaining power in a Nash cooperative bargain, will lead to a decrease in

the real wage in the short run, but to an increase in employment and an unchanged real wage in the long run in the Blanchard and Giavazzi model.

3. For recent micro evidence on foreign competition and trade reform see Pavcnik (2002), Harrison and Revenga (1995), Harrison (1994), Levinsohn (1993). For cross-country evidence on trade liberalization see Rodriguez and Rodrik (2001), Vamvakidis (2002), and Yanikkaya (2003).

4. Cross sectional cross-country evidence supports the existence of a positive relationship between cumulated GDP losses and the stringency of regulation, controlling for the volatility of shocks affecting the economy, captured by the standard deviation of the terms of trade and of domestic inflation.

5. See also Holmstrom (1982), Nalebuff and Stiglitz (1983), and Mookherjee (1984).

6. See also Parente and Prescott (1994) who argue that the productivity gap across countries is due to excessive regulation that discourages the adoption of new technologies and protects poorly performing firms, thereby slowing the convergence to the world technology frontier.

7. In the endogenous growth models reviewed here, regulatory reform can be though of as increasing the price elasticity of demand, or decreasing the cost of entry (increasing the probability of entry), or decreasing the cost at which a competitive fringe can produce.

8. However, minor modifications to the cost of introducing an innovation could eliminate this scale effect (Jones (1999)).

9. See also Vives (2006) for a discussion of the effect of competition on innovation in a variety of models of imperfect competition. The paper makes the point that the theoretical predictions depend upon the measure of competitive pressure used (degree of product substitutability, ease of entry, number of competitors, market size), upon whether one considers markets with restricted (exogenous market structure) or free (endogenous) entry, and upon whether one focuses on product or process innovation. In markets with free entry, decreasing entry costs increases the number of firms (variety) but decreases R&D effort per firm finalized to cost reduction. However, typically total R&D effort increases. Increasing product substitutability tends to increase R&D effort per firm, but the number of varieties may decrease. In markets with restricted entry an increase in the number of firms tends to reduce R&D effort at the firm level, while increasing product substitutability tends to increase R&D effort.

10. See also Jaganathan and Srinivassan (2000) for a different way of testing the effect of competition on agency problems, based on the relationship between leverage and profits.

11. For evidence on the effect of the EU Single Market Program on markups and productivity, see also Gagnepain and Marin Uribe (2003), Goldberg and Verboven (2005) among others. See also Martins, Scarpetta and Pilat (1996) on markups in the OECD. For a review, see Ahn (2002), pp. 17-18, Ahn (2001), pp. 24-25, and Faini et al. (2005).

12. See Haltiwanger (2000) and Ahn (2001) for a review. In some decompositions, in addition to the "within", "between" and entry/exit components there is also a "cross" component.

13. See Heckman and Pages (2003) on the effect of labor market regulation in Latin America. See also Eslava, Haltiwanger, Kugler, and Kugler (2005) for evidence on the effect of factor market reform on employment adjustment, capital adjustment, and productivity using a panel of plants in Colombia.

14. See Ahn (2002) for a review. See also Geroski (1995)

15. See Cohen and Levin (1989).

16. See for instance Basu and Kimball (1997) on the problems in measuring productivity growth.

17. See Conway and Nicoletti (2006). See also Conway, Janod, and G. Nicoletti (2005) and Nicoletti, Scarpetta and Boylaud (1999) for economy-wide indicators of product market regulation.

18. See Nicoletti and Pryor (2006) for evidence that the OECD economy-wide indicators and the Fraser Institute indicators are highly correlated, in spite of the different methodology used in their construction.

19. See www.enterprisesurveys.org.

20. It also contains retrospective information for three years on basic balance sheet items.

21. See also Crafts (2006) for an overview of regulation and its effect on productivity.

22. See IMF's *World Economic Outlook*, 2004, ch. III "Fostering Structural Reforms in Industrial Countries."

23. A contemporaneous bad year increases labor market regulation, and past weak growth is associated with tighter financial regulation.

24. For instance, the data for firm demographics refer to the period 1997-2003 for most countries in Cincera and Galgau (2005), and to 1998 and 1999 in Klapper et al. (2004). In Loayza et al. (2009b) the period is somewhat longer for some countries, but not for others.

25. In the estimating equation, the author controls for lagged entry, capital, and R&D intensity as a measure of barrier to entry, and other market structure variables as a measure of opportunities, in addition to year, country, and sector effects. Note that the use of the within estimator even in a dynamic equation with short T is not appropriate.

26. Klapper et al. use the time-invariant measures on barrier to entry in Djankov et al. (2002). The equations contain also country, industry, size, and year effects. In one specification regulation is instrumented by country of origin, with no fundamental change to the results.

27. Loayza et al. construct time-invariant measures of regulation related to the areas of firm entry, bankruptcy, trade, finance, and judicial administration. The information is obtained from the World Bank, the Heritage Foundation, and the Fraser Institute. The statistics for firm demographics

and productivity for the various countries cover different subperiods of the 1980s and 1990s. The equations contain also industry effects. The paper also studies the effect of labor market regulation and fiscal burden.

28. The model allows for quadratic adjustment costs in capital.

29. See Nickell, Nunziata, and Oechel (2005) and Bassanini and Duval (2006) as an example of recent econometric work on the effects on unemployment/employment of labor market polices and institutions. Se also Blanchard and Wolfers (2000) for an emphasis on how labor market regulation influences the effect of macro shocks. For a critical discussion of standard ways to measure labor market regulation and for evidence for developing countries, see Heckman and Pages (2003). For a (particularly) critical assessment of the studies emphasizing the negative effect of protective labor market institutions see Howell, Baker, Glyn, and Schmidt (2007).

30. Griffith, Harrison, and McCartney (2007) and Amable, Demmou, and Gatti (2007) find that high labor market regulation enhances the effect of product market deregulation, while Bassanini and Duval (2006) and Berger and Danninger (2006) find the opposite.

31. Brandt (2004) also present correlation between entry and measures of economic performance, but given the endogeneity problem, it is difficult to figure out what to make of them.

32. Very recent empirical work conducted at the Institute for Fiscal Studies (still in a draft stage) confirms that the inclusion or exclusion of Scandinavian countries affects deeply the shape of the relationship between the markup and innovation. I thank R. Griffith for useful comments and information on this point.

33. The only significant effect is on employment growth.

34. Note that the results for the effect of regulation on productivity in Nicoletti and Scarpetta (2003) subsume and extend the ones in Scarpetta, Hemming, Tressel, and Woo (2002).

35. Legal origin, fraction of the population that speaks a major European language, and initial per capita GDP are used as instruments. The test of over-identifying restrictions does not suggest misspecification. Concerns about the power of such tests, however, should not be forgotten.

36. Remember that the cross term reflects the extent to which more efficient firms have greater market shares.

37. See also Galindo, Schiantarelli, and Weiss (2007) for micro evidence on the impact of financial reform on the efficiency of allocation of investment funds and Banerjee and Duflo (2005) for a general review of the causes and empirical evidence on resource misallocation

38. Note that higher markups are associated also with more R&D spending.

39. See Neiss (2001) for cross-sectional evidence on the relationship between the markup and inflation in OECD countries and Cavelaars (2002) for a cross-sectional analysis of the effect of product market regulation.

References

Aghion, P., N. Bloom, R. Blundell, R. Griffith, and P. Howitt. 2005. "Competition and Innovation: An Inverted U Relationship." *Quarterly Journal of Economics* May: 701–728.

Aghion, P., R. Blundell, R. Griffith, P. Howitt, and S. Prantl. 2006a. "The Effects of Entry on Incumbent Innovation and Productivity." Discussion Paper 5323, CEPR.

Aghion, P., R. Burgess, S. Redding, and F. Zilibotti. 2006b. "On the Unequal Effects of Liberalization: Evidence from Dismantling the License Raji in India." Discussion Paper 5492, CEPR.

Aghion, P., M. Dewatripoint, and P. Rey. 1999. "Competition, Financial Discipline and Growth." *Review of Economic Studies* 66: 825-852.

Aghion, P., and R. Griffith. 2005. *Competition and Growth; Reconciling Theory and Evidence.* Cambridge, MA: MIT Press.

Aghion, P., C. Harris, P. Howitt, and J. Vickers. 2001. "Competition, Imitation and Growth with Step-by-Step Innovation." *Review of Economic Studies* 68: 467–492.

Aghion, P., C. Harris, and J. Vickers. 1997. "Competition and Growth with Step-by-Step Innovation: An Example." *European Economic Review, Papers and Proceedings* 771–782.

Aghion, P., and P. Howitt. 1992. "A Model of Growth through Creative Destruction." *Econometrica* 60: 323–351.

Ahn, S. 2001. "Firm Dynamics and Productivity Growth: A Review of Micro Evidence from OECD Countries. Economics Department Working Paper 297, OECD, Paris.

———. 2002. "Competition, Innovation and Productivity Growth: A Review of Theory and Evidence." Economics Department Working Paper 317, OECD, Paris.

Alesina, A., S. Ardagna, G. Nicoletti, and F. Schiantarelli. 2005. "Regulation and Investment." *Journal of the European Economic Association* June: 1–35.

Amable, B., L. Demmou, and D. Gatti. 2007. "Employment Performance and Institutions: New Answers to an Old Question." IZA Discussion Paper 2731.

Arnold, J., G. Nicoletti, and S. Scarpetta. 2008. "Regulation, Allocative Efficiency and Productivity in OECD Countries: Industry and Firm-Level Evidence." Economics Department Working Paper 616, OECD, Paris.

Baily, M.N., C. Hulten, and D. Campbell. 1992. "Productivity Dynamics in Manufacturing Plants." *Brookings Papers on Economic Activity: Microeconomics* 187–249.

Banerjee, A., and E. Duflo. 2005. "Growth Theory through the Lens of Development Economics." In *Handbook of Economic Growth*, Vol. 1A, ed. P. Aghion and S. Durlauf. North Holland, Amsterdam.

Bartelsman, E.J, J. Haltiwanger, and S. Scarpetta. 2004a. "Microeconomic Evidence of Creative Destruction in Industrial and Developing Countries." Discussion Paper TI 20004-114/3, Tinbergen Institute.

———. 2004b. "Microeconomic Evidence of Creative Destruction in Industrial and Developing Countries." World Development Report background paper, World Bank, Washington, DC.

Bassanini A., and R. Duval. 2006. "Employment Patterns in OECD Countries: Reassessing the Role of Policies and Institutions." Economics Department Working Paper 486, OECD, Paris.

Bassanini, A., and E. Ernst. 2002. "Labor Market Institutions, Product Market Regulation, and Innovation: Cross-Country Evidence." Economics Department Working Paper (2002) 2, OECD, Paris.

Basu, S., and M. Kimball. 1997. "Cyclical Productivity with Unobserved Input Variation." Working Paper 5915, NBER, Cambridge, MA.

Berger H., and S. Danninger. 2006. "The Employment Effects of Labor and Product Market Deregulation and their Implications for Structural Reforms." Working Paper 1709, CESifo.

Bergoeing, R., N. Loayza, and A. Repetto. 2004. "Slow Recoveries." *Journal of Development Economics* 75: 473–506. (Also reprinted in this volume.)

Bernard, A.B., J. Eaton, J.B. Jensen, and S. Kortum. 2003. "Plants and Productivity in International Trade." *American Economic Review* 93(4): 1268–1290.

Blanchard, O., and F. Giavazzi. 2003. "Macroeconomic Effects of Regulation and Deregulation in Goods and Labor Markets." *Quarterly Journal of Economics* 118: 1369–1413.

Blundell, R., R. Griffith, and J. Van Reenen. 1999. "Market Share, Market Value and Innovation in a Panel of British Manufacturing Firms." *Review of Economic Studies* 66: 529–554.

Bottasso, A., and A. Sembenelli. 2001. "Market Power, Productivity, and the EU Single Market Program: Evidence from a Panel of Italian Firms." *European Economic Review* 45(1): 167–186.

Brandt, N. 2004. "Business Dynamics, Regulation, and Performance." Directorate for Science Technology and Industry Working Paper 2004/3, OECD, Paris.

Caballero, R., and M. Hammour. 1994. "The Cleansing Effects of Recessions." *American Economic Review* 84(5): 1356–1368.

———. 1996. "On the Timing and Efficiency of Creative Destruction." *Quarterly Journal of Economics* 111(3): 805–852.

———. 1998. "The Macroeconomics of Specificity." *Journal of Political Economy* 106: 724–767.

Card, D., and R. Freeman. 2004. "What Have Two Decades of British Economic Reform Delivered?" Working Paper 8801, NBER, Cambridge, MA.

Cavelaars, P. 2002. "Does Competition Enhancement have Permanent Inflation Effects?" DNB Staff Reports 92/2002.

Cincera, M., and O. Galgau. 2005. "Impact of Market Entry and Exit on EU Productivity and Growth Performance." Economic Papers 222, February, European Economy, European Commission, Directorate General Economic and Financial Affairs.

Cohen W.M., and R. Levin. 1989. "Empirical Studies of Innovation and Market Structure." In Handbook of Industrial Organization, Vol. II, ed. R. Schmalensee and R.D. Willig. North Holland, Amsterdam.

Conway, P., J. Janod, and G. Nicoletti. 2005. "Product Market Regulation in OECD Countries: 1998 to 2003." Economics Department Working Paper 419, OECD, Paris.

Conway, P., and G. Nicoletti. 2006. "Product Market Regulation in the Non-manufacturing Sectors of OECD Countries." Economics Department Working Paper 530, OECD, Paris.

Crafts, N. 2006. "Regulation and Productivity Performance." Oxford Review of Economic Policy 22(2): 186–201.

Disney, R., J. Haskel, and Y. Heden. 2000. "Restructuring and Productivity Growth in UK Manufacturing." Discussion Paper 2463, May, CEPR.

Djankov, S., R. La Porta, F. Lopes de Silanes, and A. Shleifer. 2000. "The Regulation of Entry." Quarterly Journal of Economics February: 1–37.

Eslava, M., J. Haltiwanger, A. Kugler, and M. Kugler. 2005. "Employment and Capital   Adjustment after Factor Market Deregulation: Panel Evidence from Colombian Plants." Unpublished, World Bank, Washington, DC.

Faini, R., J. Haskel, G. Barba Navaretti, C. Scarpa, and C. Wey. 2005. "Contrasting   Europe's Decline: Do Product Market Reforms Help?" Unpublished.

Fiori, G., G. Nicoletti, and S. Scarpetta. 2007. "Employment Outcomes and the Interaction between Product and Labor Market Deregulation: Are they Substitutes or Complements?" Department of Economics Working Paper 663, Boston College, Boston, MA.

Foster, L., J. Haltiwanger, and C.J. Krizan. 2001. "Aggregate Productivity Growth: Lessons from Microeconomic Evidence." In New Developments in Productivity Analysis, ed. E. Dean, M. Harper, and C. Hulten. Chicago, University of Chicago Press.

Fraser Institute. 2002. Economic Freedom of the World: 2002 Annual Report.

Gagnepain P., and P.L. Marin Uribe. 2003. "Competition and Efficiency in European Aviation." Unpublished, Universidad Carlos III de Madrid.

Galindo, A., F. Schiantarelli, and A. Weiss. 2007. "Does Financial Reform Improve the
Allocation of Investment? Micro Evidence from Developing Countries." Journal of Development Economics 83: 562–587.

Geroski, P. 1995. *Market Structure, Corporate Performance and Innovative Activity*. Oxford: Oxford University Press.

Goldberg, P., and F. Verboven. 2005. "Market Integration and Convergence to the Law of One Price: Evidence from the European Car Market." *Journal of International Economics* 65(1): 49–73.

Gorgens, T., M. Paldam, and A. Wurtz. 2005. "Growth, Income and Regulation: A Non-linear Approach." CAM Working Paper 2005–12, University of Copenhagen.

Green, R., and J. Haskel. 2003. "Seeking a Premier League Economy: The Role of Privatisations." In *Seeking a Premier League Economy*, ed. R. Blundell, D. Card, and R. Freeman. Chicago: University of Chicago Press.

Griffith, R., and R. Harrison. 2004. "The Link between Product Market Reform and Macro-economic Performance." Economic Papers 209, August, European Economy, European Commission, Directorate-General for Economic and Financial Affairs.

Griffith, R., R. Harrison, and G. McCartney. 2007. "Product Market Reforms, Labor Market Institutions and Unemployment." *The Economic Journal* 117(519), March: C142–C166(1).

Griffith R., S. Redding, and J. Van Reenen. 2003. "R&D and Absorptive Capacity: From Theory to Evidence." *Scandinavian Journal of Economics* 105(1): 99–118.

———. 2004. "Mapping the Two Faces of R&D: Productivity Growth in a Panel of OECD Manufacturing Industries." *Review of Economics and Statistics* 86(4), November: 883–895.

Grilliches, Z., and H. Regev. 1995. "Firm Productivity in Israeli Industry: 1979–1988." *Journal of Econometrics* 65: 175–203.

Grossman G.M., and E. Helpman. 1991. "Quality Ladders in the Theory of Growth." *Review of Economic Studies* 58(1): 43–61.

Hall, R.E. 1986. "Market Structure and Macroeconomic Fluctuations." *Brookings Papers on Economic Activity* 2: 285–322.

———. 1988. "The Relation between Price and Marginal Cost in U.S. Industry." *Journal of Political Economy* 96(5): 921–947.

Haltiwanger, J. 2000. "Aggregate Growth: What Have We Learned from Microeconomic Evidence?" Economics Department Working Paper 7741, OECD, Paris.

Haltiwanger, J., and H. Schweiger. 2005. "Allocative Efficiency and the Business Climate." Unpublished, University of Maryland, College Park, MD.

Harrison, A.E. 1994. "Productivity, Imperfect Competition and Trade Reform: Theory and Evidence." *Journal of International Economics* 36: 53–73.

Harrison, A.E., and A. Revenga. 1995. "The Effects of Trade Policy Reform: What Do We Really Know?" Working Paper 5225, NBER, Cambridge, MA.

Hart, O. 1983. "The Market Mechanism as an Incentive Scheme." *Bell Journal of Economics* 14, Autumn: 366–382.

Heckman, J., and C. Pages. 2003. "Law and Employment: Lessons from Latin America and the Caribbean." Working Paper 10129, NBER, Cambridge, MA.

Holmstrom, B. 1982. "Managerial Incentive Problems—A Dynamic Perspective." In *Essays in Economics and Management in Honour of Lars Wahlbeck*. Swedish School of Economics.

Howell, D.R., D. Baker, A. Glyn, and J. Schmitt. 2007. "Are Protective Labor Market Institutions at the Root of Unemployment? A Critical Review of the Evidence." *Capitalism and Society* 2(1): 1–71.

Hsieh, C.T., and P. Klenow. 2006. "Misallocation and Manufacturing TFP in China and India." Unpublished. University of California at Berkeley.

IMF (International Monetary Fund). 2004. *World Economic Outlook*, Ch. III, "Fostering Structural Reforms in Industrial Countries." April: 103–146.

Jagannathan, R., and S. Srinivasan. 2000. "Does Product Market Competition Reduce Agency Costs?" Working Paper 7480, NBER, Cambridge, MA.

Jones, C. 1999. "Growth with or without Scale Effects?" *American Economic Review Papers and Proceedings* 89, May: 139–144.

Klapper, L., L. Laeven, and R.G. Rajan. 2004. "Business Environment and Firm Entry: Evidence from International Data." Working Paper 10380, NBER, Cambridge, MA.

Klette, T.J. 1999. "Market Power, Scale Economies and Productivity: Estimates from a Panel of Establishment Data." *Journal of Industrial Economics* 47(4): 451–476.

Koedijk, K., and J. Kremers. 1996. "Deregulation: A Political Economy Analysis." *Economic Policy* October: 445–467.

Levinsohn, J. 1993. "Testing the Imports as Market Discipline Hypothesis." *Journal of International Economics* 35: 1–22.

Loayza, N.V., A.M. Oviedo, and L. Servén. 2009a. "Regulation and Macroeconomic Performance across the World." This volume.

———. 2009b. "Regulation and Microeconomic Dynamics." This volume.

Martins, J., S. Scarpetta, and D. Pilat. 1996. "Mark-up Ratios in Manufacturing Industries: Estimates for 14 OECD Countries." Working Paper 162, OECD, Paris.

Melitz, M. 2003. "The Impact of Trade on Intra-industry Reallocations and Aggregate Industry Productivity." *Econometrica* 71(6), November: 1695–1725.

Melitz, M., and S. Polanec. 2008. "Dynamic Olley-Pakes Decomposition with Entry and Exit." Unpublished, Princeton University, Princeton, NJ.

Mookherjee, D. 1984. "Optimal Incentive Schemes with Many Agents." *Review of Economic Studies* 51, July: 433–446.

Moulton, B.R. 1990. "An Illustration of the Pitfall in Estimating the Effects of Aggregate Variables on Micro Units." *Review of Economics and Statistics* 72(2): 334–338.

Nalebuff, B., and J. Stiglitz. 1983. "Information, Competition and Markets." *American Economic Review* 73: 278–283.

Neiss, K.S. 2001. "The Markup and Inflation: Evidence in OECD Countries." *Canadian Journal of Economics* 34(2): 570–587.

Nickell, S. 1996. "Competition and Corporate Performance." *Journal of Political Economy* 104: 724–746.

Nickell, S., D. Nicolitas, and N. Dryden. 1997. "What Makes Firms Perform Well?" *European Economic Review* 41: 725–796.

Nickell, S., L. Nunziata, and W. Ochel. 2005. "Unemployment in the OECD since the 1960's: What Do We Know?" *The Economic Journal* 115(500), January: 1–27.

Nicoletti, G., and F. Pryor. 2006. "Subjective and Objective Measures of Governmental Regulations in OECD Nations." *Journal of Economic Behaviour and Organization* 59(3): 433–449.

Nicoletti, G., and S. Scarpetta. 2003. "Regulation, Productivity and Growth: OECD Evidence." *Economic Policy* 18(36): 11–72.

Nicoletti, G., S. Scarpetta, and O. Boylaud. 1999. "Summary Indicators of Product Market Regulation with an Extension to Employment Protection Legislation." Economics Department Working Paper 226, OECD, Paris.

Olley, G.S., and A. Pakes. 1996. "The Dynamics of Productivity in the Telecommunications Equipment Industry." *Econometrica* 64:6: 1263–1297.

Parente, S., and E. Prescott. 1994. "Barriers to Technology Adoption and Development." *Journal of Political Economy* 102(2): 298–321.

Pavcnik, N. 2002. "Trade Liberalization, Exit and Productivity Improvements: Evidence from Chilean Plants." *Review of Economic Studies* 69: 245–276.

Restuccia, D., and R. Rogerson. 2003. "Policy Distortions and Aggregate Productivity with Heterogeneous Plants." Unpublished, University of Toronto.

Rodriguez, F., and D. Rodrik. 2001. "Trade Policy and Economy Growth; A Skeptic's Guide to the Cross-national Evidence." In *Microeconomics Annual 2000*, ed. B. Bernanke and K.S. Rogoff. Cambridge, MA: MIT Press for NBER.

Romer, P. 1990. "Endogenous Technical Change." *Journal of Political Economy* 98(5), Part 2: "The Problem of Development": S71–S102.

Scarpetta, S., P. Hemmings, T. Tressel, and J. Woo. 2002. "The Role of Policy and Institutions for Productivity and Firm Dynamics: Evidence from Micro and Industry Data." Economics Department Working Paper (2002)15, OECD, Paris.

Scharfstein, D. 1988. "Product Market Competition and Managerial Slack." *Rand Journal of Economics* Spring: 147–155.

Schmidt, K. 1997. "Managerial Incentives and Product Market Competition." *Review of Economic Studies* 64(2): 191–213.

Schumpeter, J.A. 1942. *Capitalism, Socialism and Democracy.* New York: Harper and Brothers.

Srivastava, V. 1996. *Liberalization, Productivity and Competition.* Delhi: Oxford University Press.

Vamvakidis, A. 2002. "How Robust is the Growth-Openness Connection? Historical Evidence." *Journal of Economic Growth* 7(1), March: 57–80.

Wooldridge, J.M. 2003. "Cluster-Sample Methods in Applied Econometrics." *American Economic Review, Papers and Proceedings* 93(2): 133–138.

World Bank. "Doing Business Database." Available at http://www.doing-business.org.

Yanikkaya, H. 2003. "Trade Openness and Economic Growth: A Cross-Country Empirical Investigation." *Journal of Development Economics* 72, October: 57–89.

3

Regulation and Macroeconomic Performance

Norman V. Loayza, Ana María Oviedo, and Luis Servén

Introduction

Regulation of goods and factor markets is enacted purportedly to serve specific social purposes. The rationale for regulation is provided by the existence of market failures arising from informational asymmetries, economies of scale in production, incomplete markets, and externalities. Under such circumstances, economic agents may not fully internalize the social costs and benefits of their actions, and adequate market regulation can raise social welfare.

This research has been supported by the World Bank's Latin America Regional Studies Program and the Poverty Reduction and Economic Management Network. We are very grateful to Raphael Bergoeing, Caroline Freund, John Haltiwanger, Patricia Macchi, Andrea Repetto, Roberto Zagha, and participants in the EGDI-WIDER Conference on the Informal Sector (Helsinki, 2004) and seminars at the IMF and the World Bank for useful comments and data. The views expressed herein are those of the authors and do not necessarily represent those of the institutions to which they are affiliated.

However, this presumes that the actions of the regulatory author-
ity are solely motivated by the public interest. In reality, regulation
obeys a more complex political economy process, where legitimate
social goals may become entangled with the objectives of particular
interest groups concerning the level and distribution of rents. As a
result, regulation may be biased in favor of special interests, a view
stressed by the "regulatory capture" literature (e.g., Laffont 1999,
Newbery 1999). It may also become hostage to "political capture,"
which distorts the regulatory goals to pursue political ends (Stiglitz
1998).

The effects of regulation on aggregate economic performance
have attracted increasing attention in recent years in both industrial
and developing countries. According to a commonly held view,
excessive regulation is the prime cause of Europe's macroeconomic
underperformance over the last decade vis-à-vis the United States
(see Blanchard 2004). Likewise, intricate regulation and its arbitrary
enforcement are listed by the World Bank (2004) among the key
obstacles to growth in many developing countries.

Regulation can be thought of as a set of rules that constrain the
actions of economic agents in (true or purported) pursuance of social
goals. The effects of regulation on aggregate economic performance
arise from the action of such constraints. Those effects may take a
variety of forms, as described in the preceding chapter for the case
of product market regulation. Broadly speaking, regulation may
affect the (static) efficiency of resource allocation across firms and
industries, and this may have sizeable consequences for aggregate
productivity, as found for example by Hsieh and Klenow (2007) in
the cases of China and India. Regulation may also affect within-firm
efficiency by changing firms' exposure to competitive pressure in
input and output markets. Last, regulation can impact on aggregate
growth by changing the incentives for process and product innovation—and thus productivity growth—as well as capital accumulation and job creation.

Recent empirical literature has examined the impact of various
kinds of regulation on GDP growth through its proximate determinants—total factor productivity, investment, and employment—
finding for the most part negative effects. Much of this literature was
surveyed in chapter 2, so we shall mention only a few relevant studies here.[1] Among them, Nicoletti and Scarpetta (2003) find that
product market regulation lowers multifactor productivity growth
in OECD countries, while Bassanini and Ernst (2002) report a negative effect of regulation on innovation, as measured by R&D spending. However, Griffith and Harrison (2004) report the opposite
result. As for productive inputs, Alesina et al. (2005) find that prod-

uct market regulations have a negative effect on private investment in OECD economies. In turn, Nicoletti et al. (2001a, b) provide empirical evidence that anticompetitive regulation reduces employment in a panel of industrial countries, while in CEPR-IFS (2003) increased product market competition encouraged by deregulation raises both investment and employment in a panel data set covering OECD countries.[2] Regarding labor regulation, Blanchard and Wolfers (2000) and Heckman and Pagés (2000) find that hiring and firing restrictions discourage employment creation in European and Latin American economies, respectively. In turn, Haltiwanger, Scarpetta, and Schweiger (2006) document empirically the negative impact of labor market regulation on job creation and destruction at the firm level in 16 industrial and developing countries. Moreover, simulations for OECD economies suggest that the effects of output and labor regulation on aggregate investment and employment growth are quantitatively considerable (Bayoumi, Laxton, and Pesenti 2004).

A few empirical studies tackle the impact of regulation and deregulation on aggregate growth in a cross-country setting. Koedijk and Kremers (1996) find a negative association between measures of product market regulation and GDP growth among 11 European countries. In contrast, they find that labor regulations have no significant association with growth performance. Dutz and Hayri (1999) apply extreme-bounds analysis to estimate the contribution to growth of a variety of (mostly subjective) regulation and competition indicators in a sample of industrial and developing countries. They find significant effects of measures of antitrust policy and the average age of large firms (taken as proxy for entry and exit barriers). However, Card and Freeman (2002) fail to find any significant association between subjective measures of economic regulation and growth performance in a panel regression covering OECD countries over 1970–99.

In this chapter we present a comprehensive empirical assessment of the macroeconomic effects of regulation in a large sample of industrial and developing countries. We focus on two key measures of macroeconomic performance, namely, the growth and volatility of real GDP. Our empirical strategy relies on the inclusion of suitable indicators of regulation into simple empirical equations relating these aggregate performance measures to standard control variables taken from the macroeconomics and growth literature. While we do not characterize the specific channel through which the aggregate impact of regulation unfolds—a task pursued in later chapters in this volume— our approach allows us to obtain a summary measure of the magnitude of such impact that combines the action of the various intervening mechanisms—factor reallocation, capital accumulation, competition, and innovation—considered in the literature.

The paper extends the literature along four dimensions. First, we provide a broad characterization of business regulation around the world. Drawing from a variety of data sources, we build a set of synthetic indicators capturing the regulations that firms face in the multiple dimensions of their activity: entry and exit, trade, taxes, contract enforcement, labor, and finance. Using this information, we document the stylized facts of regulation across the world, regarding the extent of regulation in different countries, its relation with per-capita income, and the observed relationship between different types of regulation.

Second, unlike the existing literature on the macroeconomic impact of regulation, which has focused almost exclusively on aggregate growth or its proximate determinants, we also examine the effect of regulation on aggregate volatility. This is of independent interest for several reasons. On the one hand, recent literature suggests that excessive regulation can lead to microeconomic inflexibility (Caballero, Engel, and Micco 2004). This tends to hamper the economy's ability to absorb shocks requiring microeconomic reallocation, thus amplifying their aggregate impact. In particular, factor market rigidities may exacerbate volatility by impeding the redeployment of inputs across firms and industries in response to microeconomic and sector-specific disturbances (Loayza and Raddatz 2007). On the other hand, certain kinds of product market regulations—such as those on entry and exit—act as barriers to firm creation and destruction and might have the opposite effect, attenuating cyclical output fluctuations. Hence, the impact of regulation on volatility is a priori ambiguous, and can be established only empirically. To our knowledge, this is the first paper addressing this issue.

Third, we take into account the fact that the effects of regulation are likely to depend not only on the quantity of regulation, but also on its quality. There are good reasons for this. On analytical grounds, certain types of regulations—such as those designed to enhance competition in goods or financial markets—should be expected to exert beneficial effects, rather than adverse ones, on economic performance.[3] More generally, countries with better institutions tend to create regulatory environments genuinely aimed to improve business conditions rather than bestow privilege on a few interest groups. They are also more likely to enforce regulation in a transparent and even-handed manner, limiting the regulator's margin for arbitrariness and corruption that can place many firms at a disadvantage, sometimes forcing them to operate in the informal sector.[4] All of these arguments suggest that the quality of regulation is likely to be closely related to overall quality of governance, and thus in our experiments we use standard governance indicators to capture regulatory quality. [5]

Fourth, our empirical approach also allows for the possibility that aggregate performance may itself be one of the factors weighing on policy makers' decisions to adopt regulatory measures. Low growth or excessive macroeconomic volatility may make it more likely for the authorities to introduce or tighten regulation, e.g., adopting strict labor regulations or raising firm exit barriers in the hope of containing job and output losses in downswings. Thus, any observed association between regulation and macroeconomic performance could reflect causality from the latter to the former rather than (or in addition to) the reverse. To attempt to capture the causal effect of regulations on growth and volatility, we also report empirical results from instrumental variable estimations.

Before proceeding, we should note one important caveat of our analysis. Our objective is limited to studying the macroeconomic consequences of regulation. In this chapter we do not intend to evaluate the success of specific regulations at meeting their stated objectives, nor do we pretend to judge the impact of regulation on social welfare dimensions beyond the influence of economic growth and volatility.

The remainder of this chapter is organized as follows. The next section describes the synthetic regulation indicators and presents some stylized facts concerning the patterns of regulation across industrial and developing countries. The following section reports estimates of the impact of regulation on growth and aggregate volatility, and the final section offers some concluding remarks.

Business Regulation around the World

We now turn to a description of the nature and extent of business regulation around the world. In this section, we first give an account of the areas of economic activity on which we focus and describe how we measure regulation in each of them. Next, we discuss differences in regulation intensity across regions of the world and give a preview of the overall relationship between regulation and macroeconomic variables.

A typology of regulation

Our departure point is the assumption that the macroeconomic impact of business regulation arises from its effects on the creation, growth, and renewal of firms. Therefore, we select the relevant areas of business regulation by looking for them at the three stages of the life of a firm: entry, growth, and exit. In most countries, all three are regulated to some degree. For instance, in virtually all countries entrepreneurs need to follow a number of procedures to start a firm, but the burden of the administrative process varies widely across countries.[6] Once a firm is legally registered and allowed to operate, its decisions are conditioned by regulations on hiring and firing workers, taxes, safety standards, environmental regulations, interest rate controls, trade barriers, legal procedures, etc.[7] Finally, a firm going out of business must again follow a sometimes costly and lengthy procedure.

How does regulation alter firm renewal?

Regulation certainly affects firms' decisions, but does it improve the conditions for their activities or, on the contrary, does it impose unnecessary restrictions that increase costs and reduce productivity? Although we do not rule out the first option, we should recognize the potentially distorting effects of regulation on firms' decisions and ultimately on macro performance. Moreover, the answer to this question may well vary across different types of regulation.[8] In this section, we consider seven main areas of a firm's activity that are subject to regulation: entry, exit, labor markets, fiscal burden, international trade, financial markets, and contract enforcement; for each area, we construct an index of the severity of regulation. Rather than restricting our measures of regulation strictly to legal directives, we want to account for the practical restrictions and complications brought about by certain rules. The regulation of entry index, for example, aims at capturing the actual difficulty an entrepreneur faces to start a business, from a legal perspective as well as in practice. The index of bankruptcy regulation should reflect the speed and efficiency of the process to close down a firm. With the labor market regulation index, we want to measure how difficult it is for a firm to adjust its labor force. The index of fiscal regulation aims at measuring the burden to firms imposed by taxation and fiscal spending. With the trade regulation index we look at how much countries selectively protect domestic producers. The financial markets regulation index should capture the extent of credit restrictions and preferential interest rates that may distort a firm's access to capital markets. Last, the judicial administration index measures the hurdles and red tape facing firms that turn to their countries' justice system and its bureaucracy, in general, to resolve legal disputes and enforce contracts.

Measuring regulation

We use five data sources for the construction of our indices: Doing Business (The World Bank Group), Index of Economic Freedom (The Heritage Foundation), Economic Freedom of the World (The Fraser Institute), The Corporate Tax Rates Survey (KPMG), and International Country Risk Guide (The PRS Group). These sources cover the largest number of countries and areas under regulation, and their measures are straightforward and are derived from clear methodologies. All sources are public. Our sample covers 75 countries.[9] Complete details are provided in annex 3.1.

In most cases, data are based on surveys conducted in a single year (in the late 1990s) in a large group of countries; for components with observations for more than one year, we use average values over the period. Therefore, our indices best represent average regulation levels in the late 1990s. We should note, however, that regulation tends to stay constant over long periods of time.[10]

Each index measures the intensity of the regulatory system on a scale from 0 to 1 (1 representing the heaviest regulation). To combine the components of each index, each component is standardized according to the formula:

$$\frac{X_i - X_{min}}{X_{max} - X_{min}} , \text{ if higher values of } X \text{ indicate heavier regulation, and}$$

$$\frac{X_{max} - X_i}{X_{max} - X_{min}} , \text{ if lower values of } X \text{ indicate heavier regulation}$$

The availability of different regulation datasets with ample country coverage offers a rich and detailed source of regulation indicators for a large number of countries. This notwithstanding, the dataset is not complete for all indicators, which poses the issue of dealing with missing values. For most individual regulatory indicators, the number of missing data points is fairly small, but the result from combining them all is the loss of a substantial number of observations.[11] In order to retain a sufficiently large sample size for econometric estimation, we decided not to discard country observations if they were missing only a few indicators. Instead, to fill in the gaps, we applied an imputation procedure that estimates a missing value as the projection of related indicators.[12] We then obtained an index of regulation for each area of business activity outlined above by averaging the indicators of the same category/activity. When we discuss the robustness of the results to alternative specifications (at the end of the section on regulation and macroeconomic performance, below), we will consider the possibility of using only the sample of countries with complete (nonimputed) data.

The *entry* regulation index combines the number of legal steps required to register a new business with an indicator of the overall legal burden of registration and willingness of the government to facilitate the process and intervene minimally. The index of *labor* regulation combines indicators of the presence of a minimum wage, the flexibility of hiring and firing laws, the unionization rate, the amount of unemployment benefits, the use of conscription in the military, and minimum mandatory working conditions. The index of *fiscal* regulation measures direct taxation—that is, the maximum tax rate applied to individuals and businesses—and the volume of fiscal spending. The index of *trade* regulation combines indicators of average tariffs, other import barriers, and the cost of importing generated by mandatory administrative procedures (e.g., license fees, bank fees, etc.). The index of *financial markets* regulation measures the degree of government intervention through interest rate controls, ownership of banks, entry barriers, restrictions in securities markets, and constraints on foreign banks. The index of *judicial administration* combines a measure of the complexity of court procedures with a measure of bureaucracy's red tape for policy formulation and routine administrative functions. Finally, the index of *bankruptcy* regulation combines measures of the time and cost of the liquidation procedure, the enforcement of priority of claims, the extent to which an efficient outcome is achieved, and the degree of court involvement in the process.

We should note that the resulting indices, as well as their components, do not provide full information about the quality of regulation; in particular, they do not reflect completely either the extent to which regulation corrects for market failures or the political and social context in which regulation is implemented. These distinctions are important because, as already noted, the economic impact of regulation may be dependent on institutional country characteristics.[13] We will return to this issue in the econometric section of the paper.

Regulation around the world

How do entry, growth, and exit regulations vary across world regions? Although governments oversee and extract revenues from business activities in all countries (and quite heavily in many), there is considerable variation in the intensity of regulation across regions. Table 3.1 presents the summary statistics of the seven indices mentioned above. Industrial countries tend to adopt heavy fiscal regulation, medium labor regulation, and low regulation in trade, financial markets, entry, bankruptcy, and judicial administration. The developing world cannot be characterized as simply as the OECD, as it shows varying regulation patterns across regions. For example, with respect to the OECD, labor regulation is slightly lower in Asia and in Sub-Saharan Africa, while it is higher in Latin America and the Middle East. Fiscal regulation is also typically lower in developing regions, but here again differences across regions are substantial, from about 5 percent below the OECD average in the Middle East to more than 30 percent below it in Latin America. Regarding the remaining areas, all developing regions tend to have heavier regulations than OECD countries, and we find the largest gap in trade regulation, where developing countries show values roughly three times higher than those of the OECD.

Which countries regulate the most? OECD countries rank highest in fiscal regulation: Belgium ranks number one; Italy number two; and France is number three. The country with the lowest fiscal-regulation score in our sample is Paraguay. OECD countries do not have high labor regulation on average, but they do exhibit substantial dispersion, so that over the entire sample, Portugal has the highest labor-regulation score, while the United States has the lowest. In the remaining areas, OECD countries always occupy the bottom of the distribution. For instance, The Netherlands has the lowest score in financial regulation, Finland in bankruptcy and trade, Australia in judicial administration, and Canada in entry regulation. The harshest regulatory environments are in the Republic of Congo (judicial administration), Haiti (entry), the Islamic Republic of Iran and the Syrian Arab Republic (financial markets), Nigeria (trade), and the Philippines (bankruptcy).

Table 3.2 shows simple correlations between the regulation indices. The strongly positive correlations among all but the fiscal and labor indices suggest that regulation policy comes in "packages." Judging from these correlations, we can distinguish three regulation categories: "product market," which includes the entry, trade, financial markets, bankruptcy, and judicial administration indices; labor; and fiscal.[14] The product-market regulation index is computed as the simple average of the scores of these components. We also compute an "overall" regulation index by averaging the scores of all seven indices.

The arrangement of the regulation indices into these three groups receives additional statistical support from factor analysis. The first three principal components obtained from factor analysis of the seven basic indices explain, respectively, 56 percent, 15 percent, and 11 percent of their overall variance. These principal components

Table 3.1: Summary Statistics of Regulation Indices
by Region

Indicator	No. obs.	Mean	Std. dev.	Min	Max
Africa					
Entry	16	0.59	0.18	0.24	0.95
Financial markets	16	0.52	0.11	0.33	0.70
Judicial	16	0.58	0.21	0.29	1.00
Trade	16	0.73	0.16	0.42	1.00
Labor	16	0.45	0.20	0.16	0.73
Fiscal	16	0.45	0.14	0.26	0.70
Bankruptcy	16	0.66	0.17	0.42	0.97
Product market	16	0.69	0.16	0.40	0.91
Overall	16	0.72	0.17	0.44	1.00
Governance	16	0.30	0.14	0.09	0.53
East Asia and Pacific					
Entry	6	0.41	0.16	0.22	0.68
Financial markets	6	0.38	0.07	0.26	0.46
Judicial	6	0.39	0.13	0.28	0.64
Trade	6	0.54	0.22	0.36	0.95
Labor	6	0.44	0.30	0.03	0.69
Fiscal	6	0.30	0.08	0.22	0.42
Bankruptcy	6	0.66	0.22	0.36	1.00
Product market	6	0.52	0.12	0.37	0.66
Overall	6	0.53	0.13	0.33	0.68
Governance	6	0.43	0.14	0.22	0.64
Latin America and the Caribbean					
Entry	21	0.53	0.20	0.22	1.00
Financial markets	21	0.42	0.18	0.10	0.79
Judicial	21	0.66	0.20	0.29	0.96
Trade	21	0.60	0.18	0.25	0.93
Labor	21	0.68	0.22	0.23	0.96
Fiscal	21	0.24	0.15	0.00	0.49
Bankruptcy	21	0.61	0.18	0.22	0.87
Product Market	21	0.62	0.15	0.38	1.00
Overall	21	0.67	0.15	0.38	0.92
Governance	21	0.36	0.16	0.00	0.69

Indicator	No. obs.	Mean	Std. dev.	Min	Max
OECD					
Entry	22	0.23	0.15	0.00	0.50
Financial markets	22	0.18	0.13	0.00	0.43
Judicial	22	0.14	0.11	0.00	0.39
Trade	22	0.12	0.07	0.00	0.29
Labor	22	0.47	0.26	0.00	1.00
Fiscal	22	0.71	0.18	0.27	1.00
Bankruptcy	22	0.31	0.22	0.00	0.89
Product market	22	0.16	0.13	0.00	0.38
Overall	22	0.30	0.18	0.00	0.58
Governance	22	0.85	0.14	0.45	1.00
Middle East and North Africa					
Entry	6	0.43	0.10	0.30	0.54
Financial markets	6	0.59	0.32	0.34	1.00
Judicial	6	0.53	0.15	0.39	0.80
Trade	6	0.85	0.10	0.67	0.95
Labor	6	0.56	0.11	0.39	0.70
Fiscal	6	0.66	0.11	0.50	0.81
Bankruptcy	6	0.57	0.12	0.44	0.77
Product market	6	0.66	0.10	0.56	0.82
Overall	6	0.77	0.09	0.67	0.91
Governance	6	0.39	0.08	0.30	0.50
South Asia					
Entry	4	0.45	0.11	0.31	0.55
Financial markets	4	0.46	0.07	0.37	0.53
Judicial	4	0.43	0.18	0.18	0.59
Trade	4	0.81	0.15	0.58	0.92
Labor	4	0.44	0.07	0.35	0.52
Fiscal	4	0.40	0.17	0.15	0.56
Bankruptcy	4	0.47	0.19	0.19	0.63
Product market	4	0.58	0.07	0.50	0.66
Overall	4	0.60	0.06	0.52	0.66
Governance	4	0.30	0.13	0.18	0.42

Source: Authors' calculations.

Table 3.2: Correlation Coefficients between Regulation Indices

	Entry	Financial markets	Judicial administration	Trade	Bankruptcy	Labor	Fiscal	Governance
Entry	1							
Financial markets	0.6471*	1						
Judicial Administration	0.6822*	0.5845*	1					
Trade	0.6684*	0.7512*	0.6131*	1				
Bankruptcy	0.5882*	0.4859*	0.5783*	0.5225*	1			
Labor	0.3836*	0.1073	0.4367*	0.1075	0.2985*	1		
Fiscal	−0.4745*	−0.2757*	−0.5954*	−0.4013*	−0.4390*	−0.1749	1	
Governance	−0.7273*	−0.6575*	−0.7778*	−0.8043*	−0.6085*	−0.2008	0.5294*	1
1st principle component	**0.8690***	0.7748*	0.8685*	0.8160*	0.7575*	0.4166*	−0.6398*	−0.8536*
2nd principle component	0.019	−0.4261*	0.1676	−0.3927*	0.0725	**0.8111***	−0.1495	0.1578
3rd principle component	0.1234	0.2874*	−0.0843	0.1079	−0.0441	0.3539*	**0.7172***	0.0468

	Product market	Labor	Fiscal	Overall	Governance
Product market	1				
Labor	0.3170*	1			
Fiscal	−0.5314*	−0.1749	1		
Overall	−0.9543*	0.5126*	−0.3385*	1	
Governance	−0.8687*	−0.2008	0.5294*	−0.7954*	1
1st principle component	**0.9838***	0.4166*	−0.6398*	0.9357*	−0.8536*
2nd principle component	−0.1393	**0.8111***	−0.1495	0.0153	0.1578
3rd principle component	0.0847	0.3539*	**0.7172***	0.3384*	0.0468

Source: Authors' calculations.
Note: * significant at 5%

have a close one-to-one match with the indices resulting from the three categories. For the first principal component, the five product-market regulation indices receive high and similar loadings, but not so the labor and fiscal regulation indices. For the second principal component, the labor regulation index receives the highest loading, while the other six indices get only low positive or negative weights. Analogously, the third principal component loads heavily only on the tax regulation index. The close connection between the principal components and our regulation categories is clearly demonstrated by the pattern of correlation coefficients shown in table 3.2.[15]

Figure 3.1 provides a regional comparison of the overall, product market, labor regulation, and fiscal indices. In addition, Figure 3.2 depicts scatter plots of these indices against the (log) GDP per capita of all countries in the sample. It's clear that labor, fiscal, and product-market regulation indices behave differently from each other. Indeed, while there seems to be little relation between a country's average income and the strength of labor regulation, the relationship is positive and significant in the case of fiscal regulation and clearly negative in the case of product-market regulation. The overall regulation index is negatively related to per-capita GDP, which is not surprising given the large weight of product-market regulation in the overall index.

Regulation and governance

The effect of regulation on firm renewal and, ultimately, macroeconomic performance is likely to depend on the institutional context in which regulation is enacted. It can be argued that countries with better government institutions create regulatory environments that try to improve business conditions rather than privilege a few interest groups and to limit the potential abuses from economic and political powers.

We use an index of "governance quality" in order to assess the quality of regulation itself and the general context that determines how regulation functions. We construct this index using measures from the International Country Risk Guide, which evaluates a country's risk for international investment. Specifically, we average the values of indicators measuring the absence of corruption in the political system, the prevalence of law and order, and the level of democratic accountability.[16] To deal with endogeneity issues in the econometric analysis, we choose measures taken in 1990, so that our index reflects the "initial" governance level of the country.

Figure 3.1: Regulation around the World

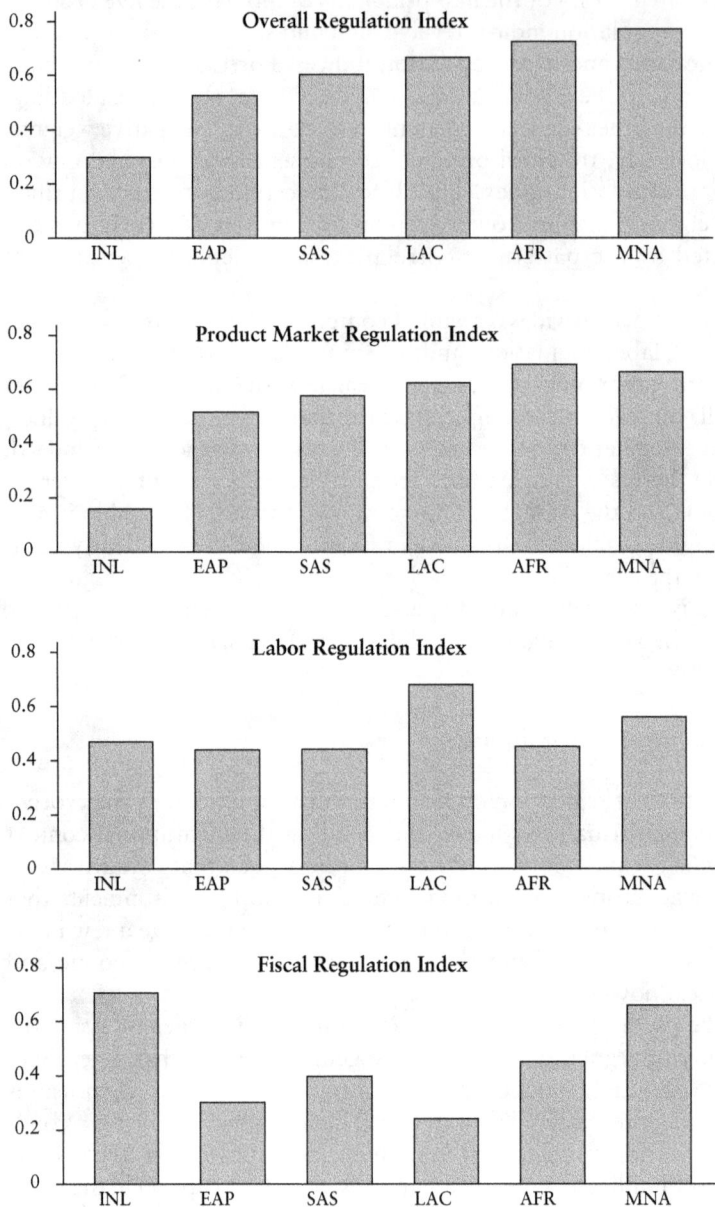

Source: Authors' calculations.

Note: Each value represents the simple average of the index values for the countries of the region. AFR: Africa region; EAP: East Asia and Pacific region; INL: industrial countries; LAC: Latin America and the Caribbean region; MNA: Middle East and North Africa region; SAS: South Asia region.

Figure 3.2: GDP per Capita vs. Regulation Indices

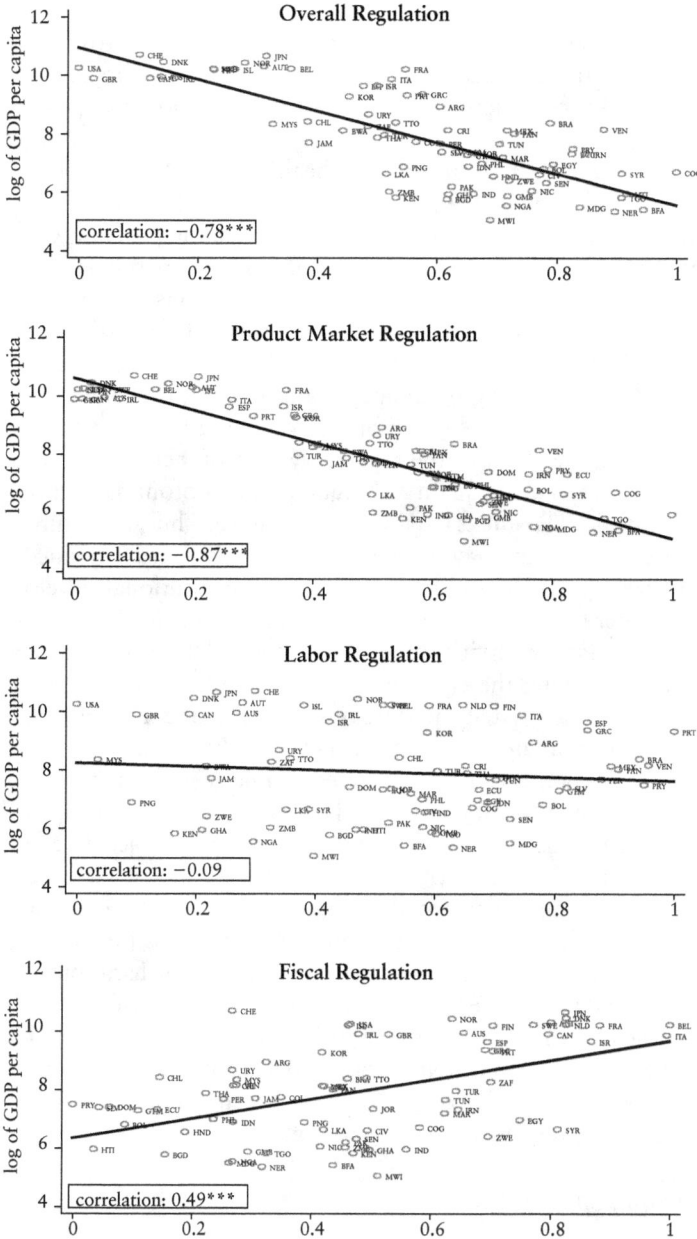

Overall Regulation

log of GDP per capita

correlation: −0.78***

Product Market Regulation

log of GDP per capita

correlation: −0.87***

Labor Regulation

log of GDP per capita

correlation: −0.09

Fiscal Regulation

log of GDP per capita

correlation: 0.49***

Source: Authors' calculations.
   * significant at 10%
  ** significant at 5%
 *** significant at 1%

Regulation and Macroeconomic Performance

Having described how the regulatory environment varies across countries, our objective for this section is to examine whether regulations have an impact on macroeconomic performance. Regulations are imposed for a variety of reasons. Officially, they are enacted to serve specific social purposes, from consumer health and safety to the protection of domestic employment. In reality, however, the imposition of regulation follows a more complex political economy process, where legitimate social goals are mixed with the objectives of particular interest groups (see Djankov et al. 2002). Whatever their justifications and objectives, regulations are likely to have an impact beyond their area of control. Here we examine whether they have an aggregate effect, specifically on economic growth and volatility, thus providing a comprehensive yet succinct evaluation of macroeconomic performance.

In assessing the effect of the regulatory environment, it is important to consider that the quality of regulation is profoundly affected by the institutional context in which it is imposed. Thus, the ultimate impact that regulation may have on macroeconomic performance is likely to be affected by the country's level of institutional development. In order to explore the interaction between institutional progress and regulatory environment, we extend the basic empirical analysis by allowing the effect of regulation to vary with a governance proxy, measured at the start of the period under study.

Our empirical analysis also considers the likely endogeneity of the regulatory environment. In particular, economic growth and volatility may shape to some extent the type and strength of regulation imposed in a country. For instance, governments of economies subject to external shocks and associated volatility may want to impose labor constraints in an attempt to protect domestic employment. Also, stagnant economic growth may prompt governments to increase public infrastructure spending, having to finance it with a heavier fiscal burden. Although the regulatory environment is likely to be affected by macroeconomic performance, it is not clear in what direction and to what extent the influence will be felt. In order to identify the effect of regulation on macroeconomic performance, we use instrumental variables that isolate the exogenous variation in regulation.

Sample and specification

Our empirical methodology is based on cross-country regression analysis. We conducted separate regressions for each dependent variable of interest, namely, economic growth and macroeconomic volatility. In each case, we used as explanatory variables a measure of regulation and a set of basic control variables. All variables included in the empirical exercises are briefly presented below, except the regulation indices that were introduced in the previous section.

Our sample consists of 75 countries, including 22 developed and 53 developing countries, of which 21 are in Latin America, 22 in Africa and the Middle East, and 10 in Asia. Country observations for each variable correspond to the years 1990–2003. We are constrained to this period because systematic and internationally comparable regulation measures have been broadly available only since 1990.

The dependent variables are defined as follows. As is standard in the literature, economic growth is measured as the average annual rate of per capita real GDP growth. Macroeconomic volatility is represented by the standard deviation of the output gap, obtained as the difference between actual and trend per capita real GDP. Trend output is estimated using the band-pass filter of Baxter and King (1999).

As described in the previous section, our explanatory variables of interest are indices that quantify a country's regulatory burden. We consider, in turn, the overall regulation index and its three main components, that is, the product market, labor, and fiscal regulation indices. In an extension to the basic specification, we interact the regulation index with a governance proxy, which as already noted, is constructed from information on experts' perceptions reported by the International Country Risk Guide in 1990.

The instrumental variables, used to isolate the exogenous variation in the regulation indices, are selected considering the recent literature on the determinants of the regulatory environment (see Botero et al. 2004 and Bolaky and Freund 2008). They are the initial level of per capita GDP, binary variables that denote legal origin (British, French, German, and Nordic), and proxies for the degree of Western influence based on the fraction of the population that speaks a major European language. The maintained hypothesis underlying our identification strategy is that the legal origin and Western influence variables do not enter the list of growth determinants, other than through their effect on regulation.[17]

Finally, the set of control variables for the growth regressions[18] consists of the initial level of per capita real GDP (to account for convergence effects), the initial rate of secondary enrollment (as proxy for human capital investment), the initial ratio of private domestic credit to GDP (to account for financial depth), and a Sub-Saharan dummy variable (to control for the particular conditions of civil conflict, mismanagement, and disease affecting this region).[19] The set of control variables for the volatility regressions represents exogenous causes of macroeconomic fluctuations. They are the standard deviation of terms of trade shocks and the frequency of natural disasters afflicting the country (droughts, earthquakes, floods, insect infestation, etc.). The set of controls for the growth and volatility regressions could be expanded, but in repeated robustness checks we find that they don't significantly affect the results presented in the paper.

Results and discussion

By way of illustration, we show scatter plots that represent the simple relationship between the regulation indices and, respectively, economic growth and macroeconomic volatility (see figures 3.3 and 3.4). The graphs using overall regulation consistently suggest that more heavily regulated economies tend to experience lower economic growth and higher volatility. Observations reflecting poor macroeconomic performance and high overall regulatory burden belong mostly to developing countries, while developed economies tend to occupy the other end of the distribution. The negative link between macroeconomic performance and overall regulation seems to be mainly driven by its product market component. On the other hand, the connection with fiscal regulation appears to go in the opposite direction: more fiscally regulated economies show better performance, although the association is not very strong. The simple relationship between labor regulations and, respectively, growth and volatility appears to be quite weak.

A more formal evaluation of the link between the regulation indices and the measures of macroeconomic performance requires multiple regression analysis, to which we now turn. The regression results are organized as follows. We first present the results of a basic specification where the regulation indices are taken as independent variables and their effects as unrelated to governance. Then, we allow for the effects of regulation on macro performance to vary with the quality of governance. Finally, keeping the regulation-governance interaction, we further control for the likely endogeneity of the regulation indices through an instrumental variable procedure.

Tables 3.3 and 3.4 present the basic specification results on economic growth and macroeconomic volatility, respectively. The overall index of regulation has a negative and significant association with economic growth, as does the product-market regulation index. On the other hand, the indices of fiscal and labor regulation have no significant link with economic growth. The results on macroeconomic volatility are similar except regarding the effect of fiscal regulation. The overall and product-market regulation indices are positively related to volatility, whereas labor regulation seems unconnected with it. Conversely, stronger fiscal regulation appears to be linked to lower macroeconomic volatility. Whereas some of these initial results are

Figure 3.3: Growth of GDP per Capita vs. Regulation Indices

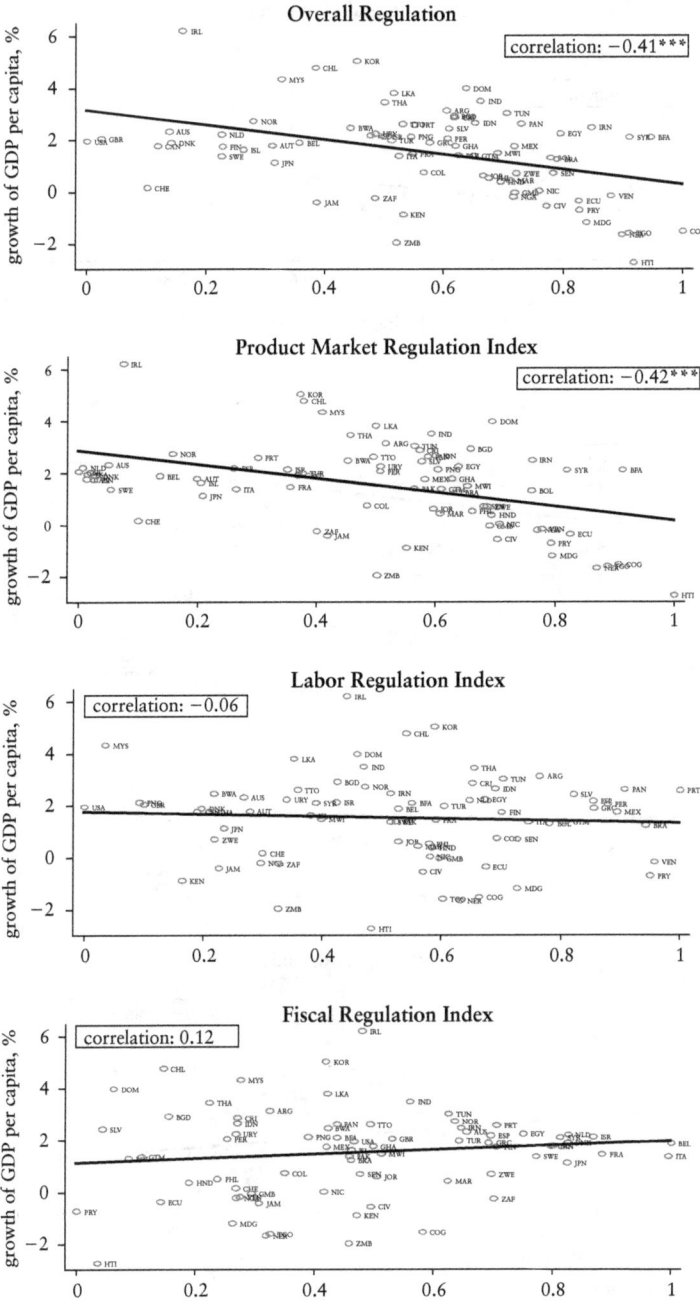

Overall Regulation

correlation: −0.41***

growth of GDP per capita, %

Product Market Regulation Index

correlation: −0.42***

growth of GDP per capita, %

Labor Regulation Index

correlation: −0.06

growth of GDP per capita, %

Fiscal Regulation Index

correlation: 0.12

growth of GDP per capita, %

Source: Authors' calculations.

Figure 3.4: Volatility of Output Gap vs. Regulation Indices

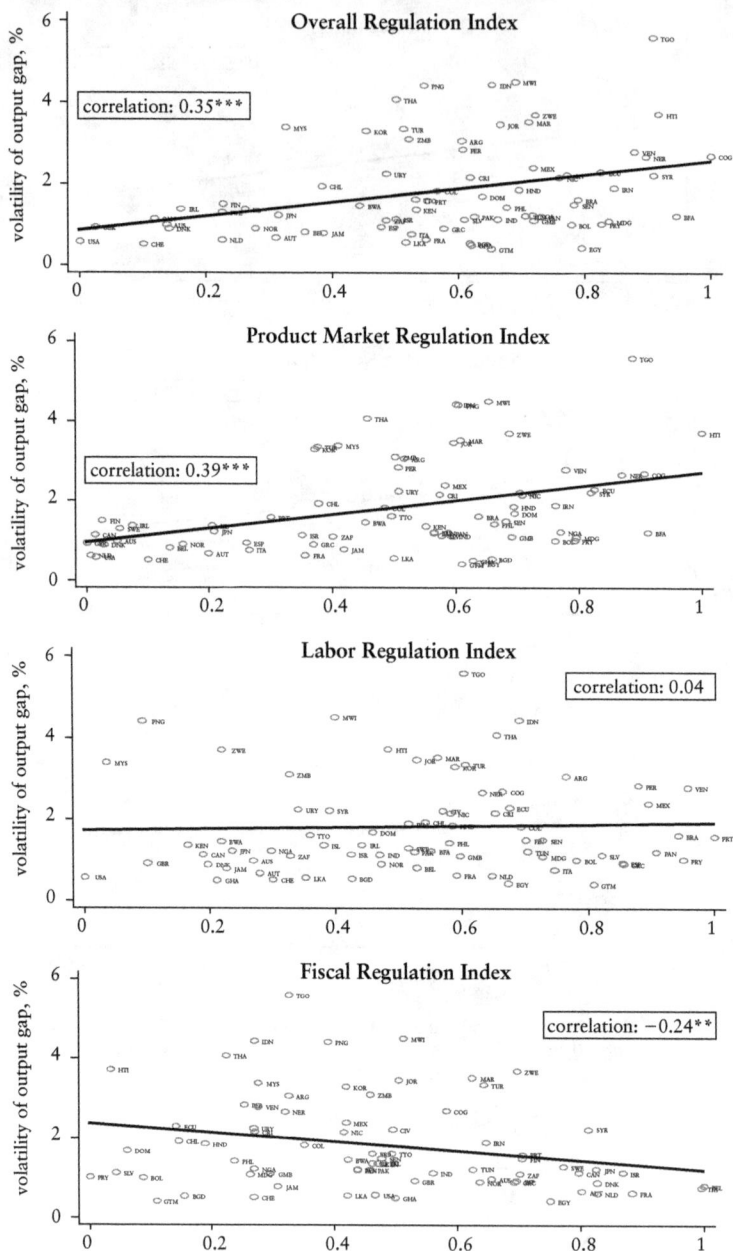

Source: Authors' calculations.
  * significant at 10%
 ** significant at 5%
*** significant at 1%

Table 3.3: Economic Growth and Burden of Regulation: Basic Specification, 1990–2003

Estimation method: ordinary least squares

Dependent variable: Economic growth: Average annual growth rate of GDP per capita

	Type of regulation index			
	Overall [1]	Product market [2]	Labor [3]	Fiscal [4]
Regulation (index ranging from 0 to 1, higher meaning more regulated)	-2.8829	-3.8652	-0.6269	0.2002
	-2.51	-2.82	-0.96	0.21
Control Variables:				
Initial GDP per capita (in logs)	-0.4878	-0.6815	-0.2136	-0.2452
	-2.18	-2.75	-0.98	-1.09
Initial education (log of secondary enrollment rate in 1990)	0.5290	0.4636	0.5397	0.5780
	1.24	1.17	1.13	1.13
Initial financial depth (log of private domestic credit / GDP in 1990)	0.1972	0.1812	0.3006	0.3523
	0.71	0.63	1.06	1.27
Sub-Saharan Africa dummy (1 if country belongs to Sub-Saharan Africa and 0 otherwise)	-1.7304	-1.8200	-1.7173	-1.6389
	-3.62	-3.94	-3.06	-2.91
Constant	4.6315	6.7602	0.7900	0.2706
	2.70	3.22	0.48	0.18
Observations (N)	75	75	75	75
R-squared	0.34	0.36	0.28	0.34

Source: Authors' calculations.

Note: The sample is 75 countries. Standard errors are robust to heteroscedasticity (Newey-West). t-statistics are presented below the corresponding coefficient.

Table 3.4: Macroeconomic Volatility and Burden of Regulation: Basic Specification, 1990–2003

Estimation method: ordinary least squares

Dependent variable: Macroeconomic Volatility: Standard deviation of the per capita GDP gap

	Type of regulation index			
	Overall [1]	Product market [2]	Labor [3]	Fiscal [4]
Regulation (index ranging from 0 to 1, higher meaning more regulated)	0.0144 2.99	0.0163 3.36	0.0022 0.41	-0.0092 -1.81
Control Variables:				
Volatility of terms of trade shocks (standard deviation of annual terms of trade growth)	0.0002 0.98	0.0001 0.47	0.0005 2.28	0.0004 1.84
Natural Disasters (average per million population, 1970–2004)	0.0021 0.47	0.0009 0.21	0.0014 0.29	-0.0013 -0.28
Constant	0.0083 3.53	0.0093 5.06	0.0135 3.83	0.0200 5.06
Observations (N)	75	75	75	75
R-squared	0.13	0.16	0.07	0.10

Source: Authors' calculations.

Note: The sample is 75 countries. Standard errors are robust to heteroscedasticity (Newey-West). t-statistics are presented below the corresponding coefficient.

strengthened in the richer regression specifications discussed next, others change radically: such is the case of the apparent irrelevance of labor regulations and the ambiguous role of fiscal regulations for macroeconomic performance.

Tables 3.5 and 3.6 present the estimation results when we allow for the effect of regulation on growth and volatility to vary with the quality of governance. In the case of economic growth, we add to the basic specification, first, the multiplication of the corresponding regulation index and the governance proxy and, second, the level of governance itself. We include the latter in order to avoid the possibility that the interaction term captures the direct effect of governance. The overall and product-market regulation indices all carry significantly negative signs and their interaction terms with governance show a positive and significant coefficient. Thus, the negative association of these regulation indices with economic growth appears to be mitigated when the quality of governance rises. Indeed, the point estimates suggest that at the maximum level of the governance proxy (equal to one), the impacts of the overall and product-market regulation indices are nil (see the test results reported in the last row of the table).[20]

The pattern of coefficient signs is the same in the case of labor regulations, that is, negative on the labor index and positive on the interaction term; however, they fail to be significant. The case of fiscal regulation is different from the rest; in fact, the pattern of signs reverses completely: positive on the tax index and negative on the interaction term, indicating a potential positive relationship between growth and taxation particularly in countries with low institutional development. Finally, regarding the effect of governance, it may appear surprising that its level carries a negative coefficient. However, the net effect (which combines the direct and interaction effects) fails to be significant for any country in the sample and any of the regulation indices considered. We will come back to this issue below, as we analyze the causal impact of regulation and governance on growth.

We turn now to the results on macroeconomic volatility (see table 3.6). Initially, we added to the basic specification the interaction term and the level of governance, just as we did in the case of the growth regressions. Unfortunately, however, the three coefficients of interest (on the levels of both governance and regulation and on the interaction between the two) were not individually significant, although they were statistically significant as a group.[21] Given our focus on regulation, we decided to exclude the level of governance from the regression, being aware that the interpretation of the interaction term becomes less clear as it may partially proxy for the direct effect of governance.[22] With this caveat in mind, we now present the results of the "restricted" interaction specification.

Table 3.5: Economic Growth and Burden of Regulation:
Governance Interactions, 1990–2003

Estimation method: ordinary least squares
Dependent variable: Economic growth: Average annual growth
rate of GDP per capita

Regulation
  (index ranging from 0 to 1, higher meaning more regulated)

Regulation-Initial Governance interaction
  (Regulation index *Governance index in 1990)

Initial Governance
  (index ranging from 0 to 1, higher meaning better governance)

Control Variables:

Initial GDP per capita
  (in logs)

Initial education
  (log of secondary enrollment rate in 1990)

Initial financial depth
  (log of private domestic credit / GDP in 1990)

Sub-Saharan Africa
  dummy (1 if country belongs to Sub-Saharan Africa and 0 otherwise)

Constant

Observations (*N*)
R-squared
P-value of Ho: sum of
  regulation coefficients = 0

Source: Authors' calculations.
Note: The sample is 75 countries. Standard errors are robust to heteroscedasticity
(Newey-West). t-statistics are presented below the corresponding coefficient.

	Type of regulation index		
Overall [1]	Product market [2]	Labor [3]	Fiscal [4]
−7.3997	−7.9946	−1.1390	2.4689
−2.79	−3.79	−0.62	1.72
7.7409	7.2765	1.2170	−4.8794
2.57	3.52	0.51	−1.70
−3.8355	−3.2259	0.1828	3.0474
−1.77	−1.97	0.08	1.65
−0.4757	−0.6315	−0.3599	−0.2799
−1.79	−2.47	−0.95	−0.86
0.4513	0.3601	0.5779	0.4794
1.11	0.93	1.08	0.95
0.2685	0.2636	0.3176	0.3572
1.01	0.97	1.07	1.30
−1.7369	−1.8114	−1.8826	−1.8892
−3.35	−3.54	−3.26	−3.36
7.2742	8.7779	1.6541	−0.2971
3.44	3.99	0.84	−0.14
75	75	75	75
0.42	0.45	0.29	0.33
0.80	0.64	0.93	0.23

Table 3.6: Macroeconomic Volatility and Burden of Regulation: Governance Interactions, 1990–2003

Estimation method: ordinary least squares

Dependent variable: Macroeconomic volatility: Standard deviation of the per capita GDP gap

	Type of regulation index			
	Overall [1]	Product market [2]	Labor [3]	Fiscal [4]
Regulation (index ranging from 0 to 1, higher meaning more regulated)	0.0160	0.0156	0.0080	0.0084
	2.51	2.20	1.12	0.97
Governance-Regulation interaction (Regulation index * Governance index in 1990) (Gov. index ranges from 0 to 1, higher meaning better governance)	−0.0067	0.0026	−0.0153	−0.0229
	−0.57	0.19	−1.71	−2.91
Control Variables:				
Volatility of terms of trade shocks (standard deviation of annual terms of trade growth)	0.0002	0.0001	0.0003	0.0002
	0.73	0.52	1.61	0.76
Natural disasters (average per million population, 1970–2004)	0.0026	0.0006	0.0018	0.0014
	0.57	0.14	0.40	0.29
Constant	0.0092	0.0092	0.0150	0.0190
	3.61	4.92	4.07	5.04
Observations (N)	75	75	75	75
R-squared	0.14	0.16	0.10	0.17
P-value of Ho: sum of regulation coefficients = 0	0.28	0.06	0.31	0.00

Source: Authors' calculationd.

Note: The sample is 75 countries. Standard errors are robust to heteroscedasticity (Newey-West). t-statistics are presented below the corresponding coefficient.

The overall and product-market regulation indices carry positive and significant coefficients, but their interaction terms with governance fail to be significant. This indicates that product-market regulations are related to macroeconomic volatility regardless of the governance level. The opposite occurs in the case of labor and fiscal regulations: the coefficients on their levels are not significant, but those on their governance interaction term are negative and significant. That is, when the quality of governance is sufficiently high, heavier labor and fiscal regulation are related to lower volatility.

Tables 3.7 and 3.8 report the results when we both allow for the governance-regulation interaction and control for the likely endogeneity of the regulation indices. Given that now reverse causation is controlled for, the interpretation of the regression coefficients goes beyond the mere association between regulation and the indices of macroeconomic performance. The coefficients can now be interpreted as the effects of regulation changes on, respectively, economic growth and macroeconomic volatility.

First, let's discuss the results on economic growth. The overall and product-market regulation indices carry negative and significant coefficients, while their respective governance interaction terms carry significantly positive coefficients. Therefore, product-market regulations appear to have a growth-reducing impact that is mitigated and eventually cancelled as governance improves. Labor regulation now appears relevant though detrimental for growth—its direct coefficient is significantly negative and its governance interaction approaches but does not reach statistical significance. The instrumental variable regressions confirm that, concerning growth effects, fiscal regulation is quite different from the rest. Its direct coefficient is significantly positive, and that on its governance interaction term is negative and almost significantly so. Heavier fiscal regulation seems to have a growth-improving effect especially in countries affected by poor governance; as the latter improves, the beneficial growth effect disappears. Finally, the net effect of the (initial) level of governance on growth is confirmed to be not significant once the regulatory regime is controlled for. This does not mean that governance is irrelevant. Our results indicate that governance has a nuanced role for growth in that it mitigates some of regulation's unintended negative effects on growth. Furthermore, a lighter regulatory burden may be another way through which better governance operates.

Regarding macroeconomic volatility, the results obtained with the instrumental variable (IV) estimator are also somewhat similar to those under ordinary least squares (OLS). The overall and product-market regulation indices carry significantly positive coefficients,

Table 3.7: Economic Growth and Burden of Regulation:
Accounting for Endogeneity and Governance Interactions,
1990–2003

Estimation method: two-stage least squares
Dependent variable: Economic growth: Average annual growth rate
of GDP per capita

Regulation
(index ranging from 0 to 1, higher meaning more regulated)

Governance-Regulation interaction
(Regulation index * Governance index in 1990)

Governance
(index ranging from 0 to 1, higher meaning better governance)

Control Variables:

Initial GDP per capita
(in logs)

Initial education
(log of secondary enrollment rate in 1990)

Initial financial depth
(log of private domestic credit / GDP in 1990)

Sub-Saharan Africa dummy
(1 if country belongs to Sub-Saharan Africa and 0 otherwise)

Constant

Observations (N)
R-squared
R-squared 1st stage
(partial due to excluded instruments)

Hansen's J-test of overidentifying restrictions (p-value)
P-value of Ho: sum of regulation plus regulation * governance coefficients = 0

Source: Authors' calculations.
Note: The sample is 75 countries. Standard errors are robust to heteroscedasticity
(Newey-West). t-statistics are presented below the corresponding coefficient.
Instruments for regulation and interaction: log of per capita GDP in 1990, binary
variable of legal origin (British, French, German, Nordic), variables indicating fraction
of population that speaks a major European language, and initial governance index.

| | Type of regulation index | | |
Overall [1]	Product market [2]	Labor [3]	Fiscal [4]
−10.0621	−11.3522	−10.8374	20.0050
−2.85	−2.97	−1.69	1.61
11.3118	10.6268	15.5534	−31.3114
1.91	2.13	1.36	−1.57
−6.0810	−4.5728	−9.8082	20.9252
−1.96	−1.64	−1.18	1.48
−0.4222	−0.8048	0.5582	−0.9811
−0.76	−1.39	0.54	−0.66
0.3611	0.2704	−0.3522	−0.6545
0.80	0.60	−0.41	−0.47
0.2644	0.2359	0.0625	0.2215
0.91	0.76	0.17	0.39
−1.6727	−1.9201	−2.1388	−4.6934
−2.37	−2.65	−2.71	−1.75
9.0004	12.3080	5.5580	0.6957
2.82	2.93	1.82	0.09
75	75	75	75
0.40	0.42	—	—
0.49	0.34	0.51	0.20
0.59	0.82	0.67	0.83
0.73	0.84	0.38	0.23

Table 3.8: Macroeconomic Volatility and Burden of Regulation: Accounting for Endogeneity and Governance Interactions, 1990–2003

Estimation method: two-stage least squares

Dependent variable: Macroeconomic volatility: standard deviation of the per capita GDP gap

Regulation
  (index ranging from 0 to 1, higher meaning more regulated)

Governance-Regulation interaction
  (Regulation index * Governance index in 1990)
  (Gov. index ranges from 0 to 1, higher meaning better governance)

Control Variables:

Volatility of terms of trade shocks
  (standard deviation of annual terms of trade growth)

Natural disasters
  (average per million population, 1970–2004)

Constant

Observations (N)
R-squared
R-squared 1st stage (partial due to excluded instruments)
Hansen's J-test of overidentifying restrictions (p-value)
P-value of Ho: sum of regulation plus regulation * governance coefficients = 0

Source: Authors' calculations.

Note: The sample is 75 countries. Standard errors are robust to heteroscedasticity (Newey-West). t-statistics are presented below the corresponding coefficient. Instruments for regulation and interaction: log of per capita GDP in 1990, binary variable of legal origin (British, French, German, Nordic), variables indicating fraction of population that speaks a major European language, and initial governance index.

	Type of regulation index		
Overall [1]	Product market [2]	Labor [3]	Fiscal [4]
0.0197	0.0188	0.0130	0.0227
3.22	2.68	1.73	1.42
−0.0065	−0.0048	−0.0165	−0.0301
−0.50	−0.27	−1.76	−2.20
0.0001	0.0000	0.0003	0.0002
0.42	0.22	1.68	0.76
0.0028	0.0014	0.0021	0.0046
0.65	0.34	0.47	0.84
0.0075	0.0092	0.0126	0.0136
2.37	3.87	2.78	3.17
75	75	75	75
0.13	0.15	0.10	0.13
0.79	0.83	0.62	0.47
0.87	0.68	0.39	0.41
0.24	0.30	0.71	0.19

while their governance interaction terms don't seem to be significant. Therefore, product-market regulation has a volatility-inducing effect that *is not* alleviated by governance (in contrast with the case of economic growth). Concerning labor regulation, its direct coefficient is significantly positive while that of its governance interaction term is significantly negative. This result reveals that labor regulation is relevant for macroeconomic volatility, as it turned out to be for economic growth—it induces volatility, but this detrimental effect is mitigated and eventually eliminated as governance improves. Regarding fiscal regulation, its direct coefficient is positive but falls short of statistical significance, and the coefficient on its interaction term is significantly negative. Heavier fiscal regulation, then, may induce some volatility but this effect seems to be alleviated by better governance.

Next, we conduct some robustness checks on the IV results for growth and volatility. First, a possible concern is whether the results are sensitive to outlying observations. In order to address this concern, we conduct a robust estimation procedure that limits the influence of potential outliers. It consists of weighing the observations inversely to their corresponding projection error (each obtained from the regression that excludes the particular observation).[23] For economic growth, the results are qualitatively similar to those presented in table 3.7. For macroeconomic volatility, the robust results are similar to those in table 3.8, except that fiscal regulations seem to have no effect on macro volatility for any level of governance.

A second concern is whether the results are driven by the imputation procedure that allowed us to work with the 75-country sample. In order to dispel this doubt, we ran the IV regressions using only the samples of countries for which there was complete data. The sample size varies depending on the regulation index: 38 country observations for the overall index, 41 for the product-market regulation index, 64 for the labor regulation index, and 50 for the fiscal regulation index. Despite the sharp reduction in sample size, the results are remarkably robust. For economic growth, the results are basically the same as with the 75-country sample. For macroeconomic volatility, the results are qualitatively similar, except that fiscal regulations appear to have no effect on volatility.

A third concern refers to the selection of control variables. To address this concern, in the growth regression we include as additional explanatory variables the volume of international trade (as ratio to GDP), the average change in the terms of trade, and the average growth rate of the country's trading partners. The results did not change in any meaningful way. In the volatility regression, we also include as regressors the volatility of trading partners' growth rate and variables that could be regarded as jointly endogenous with macroeconomic volatility, such as a proxy for real exchange misalignment, the frequency of systemic banking crises, and the volatility of inflation. Again, the results presented above remained qualitatively the same. In summary, then, the IV results that account for governance interactions are robust to outliers, samples, and control variables. The only noteworthy exception is that the effect of fiscal regulations on volatility turns out to be rather weak.

How important are the regulation effects economically? Using the point estimates of the regression that accounts for governance interactions and controls for joint endogeneity, we can perform some illustrative exercises. First, consider the growth effects of regulation. If a country's product-market regulation index increased by one standard deviation of the cross-country sample (0.30), and its level of governance were equal to the world median (0.4), then its annual rate of per capita GDP growth would decrease by 1.84 percentage points. The detrimental effect of labor regulations is smaller but still important: If a country with the same level of governance were to increase its labor regulation index by one standard deviation (0.24), then its growth rate would drop by 1.11 percentage points. The opposite would happen if fiscal pressure were to increase: For the same country, a rise by one standard deviation of the fiscal regulation index (0.24) would lead to an increase in the growth rate by 1.81 percentage points. This might reflect the expanded supply of productive public services resulting from a larger government size. The effect is of the same order of magnitude as that of product-market regulations. In all cases, a decrease in the governance index expands the growth effect of changes in regulation: if the country experiencing the regulation change has a governance level in the 25th percentile of the world distribution, the growth effect would be –2.2 percentage points for product-market regulation, –1.6 for labor regulation, and 2.8 for fiscal regulation.

Next, let's consider the magnitude of the volatility effects. An increase in the product-market regulation index by one standard deviation would lead to a jump in macroeconomic volatility of 0.44 basis points, the equivalent of 32 percent of the typical (median) volatility in the cross-country sample. The effect of a change in product-market regulation is basically the same at any level of governance. On the other hand, governance does seem to matter for the magnitude of the volatility effect of labor regulations. In a country with a median level of governance, an increase in labor regulations by one standard deviation would lead to a rise in volatility equivalent to 11 percent of world typical (median) volatility. If the country experiencing the rise in labor regulations had a governance level in the 25th percentile, its macroeconomic volatility would rise by 15 percent of the world median volatility. With high levels of governance, the effect of labor regulations on volatility would disappear.

Concluding Remarks

Regulation is increasingly viewed as a key explanatory factor for the diversity of aggregate economic performance across countries. In this chapter we have provided an empirical assessment of the macroeconomic impact of regulation in a large sample of industrial and developing economies. For this purpose, we have built a set of synthetic regulation indicators encompassing a broad array of regulatory dimensions relevant to firms' economic activity: firm entry, trade, finance, contract enforcement, bankruptcy, labor, and taxation.

These synthetic regulation indicators allow us to characterize the stylized facts concerning regulation around the world. Two main findings emerge in this regard. First, the burden of regulation shows considerable variation across countries, but in ways that appear systematically related to countries' level of development. Fiscal regulation is heaviest in rich countries, while in all other areas developing countries show the harshest regulatory environments. Second, the overall regulatory framework can be conveniently summarized by the extent of regulation in three major dimensions: fiscal, labor, and product market, where the latter encompasses the regulation of entry, trade, financial markets, bankruptcy, and contract enforcement.

Using this summary representation of the regulatory environment, we have assessed empirically the impact of regulation on two key measures of aggregate performance, namely, the growth rate of GDP per capita and the volatility of the output gap. Our estimations take into account the fact that the quality of regulation is likely to vary considerably across countries, reflecting primarily the progress of their overall institutional framework. In addition, we also control for the potential endogeneity of regulation, which could itself be driven in part by aggregate economic performance. This allows us to interpret our empirical results as reflecting the causal impact of regulation on the macroeconomic variables of interest, rather than just mere association between the former and the latter.

Overall, our estimates suggest that increasing product-market and labor regulations tends to reduce average economic growth. Conversely, heavier fiscal regulation appears to lead to higher growth. Moreover, we find that better governance tends to mitigate and even eliminate the impact of regulation on growth. Regarding macroeconomic volatility, our results indicate that increasing product-market and labor regulation tend to induce higher volatility.

However, while better governance can dampen the volatility effect of labor regulation, it cannot alleviate the detrimental impact of product-market regulations. Fiscal regulations appear not to have a robust detrimental effect on macroeconomic volatility.

In this chapter we have not explored the mechanisms through which the regulatory framework matters for macroeconomic performance. Nevertheless, the received literature allows us to suggest that labor and, particularly, product-market regulations create rigidities that induce informality, distort the incentives for investment and innovation, introduce barriers to firm renewal, and constrain firms' ability to accommodate and respond to shocks. Fiscal regulations in principle can have similar effects on firms. However, they can also generate the resources to both improve public services and infrastructure and stabilize the economy against shocks.[24] This implies a more nuanced role for taxation than for other regulations, particularly in poor countries.

Does the negative macroeconomic effect of most regulations imply that they should be eliminated altogether? As warned in the introduction, this chapter does not intend to assess the impact of regulation on social goals that could arguably be beyond the sphere of direct influence of economic growth—broad goals such as social equity and peace, or narrow ones such as worker safety, environmental conservation, and civil security, which typically motivate specific regulations. Thus, our conclusions on the role of regulation must necessarily be weighed in a more comprehensive context before drawing definitive social welfare implications. At any rate, to the extent that economic growth and macroeconomic stability are also important goals, our findings imply that streamlining regulation and strengthening governance in highly regulated countries could have a significant payoff in terms of macroeconomic performance.

Annex 3.1: Sources and Description of the Regulation Indices' Components

ENTRY

Variable name in corresponding database (name in our database)	Scale	Description	Years	Source
Number of procedures (db_entry_proc)	Actual number	The number of different procedures that a start-up has to comply with in order to obtain a legal status, i.e. to start operating as a legal entity. The data cover (1) procedures that are always required; (2) procedures that are generally required but that can be avoided in exceptional cases or for exceptional types of businesses.	Survey conducted in 1999, updated to 2003	**Doing Business, The World Bank Group;** see Djankov, La Porta, Lopez-de-Silanes and Shleifer, "The Regulation of Entry", Quarterly Journal of Economics, 117, 1-37, Feb. 2002. http://rru.worldbank .org/doingbusiness
Number of days (db_entry_days)	Actual number	Time recorded in calendar days. It is assumed that the minimum time required to fulfill a procedural requirement is one day. The variable measures the average duration estimated necessary to complete a procedure. The fastest procedure (independent of cost) is chosen. It is assumed that the entrepreneur completes the procedure in the most efficient way, ignoring the time that the entrepreneur spends in information gathering.		
Cost (db_entry_cost)	% GNI	Costs associated with starting-up a business, based on the texts of the Company Law, the Commercial Code, or specific regulations. If there are conflicting sources and the laws are not completely clear, the most authoritative source is used. If the sources have the same rank the source indicating the most costly procedure is used. In the absence of express legal fee schedules, a governmental officer's estimate is taken as an		

official source. If several sources have different estimates, the median reported value is used. In the absence of government officer's estimates, estimates of incorporation lawyers are used instead. If these differ, the median reported value is computed. In all cases, the cost estimate excludes bribes.

		Description	Period	Source
Regulation (ief_regulation)	1 Very low	Existing regulations straightforward and applied uniformly to all businesses; regulations not much of a burden for business; corruption nearly nonexistent.	1995–2003 (annual)	The Index of Economic Freedom, Heritage Foundation Based on: Economist Intelligence Unit, Country Commerce and Country Report, 2001 and 2002, U.S. Department of State, Country Commercial Guide 24 and Country Reports on Economic Policy and Trade Practices for 2000, Office of the U.S. Trade Representative, 2002 National Trade Estimate Report on Foreign Trade Barriers, and official government publications of each country. http://www.heritage.org/research/features/index.html
	2 Low	Simple licensing procedures; existing regulations relatively straightforward and applied uniformly most of the time, but burdensome in some instances; corruption possible but rare		
	3 Moderate	Complicated licensing procedure; regulations impose substantial burden on business; existing regulations may be applied haphazardly and in some instances are not even published by the government; corruption may be present and poses minor burden on businesses		
	4 High	Government-set production quotas and some state planning; major barriers to opening a business; complicated licensing process; very high fees; bribes sometimes necessary; corruption present and burdensome; regulations impose a great burden on business		
	5 Very high	Government impedes the creation of new businesses; corruption rampant; regulations applied randomly		

TRADE

Variable name in corresponding database (name in our database)	Scale	Description	Years	Source
Trade (ief_trade)	1 Very low	Weighted average tariff rate less than or equal to 4 percent.	1995–2003 (annual)	**The Index of Economic Freedom, Heritage Foundation** Based on: The Economist Intelligence Unit, Country Report and Country Commerce, 2002; International Monetary Fund, Government Finance Statistics Yearbook and International Financial Statistics on CD-ROM, 2002; Office of the U.S. Trade Representative, 2002 National Trade Estimate Report on Foreign Trade Barriers; U.S. Department of State, Country Commercial Guide 3 and Country Reports on Economic Policy and Trade Practices for 2001 and 2002; World Bank, World Development Indicators 2002; World Trade Organization, Trade Policy Reviews, 1995 to June 2001; and official government publications of each country. For all the European Union countries, the authors have based the score on data reported by the World Bank.
	2 Low	Weighted average tariff rate greater than 4 percent but less than or equal to 9 percent		
	3 Moderate	Weighted average tariff rate greater than 9 percent but less than or equal to 14 percent		
	4 High	Weighted average tariff rate greater than 14 percent but less than or equal to 19 percent		
	5 Very high	Weighted average tariff rate greater than 19 percent.		

i Hidden import barriers (efw_bi)	0 to 10 (0= heavy regulation)	No barriers other than published tariffs and quotas.	1995, 2000, and 2001	**Economic Freedom of the World, The Fraser Institute** From Section: 4 Freedom to Exchange with Foreigners B. Regulatory Trade Barriers Based on: World Economic Forum (2001), *Global Competitiveness Report 2001-2002* (Oxford: Oxford Univ. Press). http://www.freetheworld.com/release.html
ii Costs of importing (efw_bii)		The combined effect of import tariffs, license fees, bank fees, and the time required for administrative red-tape raises costs of importing equipment by (10 = 10% or less; 0 = more than 50%). This component is based on survey responses to this question obtained from the Global Competitiveness Report 2000.		
FINANCIAL MARKETS iv. Avoidance of interest rate controls and regulations that lead to negative real interest rates (efw_aiv)	0 to 10 (0= heavy regulation)	Data on credit-market controls and regulations were used to construct rating intervals. Countries with interest rates determined by the market, stable monetary policy, and positive real deposit and lending rates received higher ratings. When interest rates were determined primarily by market forces and the real rates were positive, countries were given a rating of 10. When interest rates were primarily market-determined but the real rates were sometimes slightly negative (less than 5%) or the differential between the deposit and lending rates was large (8% or more), countries received a rating of 8. When the real deposit or lending rate was persistently negative by a single-digit amount or the differential between them was regulated by the government, countries were rated at 6. When the deposit and lending rates were fixed by the government and the real rates were often negative by single-digit amounts, countries were assigned a rating of 4. When the real deposit or lending rate was persistently negative by a double-digit amount, countries received a rating of 2. A zero rating was assigned when the deposit and lending rates were fixed by the government and real rates were persistently negative by double-digit amounts or hyperinflation had virtually eliminated the credit market.	1970–2000 (5-year) and 2001	**Economic Freedom of the World, The Fraser Institute** From Section: 5: Regulation of Credit, Labor, and Business A. Credit Market Regulations Based on: International Monetary Fund, International Financial Statistics Yearbook (various issues, as well as the monthly supplements)

FINANCIAL MARKETS (continued)

Variable name in corresponding database (name in our database)	Scale	Description	Years	Source
v. Interest rate controls (efw_av)		Reflects whether interest rate controls on bank deposits and/or loans are freely determined by the market.		Based on data provided by the World Economic Forum Global Competitiveness Report.
Banking and finance (ief_banking)	1 Very low	Government involvement in the financial sector negligible; very few restrictions on foreign financial institutions; banks may engage in all types of financial services	1995–2003 (annual)	**The Index of Economic Freedom, Heritage Foundation**
	2 Low	Government involvement in the financial sector minimal; few limits on foreign banks; country may maintain some limits on financial services; domestic bank formation may face some barriers		Based on: Economist Intelligence Unit, Country Commerce, Country Profile, and Country Report for 2001 and 2002; U.S. Department of State, Country Commercial Guide 19 ; U.S. Department of State, Country Reports on Economic Policy and Trade Practices for 2001; and official government publications of each country.
	3 Moderate	Substantial government influence on banks; government owns or controls some banks; government controls credit; domestic bank formation may face significant barriers		
	4 High	Heavy government involvement in the financial sector; banking system in transition; banks tightly controlled by government; possible corruption; domestic bank formation virtually nonexistent		
	5 Very high	Financial institutions in chaos; banks operate on primitive basis; most credit controlled by government and goes only to state-owned enterprises; corruption rampant		

JUDICIAL ADMINISTRATION

Indicator	Scale	Description	Years	Source
Number of procedures (db_contr_proc)	Actual number	Number of procedures mandated by law or court regulation that demands interaction between the parties or between them and the judge or court officer. The questionnaire covers the step-by-step evolution of a debt recovery case before local courts in the country's most populous city.	Survey conducted in 1999, updated to 2003	**Doing Business, The World Bank Group.** see Simeon Djankov, Rafael La Porta, Florencio Lopez-de-Silanes, and Andrei Shleifer, "Courts", Quarterly Journal of Economics, May 2003.
Bureaucracy Quality (icrg_bureau)	0 to 4	High points are given to countries where the bureaucracy has the strength and expertise to govern without drastic changes in policy or interruptions in government services. Countries that lack the cushioning effect of a strong bureaucracy receive low points because a change in government tends to be traumatic in terms of policy formulation and day-to-day administrative functions.	1990–2000	**International Country Risk Guide - PRS Group** http://www.prsgroup.com/icrg/icrg .html

FISCAL REGULATION

Indicator	Scale	Description	Years	Source
Fiscal Burden (ief_taxation)	1 Very low	Individual Income Tax Grading Scale Top income tax rate 0 percent. Marginal rate for the average taxpayer 0 percent.	1995–2003 (annual)	**The Index of Economic Freedom, The Heritage Foundation** Based on: Ernst & Young, 2002 The Global Executive and 2002 World- wide Corporate Tax Guide; Interna- tional Monetary Fund Staff Country Report, Selected Issues and Statistical Appendix, 2000 to 2002; Economist Intelligence Unit, Country Commerce, Country Profile, and Country Report for 2001 and 2002; U.S. Department
	2 Low	Top income tax rate greater than 0 percent and less than or equal to 25 percent. Marginal rate for the average taxpayer greater than 0 percent and less than or equal to 10 percent		
	3 Moderate	Top income tax rate greater than 25 percent and less than or equal to 35 percent. Marginal rate for the average taxpayer greater than 10 percent and less than or equal to 15 percent.		

FISCAL REGULATION (continued)

Variable name in corresponding database (name in our database)	Scale	Description	Years	Source
	4 High	Top income tax rate greater than 35 percent and less than or equal to 50 percent. Marginal rate for the average taxpayer greater than 15 percent and less than or equal to 20 percent.		of State, Country Commercial Guide 9 ; and official government publications of each country. Sources other than Ernst & Young are noted in the text. For information on government expenditures, the authors' primary sources were Organisation for Economic Co-operation and Development data (for member countries); International Monetary Fund, Government Finance Statistics Yearbook for 2001, and International Monetary Fund Staff Country Report, Selected Issues and Statistical Appendix, 2000 to 2002; Standard & Poor's, Sovereigns Ratings Analysis; Asian Development Bank, Key Indicators of Developing Asian and Pacific Countries 2001; African Development Bank, ADB Statistics Pocketbook 2002; European Bank for Reconstruction and Development, Country Strategies; Inter-American
	5 Very high	Top income tax rate greater than 50 percent. Marginal rate for the average taxpayer greater than 20 percent		
		Corporate Tax Grading Scale		
	1 Very low	Corporate tax rate less than or equal to 20 percent		
	2 Low	Corporate tax rate greater than 20 percent and less than or equal to 25 percent.		
	3 Moderate	Corporate tax rate greater than 25 percent and less than or equal to 35 percent.		
	4 High	Corporate tax rate greater than 35 percent and less than or equal to 45 percent.		
	5 Very high	Corporate tax rate greater than 45 percent.		
		Government Expenditures Scale for Developed Countries		
	1 Very low	Less than or equal to 15 percent.		
	2 Low	Greater than 15 percent but less than or equal to 25 percent		
	3 Moderate	Greater than 25 percent but less than or equal to 35 percent		

Variable	Unit	Definition	Period	Source
		4 High — Greater than 35 percent but less than or equal to 45 percent 5 Very high — Greater than 45 percent *Government Expenditures Scale for Developing Countries* 1 Very low — Less than or equal to 15 percent 2 Low — Greater than 15 percent but less than or equal to 20 percent. 3 Moderate — Greater than 20 percent but less than or equal to 25 percent 4 High — Greater than 25 percent but less than or equal to 30 percent 5 Very high — Greater than 30 percent		Development Bank; U.S. Department of State, Country Commercial Guide 10; and official government publications of each country. Sources other than the OECD and the IMF are noted in the text.
Corporate tax % (kpmg_tax)	%	Corporate tax rate. The above rates do not reflect payroll taxes, social security taxes, net wealth taxes, turnover/sales taxes and other taxes not levied on income. When 2 or more rates are reported, the highest number is chosen.	1997–2003 (annual)	**Corporate Tax Rates Survey, KPMG, Switzerland** The survey (begun in 1993) currently covers 68 countries, including the 30 member countries of the Organisation for Economic Co-operation and Development (OECD), and many countries in the Asia Pacific and Latin America regions. Local KPMG tax offices from these countries have contributed to this survey.

FISCAL REGULATION (continued)

Variable name in corresponding database (name in our database)	Scale	Description	Years	Source
1D Top marginal tax rate (efw_d)	0 to 10	Average of 1.D.i. Top Marginal Income Tax Rate and 1.D.ii. Top Marginal Income and Payroll Tax Rate. Countries with higher marginal tax rates that take effect at lower income thresholds received lower ratings. The income threshold data were converted from local currency to 1982/1984 US dollars (using beginning-of-year exchange rates and the US Consumer Price Index).	1970–2000 (5-year) and 2001	**Economic Freedom of the World, The Fraser Institute** From Section: 1: Size of government Based on: Price Waterhouse, Individual Taxes: A Worldwide Summary (various issues)
LABOR flexibility-of-hiring index (db_flex_hiring)	0 to 100, higher values indicating more rigid regulation	Availability of part-time and fixed-term contracts. Working time requirements, including mandatory minimum daily rest, maximum number of hours in a normal workweek, premium for overtime work, restrictions on weekly holiday, mandatory payment for nonworking days, (which includes days of annual leave with pay and paid time off for holidays),	Survey conducted in 1997, updated to 2003	**Doing Business, The World Bank** see Botero, Djankov, La Porta, Lopez-de-Silanes, and Shleifer, "The Regulation of Labor", Working Paper 9756, National Bureau of Economic Research, June 2003
conditions-of-employment index (db_cond_empl)	0 to 100, higher values indicating more rigid regulation	and minimum wage legislation. The constitutional principles dealing with the minimum conditions of employment are also coded.		

Variable	Range	Description	Source
flexibility-of-firing index (db_flex_firing)	0 to 100, higher values indicating more rigid regulation	Workers' legal protections against dismissal, including grounds for dismissal, procedures for dismissal (individual and collective), notice period, and severance payment. The constitutional principles dealing with protection against dismissal are also coded.	Based on: NATLEX database (International Labour Organization); Constitutions, available online on the U.S. Law Library of Congress website; International Encyclopaedia for Labour Law and Industrial Relations, and Social Security Programs Throughout the World. Legal advice from leading local law firms was solicited to confirm accuracy in all cases. Following the OECD Job Study and the International Encyclopaedia for Labour Law and Industrial Relations, the areas subject to statutory regulation in all countries were identified. Those include hiring of workers, conditions of employment, and firing of workers.
labor_fraser	0 to 10		**Economic Freedom of the World, The Fraser Institute** From Section: 5 B: Labor maket regulations Minimum wage, hiring and firing restrictions, unionization, unemployment benefits, use of conscription.

BANKRUPTCY

Variable name in corresponding database (name in our database)	Scale	Description	Years	Source
Goals-of-Insolvency Index (db_close_insolv)	0 to 100	The measure documents the success in reaching the three goals of insolvency, as stated in Hart (1999). It is calculated as the simple average of the cost of insolvency (rescaled from 0 to 100, where higher scores indicate less cost), time of insolvency (rescaled from 0 to 100, where higher scores indicate less time), the observance of absolute priority of claims, and the efficient outcome achieved. A score 100 on the index means perfect efficiency.	2003	**Doing Business, The World Bank** see Djankov, Simeon, Oliver Hart, Tatiana Nenova, and Andrei Shleifer, "Efficiency in Bankruptcy", working paper, Department of Economics, Harvard University, July 2003.
Cost Measure (db_close_cost)	%	Cost is defined as the cost of the entire bankruptcy process, including court costs, insolvency practitioners' costs, the cost of independent assessors, lawyers, accountants, etc. In all cases, the cost estimate excludes bribes. The cost figures are averages of the estimates in a multiple-choice question, where the respondents choose among the following options: 0–2 percent, 3–5 percent, 6–10 percent, 11–25 percent, 26–50 percent, and more than 50 percent of the insolvency estate value.	2003	
Court-Powers Index (db_close_court)	0 to 100	The measure documents the degree to which the court drives insolvency proceedings. It is an average of three indicators: whether the court appoints and replaces the insolvency administrator with no restrictions imposed by law, whether the reports of the administrator are accessible only to the court and not creditors, and whether the court decides on the adoption of the rehabilitation plan. The index is scaled from 0 to 100, where higher values indicate more court involvement in the insolvency process.	2003	

GOVERNANCE

Corruption (icrg_corrup)	0 to 6	This is an assessment of corruption within the political system. The most common form of corruption met directly by business is financial corruption in the form of demands for special payments and bribes connected with import and export licenses, exchange controls, tax assessments, police protection, or loans. Although our measure takes such corruption into account, it is more concerned with actual or potential corruption in the form of excessive patronage, nepotism, job reservations, 'favor-for-favors', secret party funding, and suspiciously close ties between politics and business.	1990	International Country Risk Guide, PRS Group
Law and Order (icrg_laworder)	0 to 6	The Law sub-component is an assessment of the strength and impartiality of the legal system, while the Order sub-component is an assessment of popular observance of the law. Thus, a country can enjoy a high rating – 3 – in terms of its judicial system, but a low rating – 1 – if it suffers from a very high crime rate of if the law is routinely ignored without effective sanction.		
Democratic Accountability (icrg_account)	0 to 6	Measure of the government's responsiveness to the people. The score depends on the type of regime: Alternating Democracy, Dominated Democracy, De-facto One-party State, or De-jure One-party State. Higher points are given to Alternating Democracies (see ICRG for details).		

Index on Regulatory Burden

Components	Method
ENTRY TRADE FINANCIAL MARKETS CONTRACT ENFORCEMENT BANKRUPTCY LABOR REGULATION FISCAL BURDEN	We apply the following standardization formula to each component described above: $(X_i-X_{min})/(X_{max}-X_{min})$ if higher values indicate heavier regulation and $(X_{max}-X_i)/(X_{max}-X_{min})$ if lower values indicate heavier regulation. Therefore, all values are distributed between 0 and 1, with higher values denoting heavier regulation. Next we take the simple average of the components in each category to get the corresponding partial indicator. The overall index on regulatory burden is the simple average of the partial indicators.

111

Notes

1. Crafts (2006) also surveys evidence on the impact of regulation on productivity performance. Guasch and Hahn (1999) review quantitative estimates of the costs and benefits of various forms of regulation in developing countries.

2. In contrast, Griffith and Harrison (2004) find that the impact of product market competition on aggregate productivity growth is less robust: the effect is positive only when the cross-country variation is taken into consideration, and negative when the estimates are computed using the within-country variation.

3. For instance, Klapper et al. (2004) find that certain regulations, such as entry and exit barriers, have negative effects on firm entry, whereas others, like investors' rights regulations, have positive effects.

4. See for instance De Soto (1989).

5. Jalilian, Kirkpatrick, and Parker (2007) present a related approach, regressing growth on measures of the quality of regulation, and comparing the results with those obtained when the regressions include instead measures of the quality of governance. They conclude that regulatory quality has a bigger growth impact.

6. See Djankov et al. (2002).

7. Some regulations have also "indirect" effects on firm dynamics. For instance, Berkowitz and White (2004) find that personal bankruptcy laws play an important role in small firms' access to credit in the United States.

8. The macroeconomic effects of regulation may also depend on the quality of state governance and on the productive structure of the economy. As explained below, governance turns out to be an important determinant of the effects of regulation and, therefore, the governance-regulation interaction is a prominent topic of this chapter. On the other hand, the productive structure of the economy is not a significantly influential factor for the effects of regulation. In a series of exercises (not presented in the chapter but available on request), we tested the significance of the interaction between the regulatory measures and the share of agricultural production to GDP (as proxy for a production structure based on primary activities). We almost never found it to be statistically significant in the regressions for either average growth or growth volatility. Although business regulations are more likely to affect modern activities (such as industry and services) directly, the links between the latter and traditional activities are sufficiently strong that regulations that affect the modern sector of the economy will also impact on the rest.

9. We do not consider here the heterogeneity of regulation within countries. This can be important in some cases, such as the added burden of local taxation in federal systems. At present, however, very few data sources pro-

vide information on regulation at the regional level. One of these sources is the Investment Climate Survey of The World Bank, which records data on investment climate and activities of over 86,000 firms in 110 countries.

10. See, for instance, Bolaky and Freund (2004).

11. From a total of 22 indicators, 13 have between 0 and 5 percent missing observations, 5 between 5 and 25 percent, and 4 between 25 and 45 percent. If we were to use only the countries with complete information for the 22 indicators, the sample would consist of 38 countries, that is, half the potential sample size.

12. For filling in the gaps, we used the *impute* command in STATA. It estimates the missing values in a given variable by running a linear regression of this variable on the other variables in the *same* category and then substituting the regression-predicted values for the missing ones. Only variables in the same category (say, entry barriers) are used so that the resulting indicator is not linked by construction to the other categories (say, trade or financial regulations).

13. See, for instance, Claessens and Klapper (2005).

14. We take the term "product-market" regulations from Nicoletti et al. (2000). However, our index includes measures of financial market and bankruptcy regulations, which are absent from their measure. We include them in this category because of their statistical affinity with the other components.

15. Other studies, such as Nicoletti et al. (2000) or Klapper et al. (2004) also use factor analysis to decompose regulation measures, and they further replace the indices with their principal components in the regressions. We decided to use the indices themselves in the regression analysis because of their strong and clear correlation with the principal components and because of the greater ease in interpreting their estimated effects.

16. See annex 3.1 for a more detailed description of these components.

17. This hypothesis has been widely used in the empirical growth literature, and hence we view it as fairly uncontroversial. Note that other indirect effects of legal origin might accrue through initial GDP per capita, financial depth, and governance, which enter the growth regression as control variables. This strengthens the case for the exclusion restrictions described in the text.

18. Because the empirical growth equation relates the change in per capita GDP to a set of variables including the initial level of per capita GDP, it can also be viewed as an equation describing the time path of the latter variable, which can be solved to express the long-run level of per capita income in terms of regulation and other variables. In line with the growth literature, however, we opt for interpreting the equation as a growth equation subject to an initial condition.

19. The "Africa dummy" has a long tradition in empirical growth studies; see, for example, Easterly and Levine (1997).

20. Note that the impact of regulation under the highest level of governance quality is given by the sum of the coefficients in the first two rows of the tables.

21. These results are not presented in the current tables but are available upon request.

22. In a different context, Ravallion (1997) follows a similar approach. The statistical basis for excluding the level of governance is its lack of significance in the full specification. However, on the same basis, any of the three variables of interest could have been omitted.

23. This is the "robust regression" procedure in STATA. These results are not presented in the paper but are available upon request.

24. See Galí (1994), Fatás and Mihov (2001), and Andrés, Doménech, and Fatás (2008).

References

Alesina, Alberto, Silvia Ardagna, Giuseppe Nicoletti, and Fabio Schiantarelli. 2005. "Regulation And Investment." *Journal of the European Economic Association* 3(4): 791–825.

Andrés, Javier, Rafael Doménech, and Antonio Fatás. 2008. "The Stabilizing Role of Government Size." *Journal of Economic Dynamics and Control* 32(2): 571–593.

Barro, Robert, and Jong-Wha Lee. 2000. "International Data on Educational Attainment: Updates and Implications." Working Paper 7911, NBER, Cambridge, MA.

Bassanini, Andrea, and Ekkehard Ernst. 2002. "Labor Market Institutions, Product Market Regulations, and Innovation: Cross-Country Evidence." Economics Department Working Paper 316, OECD, Paris.

Baxter, Marianne, and Robert King. 1999. "Measuring Business Cycles: Approximate Band-Pass Filters for Economic Time Series." *Review of Economics and Statistics* 81(4), November: 575–93.

Bayoumi, Tamim, Douglas Laxton, and Paolo Pesenti. 2004. "Benefits and Spillovers of Greater Competition in Europe: A Macroeconomic Assessment." International Finance Discussion Papers 803, Board of Governors of the United States Federal Reserve System (U.S.).

Berkowitz, Jeremy, and Michelle J. White. 2004. "Bankruptcy and Small Firms' Access to Credit." *The RAND Journal of Economics* 35(1): 69–84.

Blanchard, Olivier. 2004. "The Economic Future of Europe." *Journal of Economic Perspectives* 18(4): 3–26.

Blanchard, Olivier, and Justin Wolfers. 2000. "Shocks and Institutions in the Rise of European Unemployment: The Aggregate Evidence." *Economic Journal* 100: 1–33.

Bolaky, Bineswaree, and Caroline Freund. 2008. "Trade, Regulations, and Income." *Journal of Development Economics* 87(2): 309–321.

Botero, Juan, Simeon Djankov, Rafael La Porta, Florencio Lopez-de-Silanes, and Andrei Shleifer. 2004. "The Regulation of Labor." *Quarterly Journal of Economics* 119(4): 1339–1382.

Business Environment Risk Intelligence (BERI), S.A. 2003. *Business Risk Service Operations Risk Index, 2001–2003.*

Caballlero, Ricardo, Eduardo Engel, and Alejandro Micco. 2004. "Microeconomic Flexibility in Latin America." Working Paper 10398, NBER, Cambridge, MA.

Card, David, and Richard B. Freeman. 2002. "What have Two Decades of British Economic Reform Delivered?" *International Productivity Monitor*, Centre for the Study of Living Standards (5): 41–52.

CEPR-IFS. 2003. "The Link between Product Market Reform and Macroeconomic Performance," final report ECFIN-E/2002 002.

Claessens, Stijn, and Leora Klapper. 2005. "Bankruptcy around the World: Explanations of its Relative Use." *American Law and Economics Review* 7(1): 253–283.

Cook, R. Dennis. 1979. "Influential Observations in Linear Regression." *Journal of the American Statistical Association* 74: 169 –174.

Crafts, Nicholas. 2006. "Regulation and Productivity Performance." *Oxford Review of Economic Policy* 22: 186–202.

De Soto, Hernando. 1989. *The Other Path: The Invisible Revolution in the Third World.* New York: Harper & Row.

Djankov, Simeon, Oliver Hart, Tatiana Nenova, and Andrei Shleifer. 2003. "Efficiency in Bankruptcy." Working Paper, Department of Economics, Harvard University, Cambridge, MA.

Djankov, Simeon, Rafael La Porta, Florencio Lopez-de-Silanes, and Andrei Shleifer. 2002. "The Regulation of Entry." *Quarterly Journal of Economics* 117: 1–37.

———. 2003. "Courts." *The Quarterly Journal of Economics* 118(2): 453–517.

Dutz, Mark A., and Aydin Hayri. 1999. "Does More Intense Competition Lead to Higher Growth?" Centre for Economic and Policy Research Discussion Paper 2249.

Easterly, William, and Ross Levine. 1997. "Africa's Growth Tragedy." *Quarterly Journal of Economics* 112: 1203–1250.

Fatás, A., and I. Mihov. 2001. "Government Size and Automatic Stabilizers." *Journal of International Economics* 55: 3–28.

Fox, John. 1997. *Applied Regression Analysis, Linear Models, and Related Methods.* Thousand Oaks, CA: Sage Publications.

Galí, Jordi. 1994. "Government Size and Macroeconomic Stability." *European Economic Review* 38: 117–132.

Griffith, Rachel, and Rupert Harrison. 2004. "The Link between Product Market Reform and Macroeconomic Performance." European Economy Economic Papers No. 209, European Commission Directorate-General for Economic and Financial Affairs.

Guasch, J. Luis, and Robert W. Hahn. 1999. "The Costs and Benefits of Regulation: Implications for Developing Countries." *World Bank Research Observer* 14: 137–58.

Gwartney, James, and Robert Lawson. 2002. "Economic Freedom of the World—2002." Annual Report, The Fraser Institute, Vancouver, BC.

Haltiwanger, John. 2000. "Aggregate Growth: What Have We Learned from the Microeconomic Evidence?" OECD Economics Department Working Papers 267, OECD, Paris.

Haltiwanger, John, Stefano Scarpetta, and Helena Schweiger. 2006. "Assessing Job Flows across Countries: The role of Industry, Firm Size, and Regulations." Policy Research Working Paper 4070, World Bank, Washington, DC.

Heckman, James, and Carmen Pagés. 2000. "The Cost of Job Security Regulation: Evidence from Latin American Labor Markets." Working Paper 7773, NBER, Cambridge, MA.

Hsieh, Chang-Tai, and Peter J. Klenow. 2007. "Misallocation and Manufacturing TFP in China and India." Working Paper 13290, NBER, Cambridge, MA.

Jalilian, Hossein, Colin Kirkpatrick, and David Parker. 2007. "The Impact of Regulation on Economic Growth in Developing Countries: A Cross-Country Analysis." *World Development* 35: 87–103.

Kaufmann, Dani, Aart Kraay, and Pablo Zoido-Lobatón. 1999. "Governance Matters." Policy Research Working Paper 2196, World Bank, Washington, DC.

Klapper, Leora, Luc Laeven, and Raghuram G. Rajan. 2004. "Business Environment and Firm Entry: Evidence from International Data." Centre for Economic and Policy Research Discussion Paper DP4366.

Koedijk, Kees, and Jeroen Kremers. 1996. "Market Opening, Regulation and Growth in Europe." *Economic Policy* 23: 445–467.

KPMG. 2003. *Corporate Tax Rate Survey, March 1998–January 2003.* http://www.kpmg.com/Global/IssuesAndInsights/ArticlesAndPublications/Pages/Corporateindirecttaxsurvey2008.aspx

Laffont, Jean-Jacques. 1999. *Incentives and the Political Economy of Regulation.* Oxford: Oxford University Press.

La Porta, Rafael, Florencio López-de-Silanes, Andrei Shleifer, and Robert Vishny. 1999. "The Quality of Government." *The Journal of Law, Economics, and Organization* 15: 229–79.

Loayza, Norman, and Claudio Raddatz. 2007. "The Structural Determinants of External Vulnerability." *World Bank Economic Review* 21(3): 359–387.

Newbery, David. 1999. *Privatization, Restructuring and Regulation of Network Industries.* Cambridge, MA: MIT Press.

Nicoletti Guiseppe, Andrea Bassanini, Ekkehard Ernst, Sébastien Jean, Paulo Santiago, and Paul Swaim. 2001a. "Product and Labor Markets Interactions in OECD Countries." Economics Department Working Paper 312, OECD, Paris.

Nicoletti, Guiseppe, R.C.G. Haffner, Stephen Nickell, Stefano Scarpetta, and G. Zoega. 2001b. "European Integration, Liberalization, and Labor Market Performance." In *Welfare and Employment in United Europe*, ed. G. Bertola, T. Boeri, and G. Nicoletti. Cambridge, MA: MIT Press.

Nicoletti, Guiseppe, and Stefano Scarpetta. 2003. "Regulation, Productivity and Growth: OECD Evidence." *Economic Policy* 18(36): 11–72.

Nicoletti, Guiseppe, Stefano Scarpetta, and Olivier Boylaud. 2000. "Summary Indicators of Product Market Regulation with an Extension to Employment Protection Legislation." Economics Department Working Paper 226, OECD, Paris.

O'Driscoll, Gerald, Edwin Feulner, and Mary Anastasia O'Grady. 2003. "2003 Index of Economic Freedom." The Heritage Foundation and The Wall Street Journal.

PRS (Political Risk Services Group). 1999. "International Country Risk Guide – ICRG, 1999. Brief Guide to the Rating System." Available at http://www.icrgonline.com.

Rama, Martin, and Raquel Artecona. 2002. "A Database of Labor Market Indicators across Countries." Unpublished, World Bank, Washington, DC.

Ravallion, Martin. 1997. "Can High-Inequality Developing Countries Escape Absolute Poverty?" *Economics Letters* 56: 51–57.

Shleifer, Andrei, and Robert Vishny. 1993. "Corruption." *Quarterly Journal of Economics* 108(3), August: 599–617.

Stiglitz, Joseph. 1998. "Private Uses of Public Interests: Incentives and Institutions." *Journal of Economic Perspectives* 12: 3–22.

World Bank. "Doing Business Database." Available at http://rru.worldbank.org/doingbusiness.

———. 2003. *World Development Indicators.* Washington, DC.

———. 2004a. *Investment Climate Survey, 2004.* Washington, DC.

———. 2004b. *World Development Report 2005: A Better Investment Climate for Everyone.* Washington, DC.

4

Regulation and Microeconomic Dynamics

Norman V. Loayza, Ana María Oviedo, and Luis Servén

Introduction

This chapter concentrates on the dynamics of firm renewal and resource reallocation as the mechanism through which microeconomic regulations affect economic performance. Specifically, the chapter studies the relationship between regulatory burden and labor productivity growth at the sectoral level. To deepen the analysis, the chapter first examines the connecting links of this relationship, proposing firm turnover as the mechanism through which the regulatory burden affects firms' productivity growth. For these purposes, the chapter uses manufacturing productivity and firm-turnover data for

This research has been supported by the World Bank's Latin America Regional Studies Program. We thank Koichi Kume and Tomoko Wada for excellent research assistance. We are very grateful to Raphael Bergoeing, Marcela Eslava, Alejandro Micco, John Haltiwanger, Claudio Raddatz, Andrea Repetto, Stefano Scarpetta, and Fabio Schiantarelli for useful discussions. However, they bear no responsibility for any errors. The views expressed herein are those of the authors and do not necessarily represent those of The World Bank, its executive directors, or the countries they represent.

12 countries (seven OECD and five Latin American) disaggregated at the level of 13 major manufacturing sectors. The data are obtained from a recently assembled, and largely unexplored, cross-country firm-level database encompassing both industrial and developing economies (Haltiwanger, Scarpetta, and Schweiger 2008).

Why is this important? The effects of microeconomic regulation on aggregate economic performance have attracted renewed attention in policy debates. Intricate regulation and its arbitrary enforcement are singled out from among the key obstacles to growth in developing countries (World Bank 2005). Similarly, excessive regulation has likewise been blamed by many observers for Europe's lagging performance vis-à-vis the United States (Nicoletti and Scarpetta 2003). Conversely, the recent global crisis has prompted some analysts and policy makers to question the optimality of deregulation reforms, calling for stronger government intervention in the economy. In this context, this chapter offers an evaluation of microeconomic regulations from the perspective of firm renewal and resource reallocation.

A growing literature has been concerned with the impact of regulation and deregulation on aggregate growth in a cross-country setting.[1] Koedijk and Kremers (1996) find a negative association between measures of product market regulation and GDP growth among 11 European countries. They also find that labor regulations have no significant association with growth performance. Dutz and Hayri (2000) apply extreme-bounds analysis to estimate the contribution to growth of a variety of (mostly subjective) regulation and competition indicators in a sample of industrial and developing countries. They find significant effects of measures of antitrust policy and the average age of large firms (taken as proxy for entry and exit barriers).

In contrast, Card and Freeman (2002) fail to find any significant association between subjective measures of economic regulation and growth performance in a panel regression covering OECD countries over 1970–99. More recently, however, Loayza, Oviedo, and Servén (2009) explore the growth impact of synthetic indicators of product-market, labor market, and fiscal regulation, using a large cross-country sample that includes not only developed but also developing countries. On the whole, they show that product-market and labor regulations deter per capita GDP growth while fiscal regulation has an ambiguous effect. Furthermore, they also find that the adverse growth impact of regulation is exacerbated under conditions of poor governance.

While these studies summarize the empirical relation between regulation and aggregate growth performance, they are not directly informative about the mechanisms at work. Conceptually, there are several channels through which regulation may affect aggregate performance (see, for example, Griffith and Harrison 2004). First, regulation affects the allocation of resources across firms and sectors with different productivity levels, thus impacting on overall efficiency. Second, regulation also affects the level of productivity of existing firms, by changing their incentives to reduce slack and utilize factors more or less intensely. And third, regulation has an impact on firms' incentives to innovate and introduce new products and processes, and hence on the pace of expansion of the technological frontier.

The analytical literature has devoted particular attention to the allocative mechanism, the Schumpeterian process of external restructuring whereby market selection reallocates resources from low-efficiency to high-efficiency firms, through contraction and exit of the former, and expansion and new entry by the latter. Regulatory barriers that disrupt this "creative destruction" process cause a deterioration in aggregate economic performance by allowing low-productivity activities to survive too long and discouraging the adoption of new high-productivity activities (Caballero and Hammour 1998).

In turn, the theoretical literature offers conflicting predictions regarding the effect of deregulation on the incentives to innovate. On the one hand, the reduction in rents resulting from increased market contestability may discourage the introduction of new products and processes. On the other hand, incumbent firms may face an increased incentive to innovate in order to escape the pressure of competition (Aghion et al. 2005). Thus, the net effect of regulation on innovation is ambiguous on conceptual grounds, and can be determined only empirically.

In this chapter, we assess the role of firm dynamics as the mechanism linking regulation and growth using disaggregated manufacturing data for a set of OECD and Latin American countries. The results are new and interesting. We first find that productivity grows faster in countries where firm turnover is more active. Moreover, we find that the reallocation-related components of productivity growth (commonly labeled "between" and "net entry") exhibit the most significant connection with turnover. Then we turn to the question as to whether regulations affect firm turnover. For this purpose, firm turnover rates at the sectoral level are regressed on (country-specific) labor, product-market, and taxation regulation measures and their corresponding interaction with "normal" turnover (that is, turnover in the United States, as the benchmark country).[2] We find that in countries where labor and product-market regulations are more burdensome, turnover rates are correspondingly lower on average. Furthermore, this slackening effect appears to be more relevant for sectors characterized by lower normal turnover rates. In contrast to the results on labor and product-market regulations, countries with stronger taxation show higher firm turnover. Although at first this may seem a surprising result, it may be explained by the observation that tax-financed public goods and services can indeed facilitate firm renewal.

After providing support for the transmission mechanism based on firm dynamics (from regulation to turnover, and from turnover to productivity growth), the chapter turns to its basic objective—directly assessing the connection between regulation and productivity growth. It does so by using the same cross-country sectoral database as used in the preliminary exercises but by employing a different econometric methodology. This is a variation of the difference-in-difference procedure, designed to eliminate unobserved country-specific and sector-specific effects. Since the regulation measures vary only across countries, their impact on labor productivity growth could not be estimated after removing country-specific effects, unless an additional identification assumption was used. For this purpose, we follow a Rajan-Zingales type of approach, with a twist: identification is obtained by assuming that regulations have a stronger impact on labor productivity growth in sectors that normally require higher turnover.

We find that labor and product-market regulations have a negative effect on labor productivity growth. The adverse effect is stronger on the components of productivity growth that reflect reallocation of resources between firms than on the component that captures productivity growth within firms. Conversely, fiscal taxation appears to be beneficial for firms' labor productivity growth, surely mirroring both the positive relationship between taxation and firm turnover and the beneficial productivity effect of public goods and services.

The chapter is closely related to other recent attempts to shed light on the link between regulation and aggregate performance. Griffith and Harrison (2004) study product-market regulatory reform, but rather than firm turnover, they stress instead the role of markup variations. Their implicit assumption is that regulatory reforms impact on performance only through their effect on the degree of competition among firms, as captured by markup levels. Their empirical tests, using data from OECD countries, yield mixed results: decreased regulation does lead to lower markups, but these in turn seem to be associated with lower, rather than higher, levels and growth rates of productivity and R&D effort. Moreover, in many cases, they find that regulatory variables appear to have an independent effect on aggregate performance, above and beyond the effect occurring through the markup.

Other papers focus instead on the Schumpeterian mechanism of firm entry and exit, as we do here. Klapper, Laeven, and Rajan (2006) assess the effects of regulation on firm entry using firm-level data for developed and transition European countries. On the whole, they find that regulation deters entry and also hampers industry-level productivity growth. Cincera and Galgau (2005) are likewise concerned with firm entry and exit. They assess the impact of (subjective) product-market regulation measures on entry and exit rates by sector in nine OECD countries, and also examine the effect of entry and exit on sector-wise productivity. On the whole, their results indicate that product market deregulation increases entry and exit rates, while these in turn have a (weakly) positive impact on the growth of output and labor productivity.

This chapter expands this literature in several dimensions. First, unlike most previous studies, which have focused on selected OECD economies, we consider both industrial and Latin American countries. Second, rather than confining the analysis to product-market regulation alone, which is the concern of the recent literature, we consider three different kinds of regulations: those affecting the product market, those affecting the labor market, and fiscal regulations. Third, we distinguish among the various components of observed productivity growth—i.e., those due to entry, exit, reallocation among incumbent firms, and productivity growth within incumbent firms—to assess whether they are affected in different ways by regulation.

The rest of the chapter is organized as follows. The next section provides a description of the business regulation measures used in the analysis and their behavior in our sample of Latin American and industrial countries. Similarly, the following section introduces the new data set on firm dynamics and productivity growth and describes its basic patterns in the sample of countries. This is followed by a section that lays out the main analytical questions, presents the estimation strategy, and discusses the results. The final section concludes the discussion.

Business Regulation across Countries

To begin our assessment of regulation and productivity, we make a static comparison of the severity of business regulation in the sample of countries that we later use in our regression analysis.[3] We use the regulation indices presented in Loayza, Oviedo, and Servén (2009), which combine de jure and de facto measures of regulation in seven areas of business operations: entry, financial markets, labor regulation, judicial quality, ease of trade, ease of closing a business, and fiscal burden (taxation and spending), thus accounting for the practical restrictions and complications brought about by certain rules.[4] Each index measures the intensity of the regulatory system on a scale from 0 to 1 (1 representing the lightest regulation).[5]

We also construct a composite regulation index that includes product-market and labor regulations. This is the simple average of individual regulation indicators in the six areas excluding fiscal burden. This composite index summarizes regulation in the areas for which the rankings across countries are highly correlated, suggesting that governments treat them similarly.[6] The index of fiscal burden measures direct taxation—that is, the maximum tax rate applied to individuals and businesses—and fiscal spending. For ease of comparison, we split our sample countries by level of development into two groups: Latin America and OECD countries.

Figure 4.1 presents each regulation index by country and region. The Latin American sample shows substantially higher product-market and labor regulations than does the OECD sample. On the other hand, taxation is significantly higher in the OECD sample.

Figure 4.1: Regulation Indices, Average per Region

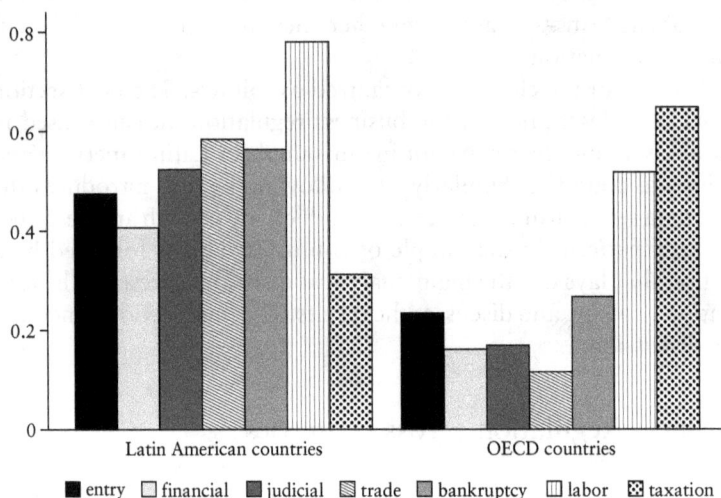

Source: Indices from Loayza, Oviedo, and Servén (2009).
Note: The scale of the original indices is inverted so that all indices take values from 0 to 1, where 1 represents the highest regulation (i.e., the most stringent).

Firm Dynamics and Labor Productivity Growth

Our main source of firm dynamics and labor productivity data is the harmonized data set collected by Bartelsman, Haltiwanger, and Scarpetta (2004), and later updated by Haltiwanger, Scarpetta, and Schweiger (2008). This data set has two parts: the first part provides demographic data, such as the number and total employment of entrants, continuers, and exiting firms by (ISIC two-digit) industry, size class, and year. The second part reports the five-year labor productivity average (level and) growth rate by (ISIC two-digit) industry and year, together with the labor productivity growth decomposition into the contribution of entering, continuing, and exiting firms computed following Foster, Haltiwanger, and Krizan (2001), and Griliches and Regev (1995), that we describe in more detail below.[7] For most countries, the data cover roughly the period from the mid-1980s to the mid-1990s.[8] Our sample includes all countries available in both datasets, resulting in 12 countries (five Latin American and seven OECD countries) and 13 manufacturing two-digit sectors.[9] In order to control for variations in firm dynamics and productivity due to cyclical factors, throughout the chapter we use the (time) average values over the period over which data are available for each country.

Firm entry, exit, and turnover

Numerous studies have documented the high degree of heterogeneity in firm-level productivity as well as the intensive reallocation of resources across firms in industrial countries (see, for example, Dunne et al. 1989, Bartelsman and Doms 2000). All find an active pace of reallocation in both the United States and Europe. For instance, Bartelsman et al. (2003) report that, on average, close to 20 percent of firms enter and exit the market every year in 10 OECD countries. In addition, productivity varies greatly across firms, even within narrowly defined industries (see Foster et al. 2001). A few studies have also looked at firm dynamics in developing countries and have found, perhaps surprisingly, that reallocation and productivity dynamics are in fact similar to those observed in industrial countries (see, for instance, Roberts and Tybout 1996).

Figure 4.2 depicts turnover rates for manufacturing sectors in our Latin American and OECD sample over various periods, depending on the country (see annex 4.1). To control for firm size, throughout this chapter we use firm turnover weighted by employment.[10] From the figure, it is not evident that the turnover rates in Latin America are very different from the rest of the countries (except perhaps the

Figure 4.2: Firm Turnover in Latin America and OECD
Countries

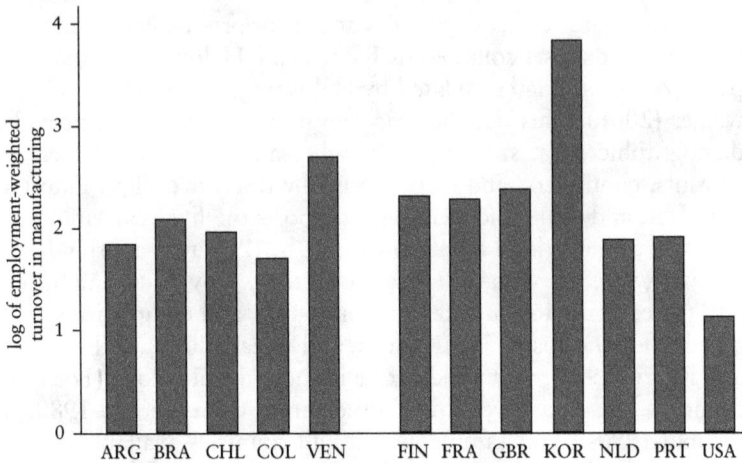

Source: Authors' calculations.
Note: For a list of countries and their 3-letter codes, please see annex 5.1.

Republic of Korea). However, if we look at average turnover rates
across the two country groups, the OECD sample exhibits a slightly
higher average turnover than the Latin American sample.

Labor productivity growth

A natural question that arises from observing firm dynamics concerns
the implications of having a more or less rapid turnover of firms on
productivity gains at the firm and industry level. Indeed, a large number of firms leaving and entering the market each year is not per se a
desirable outcome; it only becomes so if, as a result of this process,
the firms that stay in the market experience productivity gains, if not
in the short run, at least in the medium to long term.[11]

In this chapter we look at total labor productivity growth, divided
into three "components" following the identity proposed by Griliches and Regev (1995):

$$\Delta P_t = \underbrace{\sum_{i \in C} \overline{\theta}_i \Delta p_{it}}_{within} + \underbrace{\sum_{i \in C} \Delta \theta_{it} \left(\overline{p}_i - \overline{P} \right)}_{between}$$

$$+ \underbrace{\sum_{i \in N} \theta_{it} \left(p_{it} - \overline{P} \right) - \sum_{i \in X} \theta_{it-k} \left(p_{it-k} - \overline{P} \right)}_{net\ entry} \qquad (1)$$

where P is productivity at the industry level, p_i is productivity at the firm level, and θ_i is the share of firm i in the industry (in terms of output). The first term in the decomposition represents the "within" contribution to productivity growth, that is, the amount of productivity growth coming from productivity increments within continuing firms (due, for instance, to technological progress). The remaining terms in the decomposition capture the reallocation of resources: the second term is the "between" contribution, or the addition to productivity coming from reallocation of resources from less productive to more productive firms; and the last two terms represent the "net entry" contribution, or the portion of productivity growth coming from the entry and exit of firms in the industry. The upper bar over each variable represents the average value between the base and end years (five years in this case).

Empirically, it is important to keep in mind that the characteristics of available data affect the interpretation of this decomposition of productivity growth. The reason is that even within firms there is reallocation going on—across products, processes, and projects. However, such reallocation is typically unobservable. As a result, empirical applications of the productivity decomposition in (1)—or other similar decompositions—may understate the true role of resource reallocation for productivity growth.

With this caveat in mind, Figure 4.3 depicts the total growth rate of labor productivity and the respective within, between, and net entry components.[12] It is clear that average labor productivity growth is higher in the OECD sample than in the Latin American sample, although countries like Colombia and Argentina have experienced growth rates similar to those of Finland, the United Kingdom, or the Netherlands over the period. However, we should note again that the time coverage of the data is quite limited, so that the numbers for each country are not strictly comparable, if only for the different years they cover.[13] In addition, measured surges in labor productivity could in fact reflect temporary changes in utilization in response to shocks, rather than actual productivity gains (see, for instance, Basu, Fernald, and Kimball 2004), especially in the presence of adjustment costs. This should be the case particularly in countries where regulatory barriers to adjustment add to the natural adjustment costs.

Regulation, Microeconomic Dynamics, and Labor Productivity Growth

Having described both the regulatory environment and the characteristics of firm dynamics and productivity in our sample, we now

Figure 4.3: Labor Productivity Growth Rate Decomposition in Manufacturing

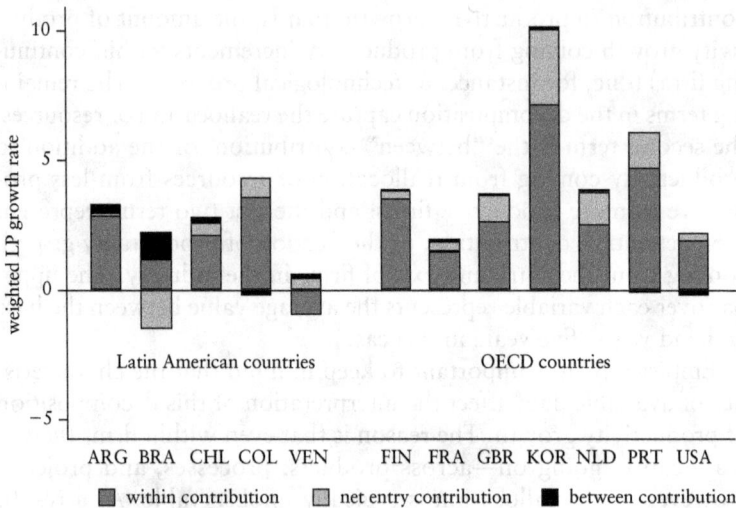

Source: Authors' calculations.

Note: The productivity decomposition shown is calculated following Griliches and Regev (1995). Labor productivity is a weighted average of firm productivity (weighted using value added), and the growth rate shown in the graphs corresponds to an average annual growth rate, based on the 5-year growth rate. For a list of countries and their 3-letter codes, please see annex 5.1.

turn to the impact of regulation on productivity growth performance. As a preliminary step, however, we examine the connecting links of this relationship. That is, we first study the link between labor productivity growth and firm turnover, and then the relationship between firm turnover and the regulatory burden. Our empirical methodology is based on cross-country, cross-sector regression analysis.[14] Let's start with the link between productivity and turnover, for which we estimate the following regression:

$$y_{i,c} = \alpha_0 + \alpha_1 I_i + \alpha_{21} p_{0c,i} + \beta turnover_{c,i} + \varepsilon_{c,i} \tag{2}$$

where $y_{i,c}$ is labor productivity growth in country c and industry i, $p_{0c,i}$ is the labor productivity level in the initial period of the sample, and $turnover_{c,i}$ is the (log) firm turnover rate in the same country and industry. We include sector fixed effects (I_i) to control for the industrial composition of each country, and we also cluster error terms by country to allow for within-country error correlation.

Table 4.1 reports the results of this regression for total labor productivity growth and for each of its components as the dependent variable. We find that higher firm turnover is positively associated with a higher labor productivity growth rate, and more importantly, we find that the positive effect comes almost exclusively from the entry and exit of firms, and to a lesser extent from the reallocation between continuing firms. Figure 4.4 also depicts a scatter plot of regression (2).

We now examine the effect of regulation on firm turnover. This is the second connecting link in the relationship between regulation and productivity. It establishes the impact of regulation on productivity through firm entry and exit, and reallocation from contracting to expanding firms. We estimate the following regression:

$$
\begin{aligned}
turnover_{c,i} = \alpha_0 + \alpha_1 I_i + \beta_1 R_c + \beta_2 \left(R_c \times turnover_{US,i} \right) \\
+ \gamma_1 growthsd_c + \gamma_2 totgrsd_c + \varepsilon_{c,i}
\end{aligned}
\tag{3}
$$

where $turnover_{c,i}$ is the (log) employment-weighted firm turnover rate in country c and industry i, R_c is the regulation index in country c, $growthsd_c$ is the standard deviation of the GDP growth rate over the respective period in country c, and $totgrsd_c$ is the standard deviation of the terms-of-trade growth rate over the respective period in country c. We allow errors to be correlated within countries, and therefore we cluster them at the country level. To diminish the potential influence of outliers on the estimates, we employ weighted least squares estimation that is robust to the presence of outliers.[15]

In equation 3, we interact regulation with the average (log) employment-weighted turnover rate in the corresponding industry in the United States in order to obtain the sectoral effect. Hence, the coefficient β_1 gives us the average (country) effect of regulation, whereas β_2 tells us whether (or not) the effect of regulation is stronger in sectors that have a naturally high firm turnover. That is, we calculate both the absolute and relative effects of regulation on turnover.

Table 4.2 presents the results of the estimation of equation (3) for firm turnover. Columns 1–7 include one single regulation index per specification, looking in turn at the effect of regulation in each of the seven areas on firm turnover. Column 8 includes both the composite regulation index and the fiscal burden (taxation) index. As described above, each regulation index is included alone and interacted with the turnover rate in the corresponding sector in the United States.

The first thing to notice is that across all specifications, the signs of the average effects are negative for six of the regulation indices, and positive only for fiscal burden. The results are statistically significant for all regulation indices, except bankruptcy regulation. Although at first the effect of the fiscal burden can appear surprising,

Table 4.1: Labor Productivity and Firm Dynamics

Estimation method: weighted least squares (robust to outliers)
Sector fixed effects were included (coefficients not reported)

Dependent variable	[1] Labor productivity growth	[2] Within component	[3] Between component	[4] Net entry component	[5] Entry component	[6] Exit component
Firm Dynamics						
Turnover (employment-weighted, in logs)	1.813**	0.969	0.093**	0.636***	0.012	−0.623**
	[0.708]	[0.561]	[0.042]	[0.193]	[0.094]	[0.233]
Control variable						
Initial labor productivity (in logs)	−0.232	−0.227	0.051***	−0.085	−0.012	0.100
	[0.173]	[0.139]	[0.016]	[0.057]	[0.044]	[0.060]
Observations	150	150	150	150	150	150

Source: Authors' calculations.

Note: The sample is 12 countries, 13 sectors (see annex 4.1 for the complete list of countries and sectors). Numbers in brackets are the corresponding robust standard errors. Errors are clustered by country.

    * significant at 10%

   ** significant at 5%

  *** significant at 1%.

Figure 4.4: Labor Productivity Growth and Firm Turnover

12 countries and 13 manufacturing sectors

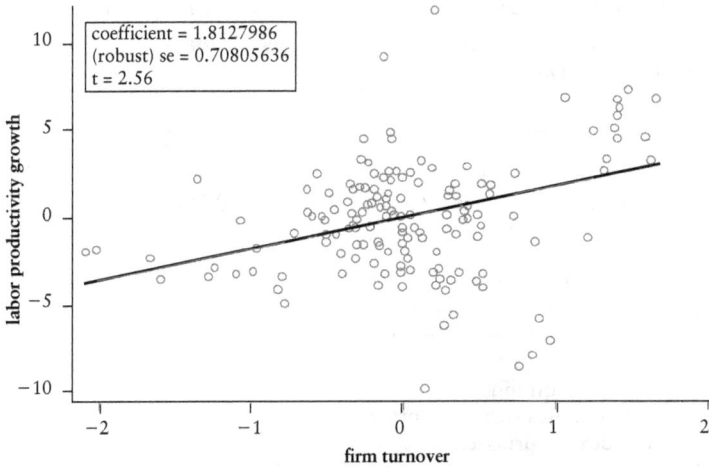

Source: Authors' calculations.

Note: Controlling for initial labor productivity and sector dummies. Errors clustered by country. Robust to outliers.

it may be explained by the observation that tax-financed public goods and services can indeed facilitate firm renewal.

Second, the coefficients of the term interacting regulation and turnover in the United States are positive and significant for all regulation indices, except bankruptcy and fiscal burden. As explained before, this coefficient can be interpreted as a relative effect, that is, it indicates in which sectors regulation has a stronger impact. The fact that all (statistically significant) coefficients turn out to be positive suggests that regulation actually affects sectors that have naturally *low* turnover rates relatively more. This is plausible, for instance, for sectors that have naturally low turnover because their activity has high sunk costs, and stringent regulation amounts to increased costs for entrants, thus discouraging firm entry, and keeping incumbent firms in the sector longer than they would otherwise remain.

In order to assess the combined effect of regulation (both absolute and relative) on turnover, we perform a simple exercise. We evaluate the combined effect at the lowest, average, and highest turnover rates (equal to 0.08, 1.13, and 2.01) in the United States for each regulation index. This amounts to the sum of the first coefficient and the product of the second coefficient and the corresponding turnover rate. We find that this combined effect remains negative at the average U.S. turnover for all regulation indices (except fiscal). For instance, using the coefficients presented in column 8, at the average turnover,

Table 4.2: Firm Turnover and Regulation

Estimation Method: weighted least squares (robust to outliers)
Sector fixed effects were included (coefficients not reported)

Dependent variable: Turnover (sum of employment for entry and exit divided by total employment, in logs)

Regulations	[1]	[2]
Entry	−1.936***	
(Entry regulation index)	[0.563]	
Entry-United States turnover interaction	0.798***	
(Entry index × turnover, by sector)	[0.179]	
Finance		−1.166***
(Finance regulation index)		[0.337]
Finance-United States turnover interaction		0.715***
(Finance index × turnover, by sector)		[0.161]
Judicial		
(Judicial regulation index)		
Judicial-United States turnover interaction		
(Judicial index × turnover, by sector)		
Trade		
(Trade regulation index)		
Trade-United States turnover interaction		
(Trade index × turnover, by sector)		
Bankruptcy		
(Bankruptcy regulation index)		
Bankruptcy-United States turnover interaction		
(Bankruptcy index × turnover, by sector)		
Labor		
(Labor regulation index)		
Labor-United States turnover interaction		
(Labor index × turnover, by sector)		
Taxation		
(Taxation regulation index)		
Taxation-United States turnover interaction		
(Taxation index × turnover, by sector)		
Composite index		
(average of entry, finance, judicial, trade, bankruptcy, and labor regulation indices)		
Composite-United States turnover interaction		
(Composite index × turnover, by sector)		
Control Variables		
GDP growth	−0.058**	−0.061
(standard deviation, constant, period 1985–2000)	[0.025]	[0.039]
Terms of Trade growth	0.045***	0.036**
(standard deviation, period 1985–2000)	[0.011]	[0.015]
Observations (N)	140	140

Source: Authors' calculations.

Note: The sample is 11 countries (United States excluded), and 13 sectors (see annex 4.1 for the complete list of countries and sectors). Numbers in brackets are the corresponding robust standard errors. Errors are clustered by country.

   * significant at 10%; ** significant at 5%; *** significant at 1%.

REGULATION AND MICROECONOMIC DYNAMICS

[3]	[4]	[5]	[6]	[7]	[8]
−2.426***					
[0.356]					
0.533***					
[0.135]					
	−1.366**				
	[0.447]				
	0.516***				
	[0.102]				
		−0.482			
		[0.424]			
		0.286			
		[0.172]			
			−0.737***		
			[0.133]		
			0.313*		
			[0.170]		
				1.138*	0.865**
				[0.552]	[0.350]
				−0.370	−0.030
				[0.259]	[0.195]
					−2.217***
					[0.403]
					0.703**
					[0.243]
0.031	−0.013	−0.056	−0.049	−0.016	0.021
[0.020]	[0.037]	[0.037]	[0.034]	[0.051]	[0.029]
0.068***	0.047***	0.029*	0.031**	0.038***	0.071***
[0.010]	[0.009]	[0.014]	[0.013]	[0.009]	[0.008]
140	140	140	140	140	140

the marginal effect of composite regulation index is −1.43, which implies that if, for example, the composite regulation index were to increase by one standard deviation, there would be a 29-percent decrease in firm turnover. For the industry with the highest turnover in the United States, a one-standard-deviation increase in the composite index would imply a 16-percent decrease in turnover, whereas for the industry with the lowest turnover, this increase in the composite index would reduce turnover by 43 percent. Using also column 8, we can estimate the impact of an increase in fiscal taxation. Since the coefficient on its interaction with U.S. turnover is not statistically significant, the effect of fiscal taxation is constant for all sectors. Then, a one-standard-deviation increase in fiscal taxation would lead to a jump in turnover rates of 19 percent.

Finally, we turn to our basic objective, namely, to measure the total impact of regulation on productivity growth. We do so by estimating a reduced form equation of a similar form to the difference-in-difference Rajan-Zingales methodology, designed to eliminate unobserved country- and industry-specific effects. Since regulation varies only by country, their impact cannot be estimated once we control for country unobserved effects, unless an additional identification assumption is used. For this purpose, we modify slightly the Rajan-Zingales method, since we assume that regulations will have a stronger impact on labor productivity growth in sectors that are normally subject to higher turnover rates. Hence, we estimate the following equation:

$$y_{i,c} = \alpha_0 + \alpha_1 I_i + \alpha_2 I_c + \alpha_3 p_{0c,i} + \beta\left(R_c \times turnover_{US,i}\right) + \varepsilon_{c,i} \quad (4)$$

where $y_{i,c}$ is the labor productivity growth rate, α_1 and α_2 are sector and country effects, $p_{0c,i}$ is the initial labor productivity level, and $turnover_{US,i}$ is the turnover rate in the United States in the corresponding sector. We conduct separate regressions for the growth rate of labor productivity, and its "within," "between," and "net entry" components. To diminish the potential influence of outliers on the estimates, we employ weighted least squares estimation that is robust to the presence of outliers.[16]

Next, table 4.3 presents the results of the estimations of the reduced form equation (4) using total labor productivity growth as the dependent variable. We find that the effects of regulation on total labor productivity growth are negative for the regulation indices related to labor and product markets (but not statistically significant for bankruptcy and labor regulation). These results are consistent with the notion that regulatory burden can hamper economic efficiency by reducing the incentives for conducting R&D, adopting new technologies, creating new firms with improved production processes, and letting firms leave the market if they become obsolete and their costs rise above those of competing firms.[17] Conversely, fiscal taxation carries a positive coefficient, indicating a beneficial impact for firms' labor productivity growth. This result reflects the positive relationship between taxation and firm turnover and, more generally, the beneficial productivity effect of public goods and services.

To have a better idea of the magnitude of the effect, we perform a similar exercise as before. We evaluate the effect on total productivity growth of a one-standard-deviation increase in composite regulation index at the average turnover rate in the United States. This increase implies a reduction of 0.71 percentage points in total labor productivity growth. An analogous increase in fiscal taxation would lead to an improvement of 0.47 percentage points in productivity growth.

How important is the mechanism based on firm dynamics? We can use the estimated effects of the composite index for illustration. For this purpose, we need to estimate the fraction of the calculated reduction in productivity growth that can be attributed to the firm dynamics channel. As stated earlier, a one-standard-deviation increase in composite regulation index, evaluated at the average U.S. turnover rate, is associated with a 29-percent decrease in turnover. If we multiply this reduction in turnover times the coefficient obtained in column 1 of table 4.1 (1.813), we obtain the change in total productivity growth coming from a change in turnover. We find that a 29-percent decrease in turnover is associated with a reduction in productivity growth of 0.52 percentage points. This represents 73 percent of the total change estimated with the reduced form. In short, we find that the firm dynamics channel explains a large fraction of the estimated change in productivity growth coming from a change to regulation.

Finally, we look at the results of the estimations using each component of labor productivity growth (within, between, net entry, and the latter also split between entry and exit) as the dependent variable (tables 4.4–4.6). Although the statistical significance of some regulation coefficients is not as high as it is in the total productivity growth regression, we still find a few interesting results.

First, for the within-firm component of labor productivity growth, we find that contract enforcement and trade regulations have a negative impact (again, this is relatively stronger in sectors with higher natural turnover), whereas fiscal burden has a positive effect. As in the case of turnover, it is possible that in some countries the combination of fiscal spending and taxation has a positive

Table 4.3: Labor Productivity and Regulation
Estimation method: weighted least squares (robust to outliers)
Country and sector fixed effects were included
(coefficients not reported)
Dependent variable: Labor productivity growth

Regulations	[1]	[2]
Entry	−4.165***	
(Entry index × turnover in the United States, by sector)	[1.547]	
Finance		−5.149***
(Finance index × turnover in the United States, by sector)		[1.484]
Judicial		
(Judicial index × turnover in the United States, by sector)		
Trade		
(Trade index × turnover in the United States, by sector)		
Bankruptcy		
(Bankruptcy index × turnover in the United States, by sector)		
Labor		
(Labor index × turnover in the United States, by sector)		
Taxation		
(Taxation index × turnover in the United States, by sector)		
Composite index		
(Composite index × turnover in the United States, by sector)		
Control Variable		
Initial labor productivity	−1.679**	−1.507**
(in logs)	[0.682]	[0.670]
Observations (N)	151	151

Source: Authors' calculations.
Note: The sample is 12 countries and 13 sectors (see annex 4.1 for the complete list of countries and sectors). Numbers in brackets are the corresponding robust standard errors.
  * significant at 10%
  ** significant at 5%
  *** significant at 1%.

[3]	[4]	[5]	[6]	[7]	[8]
−4.078*** [1.109]					
	−3.852*** [0.986]				
		−1.226 [0.891]			
			−0.750 [0.883]		
				3.039*** [1.050]	2.164* [1.209]
					−3.526** [1.349]
−1.947*** [0.607] 151	−1.598** [0.650] 151	−1.268** [0.632] 151	−1.325** [0.646] 151	−1.282** [0.571] 151	−1.893*** [0.606] 151

Table 4.4: Within Component of Labor Productivity and Regulation

Estimation method: weighted least squares (robust to outliers)
Country and sector fixed effects were included
(coefficients not reported)

Dependent variable: Within component

Regulation	[1]	[2]
Entry index	−1.359	
(Entry index × turnover	[0.994]	
in the United States, by sector)		
Finance index		−1.299
(Finance index × turnover		[0.983]
in the United States, by sector)		
Judicial index		
(Judicial index × turnover		
in the United States, by sector)		
Trade index		
(Trade index × turnover		
in the United States, by sector)		
Bankruptcy index		
(Bankruptcy index × turnover		
in the United States, by sector)		
Labor index		
(Labor index × turnover		
in the United States, by sector)		
Taxation index		
(Taxation index × turnover		
in the United States, by sector)		
Composite index		
(Composite index × turnover		
in the United States, by sector)		
Control variable		
Initial labor productivity	−0.196	−0.234
(in logs)	[0.438]	[0.444]
Observations (N)	151	151

Source: Authors' calculations.
Note: The sample is 12 countries and 13 sectors (see annex 4.1 for the complete list of countries and sectors). Numbers in brackets are the corresponding robust standard errors.

　　* significant at 10%
　　** significant at 5%
　　*** significant at 1%

[3]	[4]	[5]	[6]	[7]	[8]
−2.686*** [0.814]					
	−1.349** [0.660]				
		−0.507 [0.629]			
			−0.533 [0.592]		
				1.917** [0.806]	1.445* [0.863]
					−0.923 [0.963]
−0.708 [0.446]	−0.198 [0.435]	−0.180 [0.446]	−0.166 [0.433]	−0.355 [0.438]	−0.317 [0.432]
151	151	151	151	151	151

Table 4.5: Between Component of Labor Productivity
and Regulation
Estimation method: weighted least squares (robust to outliers)
Country and sector fixed effects were included
(coefficients not reported)
Dependent variable: Between component

Regulations	[1]	[2]
Entry	−1.097***	
(Entry index × turnover	[0.400]	
in the United States, by sector)		
Finance		−1.415***
(Finance index × turnover		[0.403]
in the United States, by sector)		
Judicial		
(Judicial index × turnover		
in the United States, by sector)		
Trade		
(Trade index × turnover		
in the United States, by sector)		
Bankruptcy		
(Bankruptcy index × turnover		
in the United States, by sector)		
Labor		
(Labor index × turnover		
in the United States, by sector)		
Taxation		
(Taxation index × turnover		
in the United States, by sector)		
Composite		
(Composite index × turnover		
in the United States, by sector)		
Control variable		
Initial labor productivity	−0.763***	−0.563***
(in logs)	[0.176]	[0.182]
Observations (N)	151	151

Source: Authors' calculations.
Note: The sample is 12 countries and 13 sectors (see annex 4.1 for the complete list
of countries and sectors). Numbers in brackets are the corresponding robust
standard errors.

   * significant at 10%
  ** significant at 5%
 *** significant at 1%

[3]	[4]	[5]	[6]	[7]	[8]
−0.363 [0.357]					
	−0.424 [0.277]				
		0.106 [0.268]			
			−0.576** [0.241]		
				−0.361 [0.348]	−0.470 [0.372]
					−0.810* [0.415]

−0.806*** [0.195]	−0.765*** [0.183]	−0.757*** [0.190]	−0.770*** [0.176]	−0.748*** [0.189]	−0.778*** [0.186]
151	151	151	151	151	151

Table 4.6: Net Entry Component of Labor Productivity
and Regulation

Estimation method: weighted least squares (robust to outliers)
Country and sector fixed effects were included
(coefficients not reported)

Dependent variable: Net entry component

Regulations	[1]	[2]
Entry (Entry index × turnover in the United States, by sector)	1.313** [0.565]	
Finance (Finance index × turnover in the United States, by sector)		1.539*** [0.557]
Judicial (Judicial index × turnover in the United States, by sector)		
Trade (Trade index × turnover in the United States, by sector)		
Bankruptcy (Bankruptcy index × turnover in the United States, by sector)		
Labor (Labor index × turnover in the United States, by sector)		
Taxation (Taxation index × turnover in the United States, by sector)		
Composite (Composite index × turnover in the United States, by sector)		
Control variable		
Initial labor productivity (in logs)	−0.709*** [0.249]	−0.694*** [0.251]
Observations (N)	151	151

Source: Authors' calculations.
Note: The sample is 12 countries and 13 sectors (see annex 4.1 for the complete list
of countries and sectors). Numbers in brackets are the corresponding robust
standard errors.

* significant at 10%

** significant at 5%

*** significant at 1%

[3]	[4]	[5]	[6]	[7]	[8]
0.737 [0.485]					
	0.183 [0.389]				
		−0.120 [0.362]			
			0.675* [0.342]		
				−0.412 [0.475]	−0.326 [0.520]
					0.975* [0.580]
−0.851*** [0.265]	−0.926*** [0.256]	−0.915*** [0.256]	−0.872*** [0.250]	−0.913*** [0.258]	−0.723*** [0.260]
151	151	151	151	151	151

impact on productivity growth through the provision of public
goods and services.

Second, we find that entry, financial, and labor regulations have
a statistically significant effect on the productivity growth associated
with reallocation between continuing firms and from the entry and
exit of firms; however, these regulations seem to have different effects
on each one of these components. Namely, they appear to reduce
productivity growth among continuing firms that are shifting
resources between each other, while they increase productivity
growth among entering and exiting firms.

Going further into detail in this result, we have also estimated the
regressions using the entry and exit components separately as dependent variables.[18] In both regressions the coefficients of all regulation
indices except fiscal burden are positive. They are statistically significant in the case of entering firms for all product market regulations, except bankruptcy, plus labor regulation. For exiting firms,
financial, trade, and bankruptcy regulations have statistically significant coefficients.

These results are plausible in a scenario in which high entry barriers (due to entry regulations, lack of access to finance, and high
hiring and firing costs) act as a "filter" for firms that wish to enter
the industry but whose initial productivity is below average, as well
as for firms that do not have sufficient information about their productivity. Because the risk of failure for these firms is higher, they
may decide not to enter the industry when costs are high, whereas
firms whose productivity is higher may be in a better position to
afford the entry cost. Likewise, some firms with productivity below
average might be prematurely selected out of the market in the presence of stringent regulations (as these may translate into higher oper-
ating costs), leading to the observation of higher productivity growth
among exiting firms in countries with more stringent regulations.

Conclusion

The macroeconomic impact of microeconomic regulation has
attracted renewed interest in the academic and policy debate. Recent
empirical studies have examined the effects of regulatory barriers—
particularly those in the product market—on the growth rates of
output and productivity at the aggregate level, mostly across industrial countries.

This chapter focuses on the Schumpeterian mechanism linking
regulation and labor productivity growth. For this purpose, it com-

bines two recently assembled databases: a cross-country dataset on regulatory indicators and a dataset on firm dynamics and productivity for a sample of both industrial and developing economies. Much of the analytical literature points toward the dynamics of firm entry and exit—i.e., the Schumpeterian process of creative destruction—as the main channel through which microeconomic regulatory barriers affect aggregate economic performance. The chapter offers an empirical evaluation of this view, assessing both the impact of regulation on labor productivity growth and the connecting links in this relationship, first relating regulation to firm turnover and then analyzing the effects of firm turnover on productivity growth. In contrast with most of the preceding literature, which has focused on the effects of product-market regulation in industrial countries, here we examine a variety of regulatory dimensions and consider both OECD and Latin American countries.

The chapter first observes that countries where firm turnover is more active exhibit faster productivity growth. Moreover, it finds that the reallocation-related components of productivity growth exhibit the most significant connection with turnover. Then, the chapter turns to the connection between regulation and firm dynamics, finding that in countries where labor and product-market regulations are more burdensome, firm turnover rates are correspondingly lower on average. However, in contrast to the results on labor and product-market regulations, countries with stronger taxation show higher firm turnover. This may suggest that tax-financed public goods and services can indeed facilitate firm renewal.

Having provided support for the transmission mechanism based on firm dynamics (from regulation to turnover, and from turnover to productivity growth), the chapter analyzes the relationship between regulation and productivity growth directly. It finds that labor and product-market regulations have a negative effect on labor productivity growth. The adverse effect is stronger on the components of productivity growth that reflect reallocation of resources between firms than it is on the component that captures productivity growth within firms. On the other hand, the net effect of higher taxation and related revenues appears to be an increase in firms' labor productivity growth, likely reflecting the positive relationship between taxation and firm turnover and, more generally, the beneficial effect of public goods and services.

Annex 4.1: Sample of Countries and Sectors

I. Countries (12)

	Period covered	
Country	Turnover	Labor productivity
Argentina	1996–2001	1995–2001
Brazil	1997–2000	2001
Chile	1980–98	1985–99
Colombia	1983–97	1987–98
Finland	1989–97	2000–02
France	1989–97	1990–95
Korea, Rep. of	1988	1988 & 1993
Netherlands	1993–95	1992–2001
Portugal	1983–98	1991–94 & 2000
United Kingdom	1982–98	1985–92 & 2000–01
United States	1989–91 & 1994–96	1992 & 1997
Venezuela, R. B. de	1996–98	1999

II. Sectors (13)

Food and beverages
Textiles
Wood
Paper
Chemicals and fuel
Rubber and plastics
Other non–metallic minerals
Basic metals
Fabricated metals except machinery
Machinery not elsewhere cited
Electrical and optical
Transport equipment
Recycling

Annex 4.2: Descriptive Statistics

Variable	Mean	Std. dev.	Minimum	Maximum
Turnover (in logs)	2.168	0.745	−0.375	4.109
Turnover in the United States (in logs)	1.125	0.556	0.081	2.012
Entry	0.335	0.184	0.061	0.643
Finance	0.263	0.193	0.000	0.630
Judicial	0.316	0.227	0.013	0.781
Trade	0.311	0.275	0.000	0.751
Bankruptcy	0.390	0.288	0.000	0.886
Labor	0.627	0.298	0.000	1.000
Taxation	0.508	0.220	0.145	0.883
Composite index	0.374	0.204	0.066	0.730
GDP growth (std. dev., constant)	2.963	1.566	1.025	6.386
Terms of trade growth (std. dev.)	6.115	6.180	0.812	24.551
Labor productivity growth	3.625	3.673	−7.369	17.878
Within component	2.797	2.638	−5.861	12.664
Between component	0.133	0.758	−2.309	4.911
Net entry component	0.695	1.600	−9.506	5.549
Entry component	−0.442	1.027	−7.433	1.847
Exit component	−1.132	1.158	−5.334	2.088
Initial labor productivity (in logs)	7.146	2.508	2.176	10.979

Annex 4.3: Principal Component Analysis of Seven Regulatory Indices

Principal components/correlation	Number of observations (countries) = 75
Number of components = 7	Rotation: (unrotated = principal)

Component	Eigenvalue	Difference	Explained variation	
			Proportion	*Cumulative*
Comp1	3.93243	2.88273	0.5618	0.5618
Comp2	1.0497	0.291605	0.1500	0.7117
Comp3	0.758097	0.261635	0.1083	0.8200
Comp4	0.496462	0.196924	0.0709	0.8910
Comp5	0.299538	0.0526998	0.0428	0.9337
Comp6	0.246839	0.029912	0.0353	0.9690
Comp7	0.216927	.	0.0310	1.0000

Principal components (eigenvectors) – Loadings

Variable	Comp1	Comp2	Comp3	Comp4	Comp5	Comp6	Comp7
Entry	0.4382	0.0185	0.1417	-0.1007	-0.8006	0.2956	0.2215
Finance	0.3907	-0.4159	0.3301	-0.1425	0.2236	0.3165	-0.6284
Judicial	0.438	0.1636	-0.0968	-0.2305	0.5402	0.3655	0.5418
Trade	0.4115	-0.3833	0.1239	-0.1404	0.0351	-0.7709	0.2306
Bankruptcy	0.382	0.0708	-0.0506	0.9165	0.0775	-0.0089	-0.0206
Labor	0.2101	0.7917	0.4065	-0.1391	0.0505	-0.2678	-0.2652
Taxation	-0.3226	-0.1459	0.8237	0.1934	0.0861	0.1128	0.3723

Annex 4.4: Definitions and Sources of Variables Used in Regression Analysis

Variable	Definition and construction	Source
Turnover	Log of turnover rate, averaged by sector and country over the available period (see annex 4.1). Turnover rate is employment-weighted, calculated as the sum of employment for entry and exit divided by total employment.	Authors' calculations with data from Haltiwanger, Scarpetta, and Schweiger (2008).
GDP growth	Standard deviation of real GDP growth over the period 1985–2000.	Authors' calculations with data from World Development Indicators.
Terms of trade growth	Standard deviation of terms of trade growth over the period 1985–2000.	Authors' calculations with data from World Development Indicators.
Entry	Combines the number of legal steps required to register a new business with an indicator of the overall legal burden of registration and willingness of the government to facilitate the process and intervene minimally.	Regulation and Macroeconomic Performance (Loayza, Oviedo, and Serven 2009).
Finance	Measures the degree of government intervention through interest rate controls, ownership of banks, entry barriers, restrictions in securities markets, and constraints on foreign banks.	Regulation and Macroeconomic Performance (Loayza, Oviedo, and Serven 2009).
Judicial	Combines a measure of the complexity of court procedures with a measure of bureaucracy's red tape for policy formulation and routine administrative functions.	Regulation and Macroeconomic Performance (Loayza, Oviedo, and Serven 2009).
Trade	Combines indicators of average tariffs, other import barriers, and the cost of importing generated by mandatory administrative procedures (license fees, bank fees, etc.).	Regulation and Macroeconomic Performance (Loayza, Oviedo, and Serven 2009).

(continues on the following page)

Annex 4.4: Definitions and Sources of Variables Used in Regression Analysis *(continued)*

Variable	Definition and construction	Source
Bankruptcy	Combines measures of the time and cost of the liquidation procedure, the enforcement of priority of claims, the extent to which the efficient outcome is achieved, and the degree of court involvement in the process.	Regulation and Macroeconomic Performance (Loayza, Oviedo, and Serven 2009).
Labor	Combines indicators of the presence of minimum wage, the flexibility of hiring and firing laws, the unionization rate, the amount of unemployment benefits, the use of conscription in the military, and minimum mandatory working conditions.	Regulation and Macroeconomic Performance (Loayza, Oviedo, and Serven 2009).
Taxation	Measures direct taxation—that is, the maximum tax rate applied to individuals and businesses—and the volume of fiscal spending.	Regulation and Macroeconomic Performance (Loayza, Oviedo, and Serven 2009).
Composite index	Average of entry, finance, judicial, trade, bankruptcy, and labor regulation indices.	Regulation and Macroeconomic Performance (Loayza, Oviedo, and Serven 2009).
Initial labor productivity	Log of initial value of labor productivity.	Bartelsman, Haltiwanger, and Scarpetta (2004).
Labor productivity growth	Average log difference of productivity over the available period (see annex 4.1).	Bartelsman, Haltiwanger, and Scarpetta (2004).

Between component	The addition to productivity coming from reallocation of resources between firms. Averaged over the available period (see annex 4.1).	Bartelsman, Haltiwanger, and Scarpetta (2004). Calculated following Griliches and Regev (1995).
Within component	The amount of productivity growth coming from productivity increments within continuing firms. Averaged over the available period (see annex 4.1).	Bartelsman, Haltiwanger, and Scarpetta (2004). Calculated following Griliches and Regev (1995).
Entry component	The portion of productivity growth coming from the entry of firms. Averaged over the available period (see annex 4.1).	Bartelsman, Haltiwanger, and Scarpetta (2004). Calculated following Griliches and Regev (1995).
Exit component	The portion of productivity growth coming from the exit of firms. Averaged over the available period (see annex 4.1).	Bartelsman, Haltiwanger, and Scarpetta (2004). Calculated following Griliches and Regev (1995).
Net entry component	Difference between entry and exit component. Averaged over the available period (see annex 4.1).	Authors' calculations with data from Bartelsman, Haltiwanger, and Scarpetta (2004).

Notes

1. The reader interested in a detailed account of this literature is referred to chapters 2 and 3 in this volume.

2. In addition, to help insure against simultaneity bias, the regressions control for the standard deviation of GDP growth and of terms-of-trade growth. These sources of volatility are likely to be correlated with both the country's regulatory stance and its firm turnover rates.

3. Our country sample covers five Latin American countries, namely, Argentina, Brazil, Chile, Colombia, and República Bolivariana de Venezuela, in addition to seven industrial economies: Finland, France, the Republic of Korea, the Netherlands, Portugal, the United Kingdom, and the United States.

4. Full details on the construction of these indices are given in chapter 3. To summarize, we use six data sources: Doing Business (The World Bank Group), Index of Economic Freedom (The Heritage Foundation), Economic Freedom of the World (The Fraser Institute), Labor Market Indicators Database (M. Rama and R. Artecona, 2002), The Corporate Tax Rates Survey (KPMG), and International Country Risk Guide (The PRS Group). These sources cover the largest number of countries and areas under regulation, and their measures use a clear methodology and are straightforward. Except for the Labor Market Indicators Database, all sources are public.

5. Each component was rescaled according to the following formula:

$$\frac{X_i - X_{min}}{X_{max} - X_{min}}$$

if higher values of X indicate heavier regulation and

$$\frac{X_{max} - X_i}{X_{max} - X_{min}}$$

if lower values of X indicate heavier regulation.

6. Annex 4.2 provides principal component analysis of the seven regulation indices across the entire sample of 75 countries for which the indices could be constructed; see chapter 3 for more details. The analysis shows that the six indices that we include in the composite regulation index carry positive loadings in the first principal component, while the taxation index has a negative loading.

7. Industry-wise labor productivity is calculated as a weighted average of firm-level productivity, using value added as the measure of output.

8. We refer the reader to Bartelsman et al. (2004) for a detailed description of the data collection protocol, as well as important discussions of the main indicators constructed.

9. See annex 4.1.

10. The turnover rate is the sum of employment in entering and exiting firms, divided by total employment in the current year.

11. According to theoretical explanations of the negative correlation between job reallocation and the business cycle, the job destruction that takes place during recessions is not entirely "creative destruction." In fact, in the presence of frictions, destruction can be highly inefficient (as in Caballero and Hammour, 1998). However, we expect that in the long run, a relatively frictionless economy will experience productivity gains coming from the entry and exit of firms, a fact that has been documented for several industrial countries by Foster et al. (2001), Barnes et al. (2002), and others. In addition, an economy that undergoes a liberalization process by tearing down burdensome regulation should indeed experience productivity gains from inefficient firms losing ground to efficient ones.

12. To control for industry composition at the country level, the chart presents residuals from the regression of each component on sector dummies.

13. For instance, Brazil has data for only 2001, while Chile and Colombia have data for over ten years; moreover, the respective sample periods may not overlap, as is the case for these three countries.

14. See a list of all variables and their sources in annex 4.4.

15. Our results are not fundamentally different if we employ unweighted techniques.

16. Our results are not fundamentally different if we employ unweighted techniques.

17. Although outside of the scope of this chapter, we should note that the effects of the regulatory burden on productivity growth can vary over the business cycle. In booms, the regulatory burden is likely to be less onerous and, thus, have smaller effects on productivity growth. In downturns, conversely, regulations may be more restrictive and influential, leading to an inefficient selection process with larger productivity repercussions (see Caballero and Hammour 1998 and Ouyang 2009).

18. These results are not shown in the tables but are available upon request.

References

Aghion, Philippe, Nick Bloom, Richard Blundell, Rachel Griffith, and Peter Howitt. 2005. "Competition and Innovation: An Inverted-U Relationship." *Quarterly Journal of Economics* 120 (2): 701–728.

Barnes, Matthew, Jonathan Haskel, and Mika Maliranta. 2002. "The Sources of Productivity Growth: Micro-level Evidence for the OECD." Unpublished manuscript.

Bartelsman, Eric J., and Mark Doms. 2000. "Understanding Productivity: Lessons from Longitudinal Microdata." *Journal of Economic Literature* 38(3): 569–94.

Bartelsman, Eric, John Haltiwanger, and Stefano Scarpetta. 2004. "Microeconomic Evidence of Creative Destruction in Industrial and Developing Countries." Background Paper for the WDR 2005, World Bank, Washington, DC.

Bartelsman, Eric, Stefano Scarpetta, and Fabiano Schivardi. 2003. "Comparative Analysis of Firm Demographics and Survival: Micro-level Evidence for the OECD Countries." Economics Department Working Paper 348, OECD, Paris.

Basu, Susanto, John Fernald, and Miles Kimball. 2004. "Are Technology Improvements Contractionary?" NBER Working Paper 10592, NBER, Cambridge, MA.

Caballero, Ricardo, and Mohamad Hammour. 1998. "The Macroeconomics of Specificity." *Journal of Political Economy* 106 (4): 724–767.

Card, David, and Richard B. Freeman. 2002. What Have Two Decades of British Economic Reform Delivered? NBER Working Paper 8801, NBER, Cambridge, MA.

Cincera, Michele, and Olivia Galgau. 2005. "Impact of Market Entry and Exit on EU Productivity and Growth Performance." European Economy Economic Paper 222, European Commission, Brussels.

Dunne, Timothy, Mark Roberts, and Larry Samuelson. 1989. "The Growth and Failure of U.S. Manufacturing Plants" *Quarterly Journal of Economics* 104(4): 671–98.

Dutz, Mark, and Aydin Hayri. 2000. "Does More Intense Competition Lead to Higher Growth?" Policy Research Working Paper 2320, World Bank, Washington, DC.

Foster, Lucia, John Haltiwanger, and C.J. Krizan. 2001. "Aggregate Productivity Growth: Lessons from Microeconomic Evidence." In *New Developments in Productivity Analysis*, ed. Edward Dean, Michael Harper, and Charles Hulten, 303–372. Chicago: University of Chicago Press.

Griffith, Rachel, and Rupert Harrison. 2004. "The Link between Product Market Reform and Macroeconomic Performance." European Economy Economic Paper 209, European Commission, Brussels.

Griliches, Zvi, and Haim Regev. 1995. "Productivity and Firm Turnover in Israeli Industry: 1979–1988." NBER Working Paper 4059, NBER, Cambridge, MA.

Haltiwanger, John, Stefano Scarpetta, Helena Schweiger. 2008. "Assessing Job Flows Across Countries: The Role of Industry, Firm Size and Regulations." NBER Working Paper 13920, NBER, Cambridge, MA.

Klapper, Leora, Luc Laeven, and Raghuram G. Rajan. 2006. "Entry Regulation as a Barrier to Entrepreneurship." *Journal of Financial Economics* 82 (3): 591–629.

Koedijk, Kees, and Jeroen Kremers. 1996. "Market Opening, Regulation and Growth in Europe." *Economic Policy* (23): 443–467.

Loayza, Norman, Ana María Oviedo, and Luis Servén. 2009. "Regulation and Macroeconomic Performance." This volume.

Micco, Alejandro, and Carmen Pagés, 2007. "The Economic Effects of Employment Protection: Evidence from International Industry-Level Data." Research Department Working Paper 592, Inter-American Development Bank, Washington, DC.

Nicoletti, Guiseppe, and Stefano Scarpetta. 2003. "Regulation, Productivity and Growth: OECD Evidence." *Economic Policy* 18(36): 9–72.

Ouyang, Min. 2009. "The Scarring Effect of Recessions." *Journal of Monetary Economics* 56(2): 184–199

Rajan, Raghuram G., and Luigi Zingales. 1998. "Financial Dependence and Growth." *The American Economic Review* 88(3): 559–586.

Rama, Martin, and Raquel Artecona. 2002. "A Database of Labor Market Indicators across Countries." Unpublished manuscript. World Bank, Washington DC.

Roberts, Mark J., and James R. Tybout, ed. 1996. *Industrial Evolution in Developing Countries: Micro Patterns of Turnover, Productivity, and Market Structure.* New York: Oxford University Press.

World Bank. 2003. *World Development Indicators.* Washington, DC.

———. 2005. *World Development Report.* Washington, DC.

5

Informality in Latin America and the Caribbean

Norman V. Loayza, Luis Servén, and Naotaka Sugawara

Introduction

"Informality" is a term used to describe the collection of firms, workers, and activities that operates outside the legal and regulatory frameworks.[1] While informality offers the benefit of avoiding the burdens of taxation and regulation, at the same time, its participants do not get to fully enjoy the protection and services that the law and the state can provide. Informality is sometimes the result of agents "exiting" the formal sector as a consequence of cost-benefit considerations;

For valuable comments and suggestions, we are grateful to Ibrahim Elbadawi, Pablo Fajnzylber, Fausto Hernández, Ana María Oviedo, Jamele Rigolini, Jaime Saavedra, and Klaus Schmidt-Hebbel. This chapter draws from Norman V. Loayza and Naotaka Sugawara, "The Informal Sector in Mexico: Basic Facts and Explanations," *El Trimestre Económico* (2009); and Ibrahim Elbadawi and Norman Loayza, "Informality, Employment, and Economic Development in the Arab World," *Journal of Development and Economic Policies* (2008). The views expressed in this chapter are those of the authors and do not necessarily reflect those of the World Bank, their Boards of Directors, or the countries they represent.

other times, it is the outcome of agents being "excluded" from formality as this becomes restrictive and the economy segmented.

In all cases, informality is a fundamental characteristic of underdevelopment and is best understood as a complex, multifaceted phenomenon. It is determined by both the modes of socioeconomic organization inherent in economies in the transition to modernity and by the relationship that the state establishes with private agents through regulation, monitoring, and the provision of public services. Informality is not only a reflection of underdevelopment; it may also be the source of further economic retardation. It implies the misallocation of resources and entails losing the advantages of legality, such as police and judicial protection, access to formal credit institutions, and participation in international markets.

According to the estimates presented below, there is a great deal of heterogeneity in the types of informality among the countries of Latin America. In all of them, however, informality is much more widespread than in the United States, and some countries in the region are among the most informal economies in the world. The typical country in Latin America produces about 40 percent of its GDP and employs 70 percent of its labor force informally. These are astounding statistics, which indicate that informality is a substantive and pervasive phenomenon that must be explained and addressed, particularly in the design of development policies.

This chapter studies informality in Latin America from a macroeconomic and international perspective. It uses cross-country variations on measures and potentially related variables of informality to study its causes and consequences. It then examines Latin American countries against this broad international context. In this chapter, the next section presents and discusses various measures of informality. This is followed by a section that assesses the impact of informality on economic growth and poverty. Next, we present an analysis of the main causes of informality, followed by a section that evaluates the empirical relevance of each determinant of informality to every Latin American country in the sample. Finally, we offer some concluding remarks.

Measuring Informality in Latin America and Around the World

Although the definition of informality can be simple and precise, this is not the case with its measurement. Given that it involves working outside the legal and regulatory frameworks, informality is best described as a latent, unobserved variable, that is, a variable for which accurate and complete measurement is not feasible but for which an approximation is possible through indicators reflecting its various aspects. Here we consider four such indicators, available for a relatively large collection of countries. Two of the indicators refer to overall informal activity in the country, and the other two relate in particular to informal employment. While each indicator on its own has conceptual and statistical shortcomings as a proxy for informality, taken together, they may provide a robust approximation to the subject.

The two indicators related to overall informal activity are the Schneider index of the shadow economy and the Heritage Foundation index of informal markets.[2] The Schneider index combines the DYMIMIC (dynamic multiple-indicator-multiple-cause) method, the physical input (electricity) method, and the excess currency-demand approach for the estimation of the share of production that is not declared to tax and regulatory authorities. The Heritage Foundation index is based on subjective perceptions of general compliance with the law, with particular emphasis on the role played by official corruption.

The two indicators that focus on the labor aspect of informality are the prevalence of self-employment and the lack of pension coverage. The prevalence of self-employment is determined by the ratio of self to total employment, as reported by the International Labour Organization (ILO). The lack of pension coverage is estimated through the fraction of the labor force that does not contribute to a retirement pension scheme, as reported in the World Bank's World Development Indicators. Annex 5.3 presents some descriptive statistics on the four informality indicators. In particular, it shows that, as expected, they are significantly positively correlated, with correlation coefficients ranging from 0.59 to 0.90—high enough to represent the same phenomenon but not so high as to make them mutually redundant.

Using data on these four indicators, we can assess the prevalence of informality across Latin America. For comparison purposes, figure 5.1 presents data on the four informality indicators for individual countries in Latin America and the Caribbean (LAC). The United States and Chile are used as benchmark countries. The United States is the developed country to which the region is most closely related. Chile is the Latin American country often taken as a model for economic reforms and sustained growth in the region.[3] It is clear from the figure that there is considerable variation in informality across countries in Latin America. However, in all of them, the degree of informality is much higher than it is in the United States and, for some countries (e.g., Bolivia and Haiti), it is comparable to the most

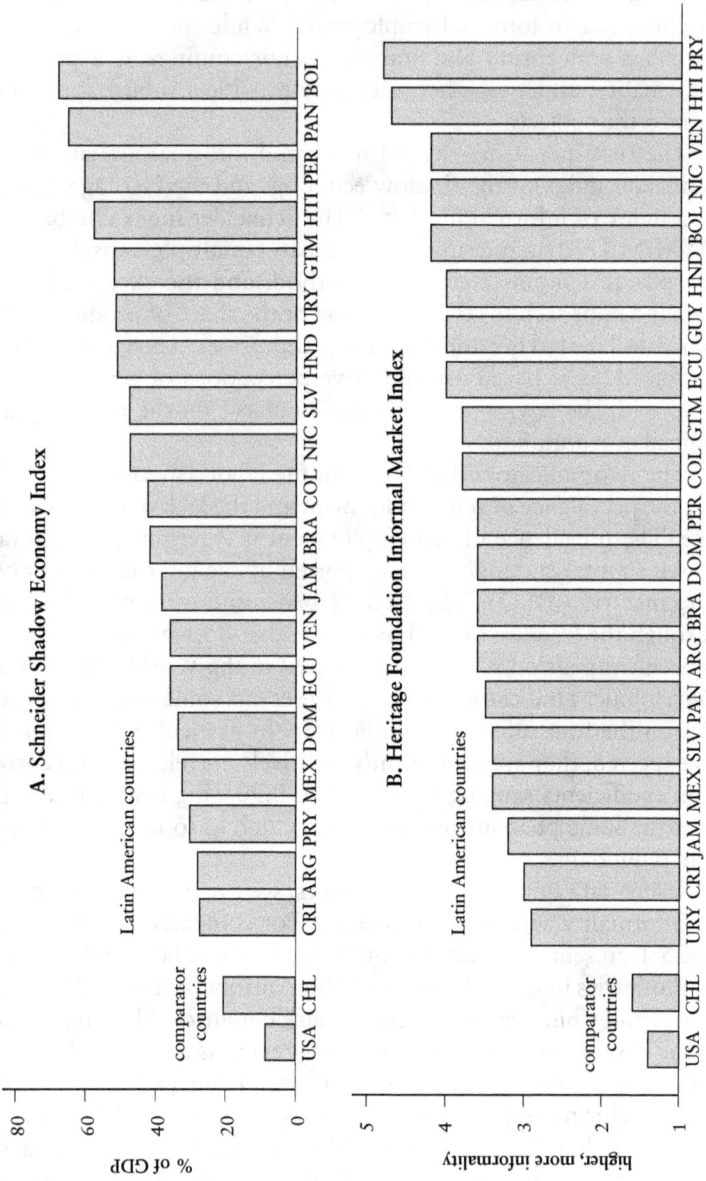

Figure 5.1: Size of Informality in Latin America, Various Measures

A. Schneider Shadow Economy Index

Latin American countries

comparator countries

% of GDP

80 60 40 20 0

USA CHL | CRI ARG PRY MEX DOM ECU VEN JAM BRA COL NIC SLV HND URY GTM HTI PER PAN BOL

B. Heritage Foundation Informal Market Index

Latin American countries

comparator countries

higher, more informality

5 4 3 2 1

USA CHL | URY CRI JAM MEX SLV PAN ARG BRA DOM PER COL GTM ECU GUY HND BOL NIC VEN HTI PRY

C. Self Employment

Latin American countries

comparator countries

% of total employment

USA CHL ARG CRI URY MEX BRA PAN SLV VEN ECU JAM GTM PER HND COL BOL DOM

D. Non-contributor to Pension Scheme

Latin American countries

comparator countries

% of labor force

USA CHL URY CRI PAN JAM BRA ARG MEX ECU VEN DOM PER SLV GTM HND PRY COL NIC BOL

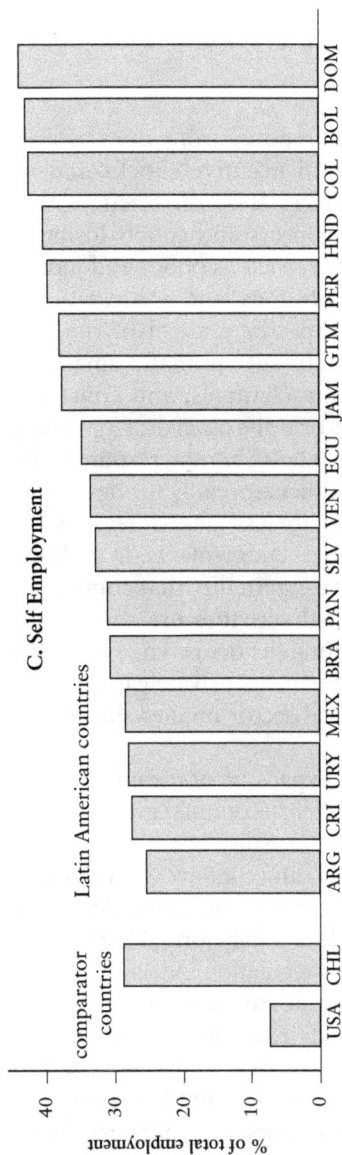

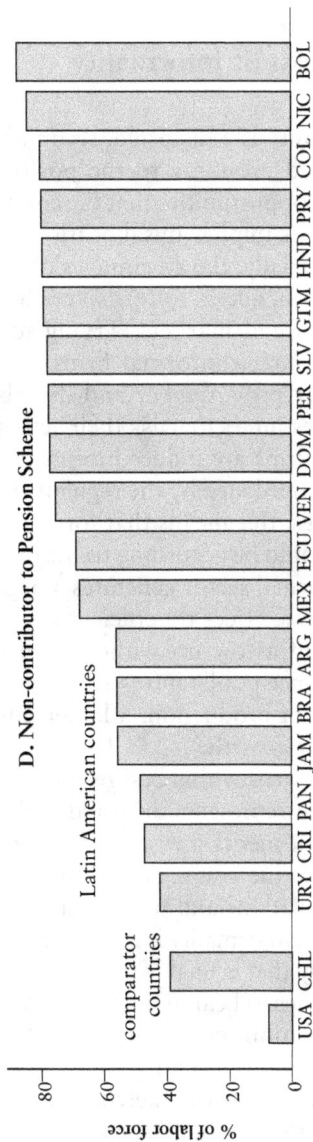

Source: Authors' calculations.
Note: For a list of countries and their 3-letter codes, please see annex 5.1.

161

informal countries in the world. For the median country in Latin
America, about 40 percent of GDP is produced informally. Informal
employment is more difficult to ascertain. Using the measure based
on pension contributions, about 70 percent of the labor force is
informal in the median country in Latin America.[4]

The Cost of Informality

Informality is a distorted, second-best response from an excessively
regulated economy to the positive and negative shocks and the
growth opportunities that the country faces. It is a distorted response
because it implies misallocation of resources and entails losing, at
least partially, the advantages of legality, such as police and judicial
protection, access to formal credit institutions, and participation in
international markets. Trying to escape the control of the state
induces many informal firms to remain suboptimally small, use
irregular procurement and distribution channels, and constantly
divert resources to mask their activities or bribe officials. Conversely,
formal firms are induced to use more intensively the resources that
are less burdened by the regulatory regime; especially for developing
countries, this means that formal firms are less labor-intensive than
they should be according to the countries' endowments. In addition,
the informal sector generates a negative externality that compounds
its adverse effect on efficiency: informal activities use and congest
public infrastructure without contributing the tax revenue to replen-
ish it. Since public infrastructure complements private capital in the
process of production, a larger informal sector implies slower productivity growth.[5]

Compared with a best response, the expansion of the informal sector often represents distorted and deficient economic growth.[6] This
statement merits further clarification: informality is suboptimal with
respect to the best scenario that occurs in an economy without excessive regulations and with adequate provision of public services. Nevertheless, informality is indeed preferable to a fully formal but sclerotic
economy that is unable to circumvent its regulation-induced rigidities.
This brings to bear an important policy implication: the mechanism of
formalization matters enormously for its consequences on employment, efficiency, and growth. If formalization is purely based on
enforcement, it will likely lead to unemployment and low growth. If,
on the other hand, it is based on improvements in both the regulatory
framework and the quality and availability of public services, it will
bring about more efficient use of resources and higher growth.

From an empirical perspective, the ambiguous impact of formalization highlights an important difficulty in assessing the impact of informality on economic growth: two countries can have the same level of informality, but if the informality has been achieved in different ways, the countries' growth rates may be markedly different. Countries where informality is kept at bay by drastic enforcement will fare worse than countries where informality is low because of light regulations and appropriate public services.

We now present a simple regression analysis of the effect of informality on growth. As suggested above, this analysis must control for enforcement, and a straightforward, albeit debatable, way to do this is by including a proxy for the overall capacity of the state as a control variable in the regression. For this purpose, we try two proxies: the level of GDP per capita, and the ratio of government expenditures to GDP. The former has the advantage of also accounting for conditional convergence, and the latter has the advantage of more closely reflecting the size of the state.[7] Another important consideration for this empirical analysis is that informality may not only affect but also be affected by economic growth. For example, faster growth could raise the profitability of production and the real wage, relative to the perceived costs of formality, thus encouraging more firms and workers to shift out of the informal sector. In order to ascertain the impact of informality on growth, we need to isolate the exogenous variation in informality. We do this through an instrumental-variable approach, where the instruments are selected among the variables that are postulated as determinants of informality—indicators of law and order, business regulatory freedom, secondary schooling, and sociodemographic factors. Since some of them have a relationship with economic growth that is independent of informality, we only use as instruments the sets of variables that comply with the exclusion restrictions, as diagnosed by the Hansen test of orthogonality between the instruments and the regression residuals (see notes on tables 5.1a and 5.1b for further explanation).

Table 5.1 presents the regression results. The dependent variable is the average growth of per capita GDP over 1985–2005. We choose a period of about 20 years for the measure of average growth in order to achieve a compromise between merely cyclical, short-run growth (which would be unaffected by informality) and very long-run growth (which could be confused with the sources, rather than consequences, of informality). We consider two alternative control variables: initial GDP per capita (table 5.1a) or initial ratio of government expenditures to GDP (table 5.1b). The explanatory variables of interest are the four informality indicators, considered one

Table 5.1a: The Effect of Informality on Economic Growth, Controlling for GDP per Capita
Dependent variable: Per capita GDP Growth, 1985–2005, country average

	OLS				IV			
	[1]	[2]	[3]	[4]	[5]	[6]	[7]	[8]
Initial GDP per capita (2000 US$, 1985, in logs)	-0.1966 / 1.29	-0.3519 / 1.54	-0.3498* / 1.88	-0.6910* / 1.98	-0.6976*** / 3.06	-0.7684*** / 2.83	-1.2819*** / 2.69	-1.7200*** / 2.95
Schneider shadow economy (% of GDP)	-0.0747*** / 3.87				-0.1479*** / 4.39			
Heritage Foundation informal market[a]		-0.8009** / 2.41				-1.3294*** / 4.05		
Self-employment (% of total employment)			-0.0657*** / 3.11				-0.1775*** / 3.21	
Non-contributor to pension scheme (% of labor force)				-0.0423*** / 2.80				-0.0872*** / 3.39
Constant	5.4231*** / 3.15	6.9131** / 2.57	6.6475*** / 3.35	9.2161** / 2.59	11.8634*** / 4.29	11.7604*** / 3.80	17.1971*** / 3.18	19.8890*** / 3.33
Observations (N)	119	127	72	91	84	87	59	68
R-squared	0.20	0.08	0.13	0.11				
Hansen J Statistic (P-value)					0.48	0.21	0.30	0.70

Source: Authors' calculations.
Note: Heteroskedasticity-robust t(z)-statistics are presented below the corresponding coefficients. See annex 5.2 for definitions and sources of variables. For IV regressions [5] to [8],
● Endogenous variable: each of four informality measures.
● Instruments: Law and order; business regulatory freedom; average years of secondary schooling.
● Sociodemographic factors not included as an instrument; they do not pass the exogeneity test using the C statistic (Difference-in-Sargan statistic).
a. Ranging from 1 to 5; the higher the number, the more informality.
* significant at 10%; ** significant at 5%; *** significant at 1%.

164

Table 5.1b: The Effect of Informality on Economic Growth, Controlling for Government Expenditure/GDP
Dependent variable: Per capita GDP Growth, 1985–2005, country average

	OLS				IV			
	[1]	[2]	[3]	[4]	[5]	[6]	[7]	[8]
Initial government expenditure (% of GDP, 1985)	-0.0340*	-0.0513**	-0.0681***	-0.0588**	-0.0593**	-0.0717***	-0.1008**	-0.0776***
	1.96	2.60	2.82	2.59	2.14	2.94	2.55	3.34
Schneider shadow economy (% of GDP)	-0.0622***				-0.0789***			
	4.76				4.31			
Heritage Foundation informal market[a]		-0.6724***				-0.6085***		
		5.52				4.18		
Self-employment (% of total employment)			-0.0557***				-0.0596***	
			3.84				2.85	
Non-contributor to pension scheme (% of labor force)				-0.0183***				-0.0203***
				3.58				3.51
Constant	4.1214***	4.5441***	4.6023***	3.5267***	5.0933***	4.6934***	5.0909***	4.1156***
	6.71	7.98	6.69	6.19	6.18	6.72	4.50	6.70
Observations (N)	112	118	69	85	88	91	59	72
R-squared	0.20	0.18	0.18	0.11				
Hansen J Statistic (P-value)					0.53	0.89	0.62	0.72

Source: Authors' calculations.
Note: Heteroskedasticity-robust t(z)-statistics are presented below the corresponding coefficients. See annex 5.2 for definitions and sources of variables. For IV regressions [5] to [8],
• Endogenous variable: each of four informality measures.
• Instruments: Law and order; business regulatory freedom; average years of secondary schooling.
• Sociodemographic factors not included as an instrument; they do not pass the exogeneity test using the C statistic (Difference-in-Sargan statistic).
a. Ranging from 1 to 5; the higher the number, the more informality.
* significant at 10%; ** significant at 5%; *** significant at 1%.

at a time. The table first presents the ordinary least-square (OLS) results and then the instrumental-variable (IV) results.

The OLS and IV regression results are basically the same regarding the sign and significance of the coefficients on the informality indicators. If anything, the IV coefficient estimates are somewhat larger in magnitude than their OLS counterparts. They clearly indicate that an increase in informality leads to a decrease in economic growth. All four informality indicators carry negative and highly significant regression coefficients. The harmful effect of informality on growth is not only robust and significant, but its magnitude makes it also economically meaningful: using the estimates from the IV regressions controlling for initial government expenditures/GDP, an increase of one standard deviation in any of the informality indicators leads to a decline of 0.7–1 percentage points in the rate of per capita GDP growth.[8] These are conservative estimates when compared to those from the regression that controls for GDP per capita—there, the growth effects of a reduction in informality are about twice as large.

There is also a close connection between poverty and informality, reflecting at least in part the negative relationship between economic growth and informality. Table 5.2 presents cross-country regression analysis with the headcount poverty index as dependent variable and, in turn, the four measures of informality as explanatory variables. In order to have a close chronological match between dependent and explanatory variables, the headcount poverty index corresponds to the latest available measure per country. As in the growth regressions, the level of GDP per capita (table 5.2a) or the ratio of government expenditures to GDP (table 5.2b) are included as control variables. Also as in previous regressions, we present both OLS and IV estimates, the latter to account for the likely endogeneity of informality with respect to poverty.

The regression results reveal a positive relationship between the prevalence of informality and the incidence of poverty. When government expenditure is controlled for, the four measures of informality carry positive and significant coefficients in the IV regressions. Similarly, when the level of GDP per capita is controlled for, three of the four informality indicators carry positive and significant coefficients (self-employment is the exception).

The significant relationship between informality, on the one hand, and economic growth and poverty, on the other, is remarkable: it underscores the importance of the issue and urges for analysis on the complex sources of informality. To this, we turn next.

Table 5.2a: The Effect of Informality on Poverty, Controlling for GDP per Capita
Dependent variable: Poverty headcount index, latest year

	OLS				IV			
	[1]	[2]	[3]	[4]	[5]	[6]	[7]	[8]
Initial GDP per capita (2000 US$, 1985, in logs)	-0.1331***	-0.1028***	-0.0995***	-0.0656**	-0.1129***	-0.0800***	-0.0796	-0.0346
	6.18	4.07	3.02	2.33	3.48	3.10	1.26	0.94
Schneider shadow economy (% of GDP)	0.0067**				0.0104*			
	2.34				1.71			
Heritage Foundation informal market[a]		0.0841**				0.1229*		
		2.38				1.89		
Self-employment (% of total employment)			0.0004				-0.0017	
			0.22				0.24	
Non-contributor to pension scheme (% of labor force)				0.0031**				0.0051**
				2.34				2.08
Constant	0.8607***	0.6053**	0.8476***	0.4127	0.5717	0.3001	0.7636	0.0436
	4.54	2.30	3.48	1.55	1.46	0.83	1.09	0.11
Observations (N)	51	51	34	46	41	42	30	38
R-squared	0.51	0.42	0.34	0.35	0.47	0.33	0.11	0.11
Hansen J Statistic (P-value)					0.47	0.33	0.11	0.69

Source: Authors' calculations.
Note: Heteroskedasticity-robust t(z)-statistics are presented below the corresponding coefficients. See annex 5.2 for definitions and sources of variables. For IV regressions [5] to [8],
• Endogenous variable: each of four informality measures.
• Instruments: Law and order; Business regulatory freedom; Average years of secondary schooling.
• Sociodemographic factors not included as an instrument; they do not pass the exogeneity test using the C statistic (Difference-in-Sargan statistic).
a. Ranging from 1 to 5; the higher the number, the more informality.
  * significant at 10%; ** significant at 5%; *** significant at 1%.

Table 5.2b: The Effect of Informality on Poverty, Controlling for Government Expenditure/GDP
Dependent variable: Poverty Headcount index, latest year

	OLS				IV			
	[1]	[2]	[3]	[4]	[5]	[6]	[7]	[8]
Initial government expenditure (% of GDP, 1985)	0.0031 0.51	0.0096 1.58	0.0114 1.09	0.0063 1.01	0.0033 0.37	0.0157* 1.86	0.0224*** 3.44	0.0123 1.54
Schneider shadow economy (% of GDP)	0.0075* 1.95				0.0240*** 2.97			
Heritage Foundation informal market[a]		0.2135*** 4.41				0.2470*** 3.47		
Self-employment (% of total employment)			0.0091 1.51				0.0230*** 3.08	
Non-contributor to pension scheme (% of labor force)				0.0064*** 4.95				0.0076*** 3.41
Constant	−0.1130 0.59	−0.7019*** 3.33	−0.2911 0.99	−0.3624*** 2.86	−0.7887** 2.45	−0.9201*** 2.77	−0.9325*** 3.34	−0.5467** 2.56
Observations (N)	48	48	32	43	40	41	29	37
R-squared	0.12	0.33	0.13	0.36				
Hansen J Statistic (P-value)					0.25	0.14	0.52	0.61

Source: Authors' calculations.
Note: Heteroskedasticity-robust t(z)-statistics are presented below the corresponding coefficients. See annex 5.2 for definitions and sources of variables. For IV regressions [5] to [8],
• Endogenous variable: each of four informality measures.
• Instruments: Law and order; Business regulatory freedom; Average years of secondary schooling; Sociodemographic factors.
a. Ranging from 1 to 5; the higher the number, the more informality.
* significant at 10%; ** significant at 5%; *** significant at 1%.

The Causes of Informality

Informality is a fundamental characteristic of underdevelopment, shaped by both the modes of socioeconomic organization inherent in economies in the transition to modernity and by the relationship that the state establishes with private agents through regulation, monitoring, and the provision of public services. As such, informality is best understood as a complex, multifaceted phenomenon.

Informality arises when the costs of belonging to the country's legal and regulatory framework exceed its benefits. Formality entails costs of entry—in the form of lengthy, expensive, and complicated registration procedures—and costs of permanence—including payment of taxes, compliance with mandated labor benefits and remunerations, and observance of environmental, health, and other regulations. The benefits of formality potentially consist of police protection against crime and abuse, recourse to the judicial system for conflict resolution and contract enforcement, access to legal financial institutions for credit provision and risk diversification, and, more generally, the possibility of expanding markets both domestically and internationally. At least in principle, formality also voids the need to pay bribes and prevents penalties and fees, to which informal firms are continuously subject. Therefore, informality is more prevalent when the regulatory framework is burdensome, the quality of government services to formal firms is low, and the state's monitoring and enforcement power is weak.

These cost and benefit considerations are affected by the structural characteristics of underdevelopment, dealing in particular with educational achievement, production structure, and demographic trends. Other things being equal, a higher level of education reduces informality by increasing labor productivity and, therefore, making labor regulations less onerous and formal returns potentially larger. Likewise, a production structure tilted toward primary sectors like agriculture, rather than to the more complex processes of industry, favors informality by making legal protection and contract enforcement less relevant and valuable. Finally, a demographic composition with larger shares of youth or rural populations is likely to increase informality by making monitoring more difficult and expensive, by placing bigger demands on resources for training and acquisition of abilities, by creating bottlenecks in the initial school-to-work transition, and by making more problematic the expansion of formal public services (see Fields 1990; Schneider and Enste 2000; ILO 2004).

Popular and even academic discussions often focus on particular sources of informality, rather than taking this comprehensive approach. Thus, some observers stress insufficient enforcement and related government weaknesses such as corruption; others prefer to emphasize the burden of taxes and regulations; yet others concentrate on explanations dealing with social and demographic characteristics.

As suggested above, all these possibilities make sense, and there is some evidence to support each of them. To illustrate this, figure 5.2 presents cross-country scatter plots of each of the four measures of informality versus proxies for the major proposed determinants of informality. The sample observations include all countries with available data; for illustration purposes, countries in Latin America and the Caribbean are highlighted in the figures. The proxies for the determinants of informality are as follows.[9] An index on the prevalence of law and order—obtained from *The International Country Risk Guide*—is used as a proxy for both the quality of formal public services and government's enforcement strength. An index of business regulatory freedom—taken from the Fraser Institute's *Economic Freedom of the World Report*—is used to represent the ease of restrictions imposed by the legal and regulatory frameworks. The average years of secondary schooling of the adult population—taken from Barro and Lee (2001)—represents the educational and skill achievement of the work force. And, finally, an index of sociodemographic factors—constructed from the World Bank's *World Development Indicators* and other databases—which includes the share of youth in the population, the share of rural population, and the share of agriculture in GDP, was selected.[10]

Remarkably, all 16 correlation coefficients (4 informality measures times 4 determinants) are highly statistically significant, with p-values below 1 percent, and of large magnitude, ranging approximately between 0.54 and 0.87. All informality measures present the same pattern of correlations: informality is negatively related to law and order, regulatory freedom, and schooling achievement, and it is positively related to factors that denote the early stages of sociodemographic transformation.

Therefore, all of these explanations may have some truth in them. What we need to determine now is whether each of them has *independent* explanatory power with respect to informality. More specifically, we need to assess to what extent each of them is relevant both in general for the cross-section of countries and in particular for a given country. We turn next to this purpose.

In what follows, we use cross-country regression analysis to evaluate the importance of each explanation regarding the origins of informality. Each of the four informality measures presented earlier serves as the dependent variable of its respective regression

Figure 5.2: Informality and Basic Determinants

A. Schneider Shadow Economy index

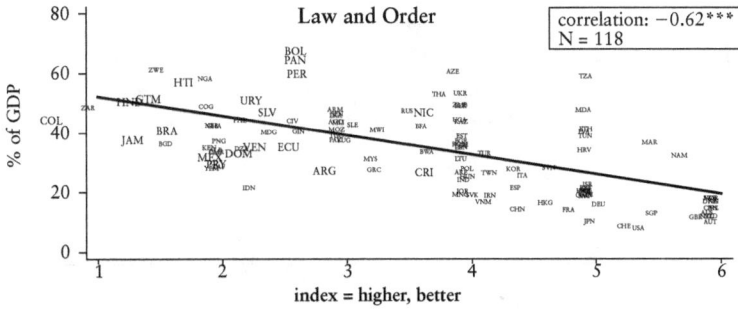

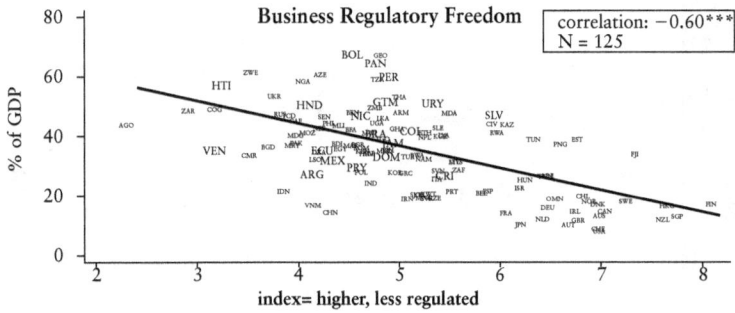

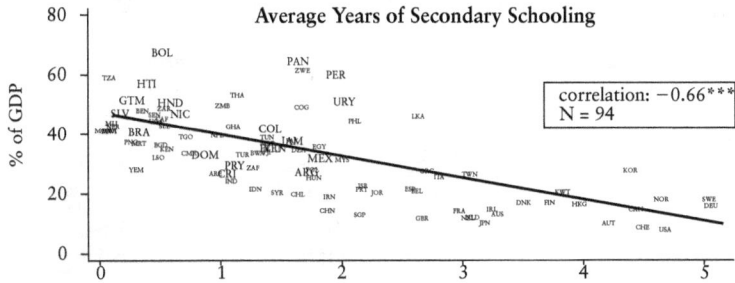

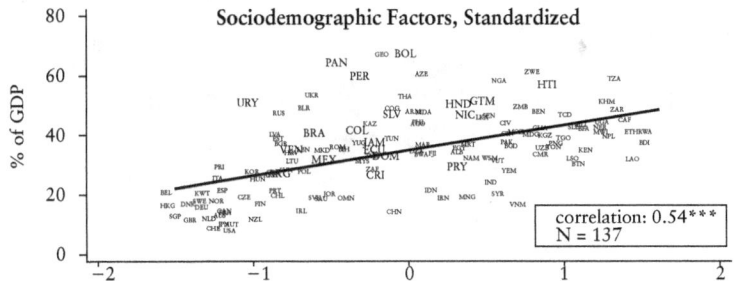

Law and Order

correlation: −0.62***
N = 118

% of GDP

index = higher, better

Business Regulatory Freedom

correlation: −0.60***
N = 125

% of GDP

index= higher, less regulated

Average Years of Secondary Schooling

correlation: −0.66***
N = 94

% of GDP

Sociodemographic Factors, Standardized

correlation: 0.54***
N = 137

% of GDP

Figure 5.2: Informality and Basic Determinants (*continued*)
B. Heritage Foundation Informal Market index

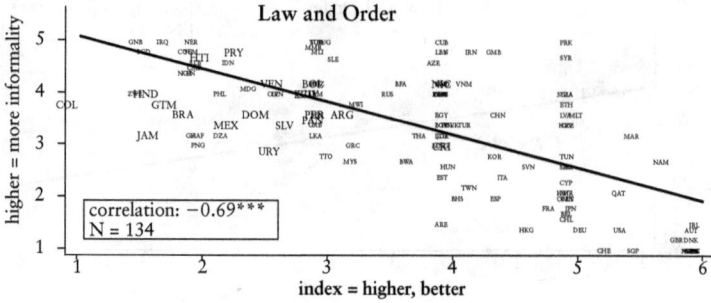

Law and Order

higher = more informality

correlation: −0.69***
N = 134

index = higher, better

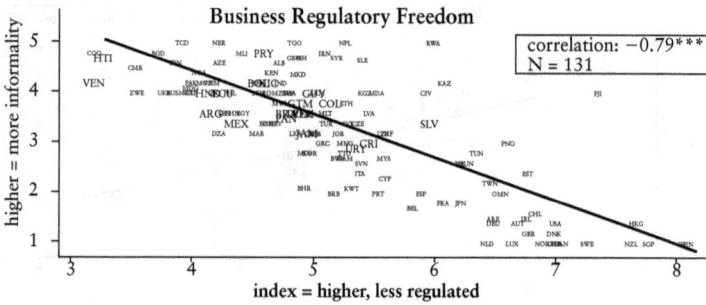

Business Regulatory Freedom

higher = more informality

correlation: −0.79***
N = 131

index = higher, less regulated

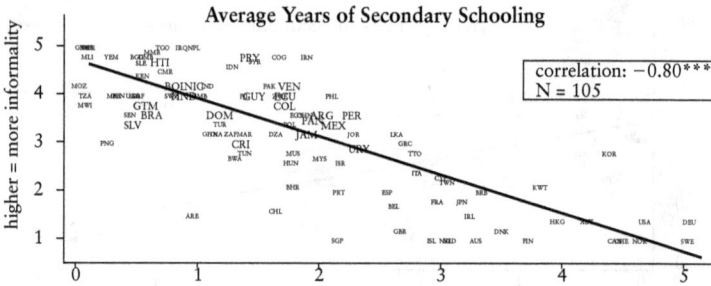

Average Years of Secondary Schooling

higher = more informality

correlation: −0.80***
N = 105

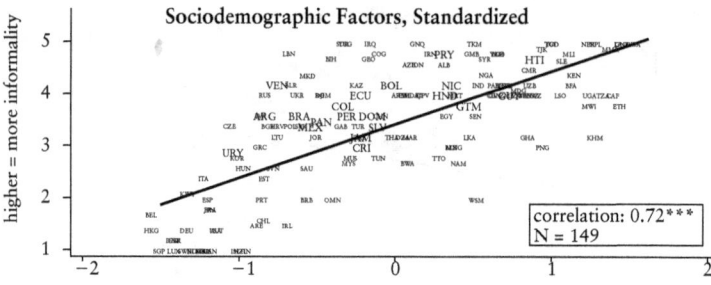

Sociodemographic Factors, Standardized

higher = more informality

correlation: 0.72***
N = 149

Figure 5.2: Informality and Basic Determinants (*continued*)
C. Self-employment

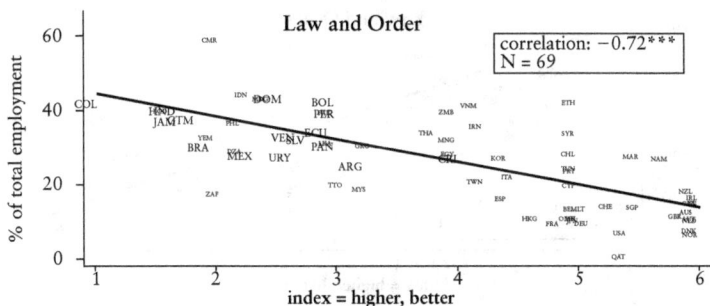

Law and Order

correlation: −0.72***
N = 69

% of total employment

index = higher, better

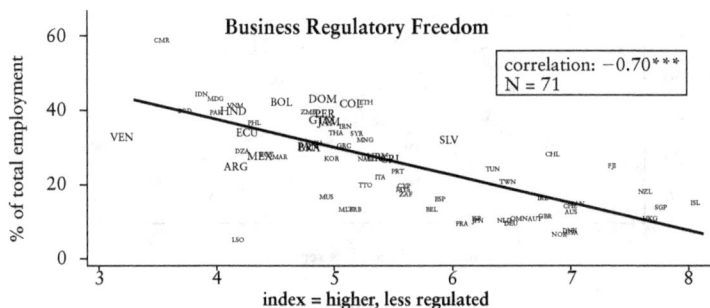

Business Regulatory Freedom

correlation: −0.70***
N = 71

% of total employment

index = higher, less regulated

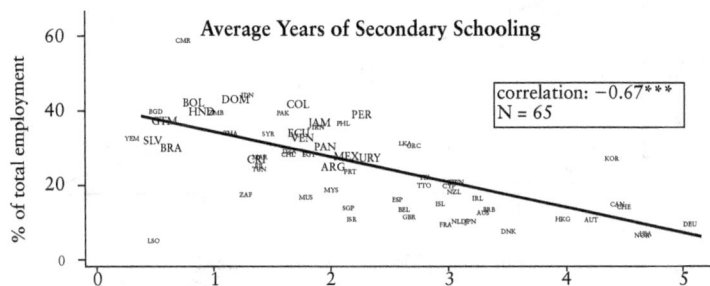

Average Years of Secondary Schooling

correlation: −0.67***
N = 65

% of total employment

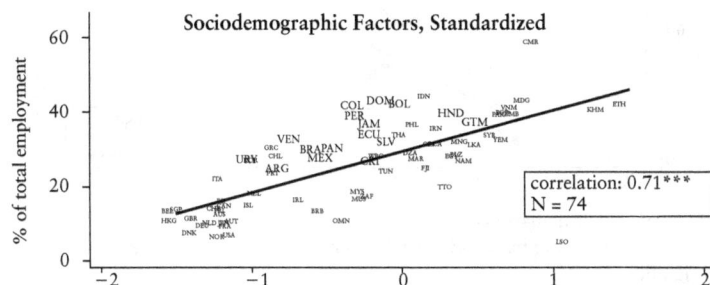

Sociodemographic Factors, Standardized

correlation: 0.71***
N = 74

% of total employment

Figure 5.2: Informality and Basic Determinants (*continued*)

D. Non-contributor to pension scheme

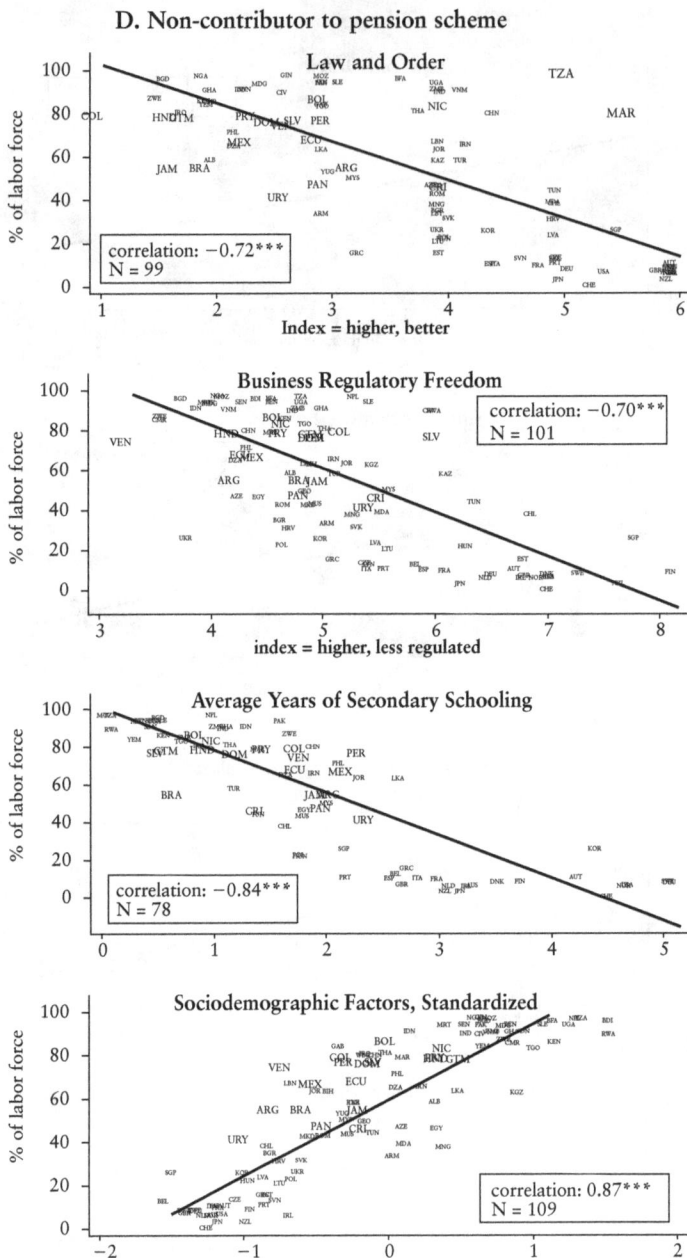

Law and Order

correlation: −0.72***
N = 99

Index = higher, better

Business Regulatory Freedom

correlation: −0.70***
N = 101

index = higher, less regulated

Average Years of Secondary Schooling

correlation: −0.84***
N = 78

Sociodemographic Factors, Standardized

correlation: 0.87***
N = 109

Source: Authors' calculations.
Note: For a list of countries and their 3-letter codes, please see annex 5.1.
*** significant at 1%

model. The set of explanatory variables is common to all informality measures and represents the major determinants of informality. They are the same variables used in the simple correlation analysis, introduced above. Then we apply these estimated relationships to the case of the Latin American and Caribbean countries with available data in order to evaluate the *country-specific* relevance of each proposed mechanism. We can do this for those countries that possess complete information on dependent and explanatory variables, or at least information on the latter, with which we can obtain *predicted* values of the dependent variable. There are 20 countries in the Latin American and Caribbean region that possess complete information on all explanatory variables, but comparable data on self-employment and pension coverage are not available for Haiti. Likewise, Nicaragua and Paraguay do not have data on self-employment, and Guyana has data on the Heritage index only. (In both cases, however, we can construct for them a predicted value based on the regression analysis using the sample of all other countries.)

The regression results are presented in table 5.3. They are remarkably robust across informality measures. Moreover, all regression coefficients have the expected sign and are highly significant. Informality decreases when law and order, business regulatory freedom, or schooling achievement rise. Similarly, informality decreases when the production structure shifts away from agriculture and when demographic pressures from youth and rural populations decline. The fact that each explanatory variable retains its sign and significance after controlling for the rest indicates that no single determinant is sufficient to explain informality. All of them should be taken into account for a complete understanding of informality.

The four explanatory variables account jointly for a large share of the cross-country variation in informality: the R-squared coefficients are 0.57 for the Schneider shadow economy index, 0.89 for the Heritage Foundation informal market index, 0.78 for the share of self-employment, and 0.88 for the share of the labor force not contributing to a pension program.

Explaining Informality in Latin American Countries

The cross-country regression analysis presented above can be used to assess the determinants of informality that are most relevant to each Latin American country. The first issue to explore is whether these countries are outliers or follow the general trend established by the cross-country regressions. Figure 5.3 presents a scatter plot

Table 5.3: Determinants of Informality
Method of estimation: Ordinary Least Squares with Robust Standard Errors
Dependent variable: Four types of informality measures, country average

Explanatory variables: Average of 2000–05 by country	Informality measures			
	Schneider shadow economy index (% of GDP) [1]	Heritage Foundation informal market index (1–5: higher, more) [2]	Self-employment (% of total employment) [3]	Non-contributor to pension scheme (% of labor force) [4]
Law and order (ICRG, index ranging 0–6: higher = better)	−3.2360** −2.57	−0.0969* −1.76	−1.6925* −1.84	−2.9764* −1.67
Business regulatory freedom[a]	−2.0074* −1.80	−0.5333*** −9.95	−2.5196** −2.17	−5.8675** −2.28
Average years of secondary schooling (Barro and Lee 2001)	−1.9684* −1.70	−0.1152** −2.00	−2.1527** −2.25	−5.8114*** −3.27
Sociodemographic factors[b]	3.8438** 2.00	0.5027*** 4.99	5.9743*** 3.77	21.6130*** 7.31
Constant	60.3429*** 10.48	6.6326*** 31.72	54.7254*** 14.06	113.3110*** 11.40
Observations (N)	84	86	57	70
Adjusted R-squared	0.57	0.89	0.78	0.88

Source: Authors' calculations.

Note: Heteroscedasticity-robust t-statistics are presented below the corresponding coefficients. See annex 5.1 for countries included in each regression and annex 5.2 for definitions and sources of variables and periods used to compute country averages of informality measures.

a. The Fraser Institute index ranges from 0 to 10; the higher the number, the less regulated.

b. Average of share of youth population, share of rural population, snd share of agriculture in GDP.

* significant at 10%; ** significant at 5%; *** significant at 1%.

Figure 5.3: Predicted and Actual Levels of Informality

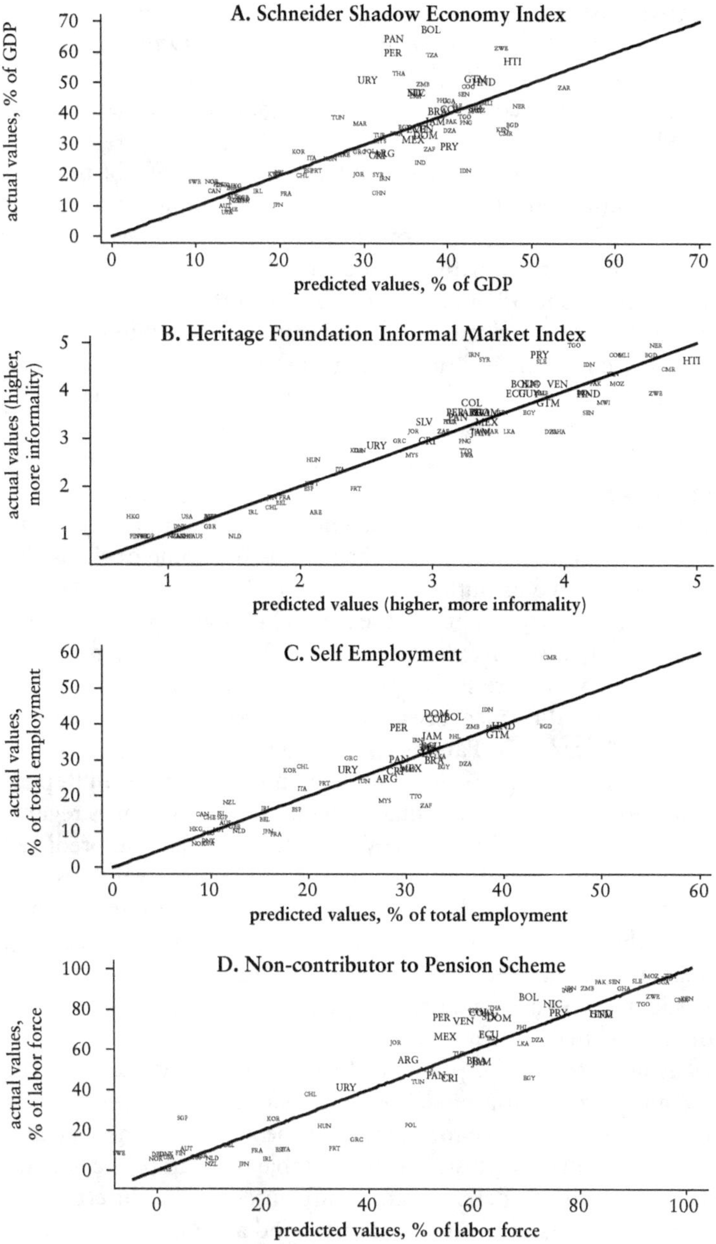

Source: Authors' calculations.

Note: In each graph, a 45-degree line is drawn to show a distance between predicted and actual levels. For a listing of countries and their 3-letter codes, please see annex 5.1.

of the actual vs. predicted values of each informality measure. (For illustrative purposes, observations corresponding to Latin American countries are highlighted in the figure). The majority of countries in the world have small residuals (i.e., the unpredicted portion of informality), a fact that is consistent with the large R-squared coefficients obtained in the regressions.

Is this also the case for the Latin American and Caribbean countries under consideration? The answer is not simple and must be nuanced by the heterogeneity of the countries in the region. Some Latin American and Caribbean countries are located around the 45-degree line, but others are quite far from it. In fact, when we include a "Latin American and Caribbean country" dummy in the regressions, its coefficient turns out to be positive in all cases and significant in three of them (the exception is self-employment).[11] The significance of the regional dummy indicates that the actual values of informality are larger than the predicted values for the majority of countries in the region. This is so for the Heritage index and the pension coverage measure. For the Schneider index, not only do the majority of countries have positive residuals but some of them also could be considered as outliers.

In terms of specific countries, the following points seem noteworthy. For Brazil, Costa Rica, Honduras, and Jamaica, the predicted values of informality are similar to their actual counterparts in all of the four informality measures. Five more countries—Argentina, Guatemala, Nicaragua, Panama, and Uruguay—join this group in all but the Schneider index. In Colombia and the Dominican Republic, while predicted values are much smaller than actual ones regarding *labor* informality (the last two indices), the actual and predicted values of *production* informality (that is, the first two indices) are quite close. Contrary to this, as clearly shown in the figure, actual values of the Schneider index are much larger than predicted ones for Bolivia, Panama, Peru, and Uruguay, which in part explains why the R-squared coefficient for this regression is smaller than those of the other informality measures.

Focusing now on the portion of informality explained by the cross-country regression model, we can evaluate the importance of each explanatory variable for the case of the 20 Latin American and Caribbean countries with sufficient available data. In particular, we can assess how each determinant contributes to the difference in informality between individual countries and a comparator one, for which we choose Chile, given its widely-recognized status of reform leader in the region. The contribution of each explanatory variable is obtained by multiplying the corresponding regression coefficient (from table 5.3) times the difference in the value of this explanatory variable between each Latin American and Caribbean country and the comparator country.

The importance of a particular explanatory variable would, therefore, depend on the size of its effect on informality in the cross-section of countries *and* how far apart the two countries are with respect to the explanatory variable in question. Naturally, the sum of the contributions equals the total difference in predicted informality between each individual country and Chile. This difference is plotted in figure 5.4. As expected, it shows that all the countries have larger (predicted) informality levels than Chile. Haiti, Honduras, and Guatemala are predicted to be the most informal (and in general show the largest difference with respect to Chile). On the other hand, Uruguay, Argentina, and Costa Rica are predicted to be the least informal among the Latin American and Caribbean countries, though they still show larger informality levels than Chile.

Figure 5.5 presents the decomposition of the difference of (predicted) informality between each of the 20 countries under analysis and Chile. The figure has four panels, corresponding to each of the four informality indicators. The most remarkable observations are the following. Policy and institutional variables related to the quality of the state are the most important factors explaining the differences in informality. Restricted regulatory freedom tends to contribute to larger informality in all Latin American and Caribbean countries for the Heritage index, self-employment, and pension coverage, while deficient law and order explains the bulk of informality for the Schneider index.

Education, measured by average years of secondary schooling, does not play a major role in explaining differences in informality with respect to Chile for any of four informality measures, even in the cases of Haiti and Honduras. Sociodemographic factors are particularly important in explaining the differences regarding *labor* informality, and less so regarding *production* informality. Moreover, in the case of labor informality, the larger the differences in informality with respect to Chile, the larger the importance of sociodemographic factors. This is the case, for instance, of Haiti and Honduras, where all determinants of informality (excluding educational level) are about as important. On the other hand, there is no such trend regarding the two *production* informality measures: for them, the variables dealing with the quality of the state are always more important, especially law and order for the Schneider index and regulatory freedom for the Heritage index.

Figure 5.4: Differences in Informality between Latin American Countries and Chile

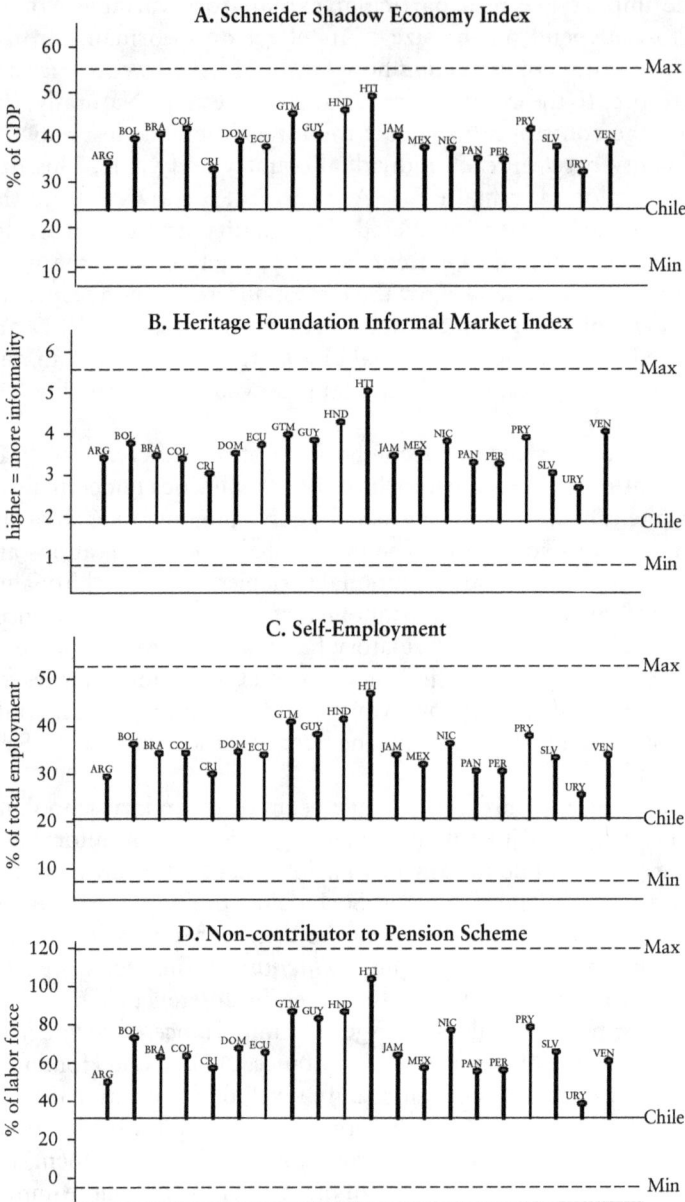

A. Schneider Shadow Economy Index

% of GDP

60 — Max
50
40   ARG BOL BRA COL DOM ECU GTM GUY HND HTI JAM MEX NIC PAN PER PRY SLV URY VEN
30
20   Chile
10 — Min

B. Heritage Foundation Informal Market Index

higher = more informality

6 — Max
5
4   ARG BOL BRA COL CRI DOM ECU GTM GUY HND HTI JAM MEX NIC PAN PER PRY SLV URY VEN
3
2   Chile
1 — Min

C. Self-Employment

% of total employment

50 — Max
40   ARG BOL BRA COL CRI DOM ECU GTM GUY HND HTI JAM MEX NIC PAN PER PRY SLV URY VEN
30
20   Chile
10 — Min

D. Non-contributor to Pension Scheme

% of labor force

120 — Max
100
80   ARG BOL BRA COL CRI DOM ECU GTM GUY HND HTI JAM MEX NIC PAN PER PRY SLV URY VEN
60
40
20   Chile
0 — Min

Source: Authors' calculations.

Note: Presented are all predicted levels, which may be above or below the actual maximum/minimum values. For a list of countries and their 3-letter codes, please see annex 5.1.

Figure 5.5a: Explanation of Differences in Informality between Latin American Countries and Chile

Schneider Shadow Economy Index

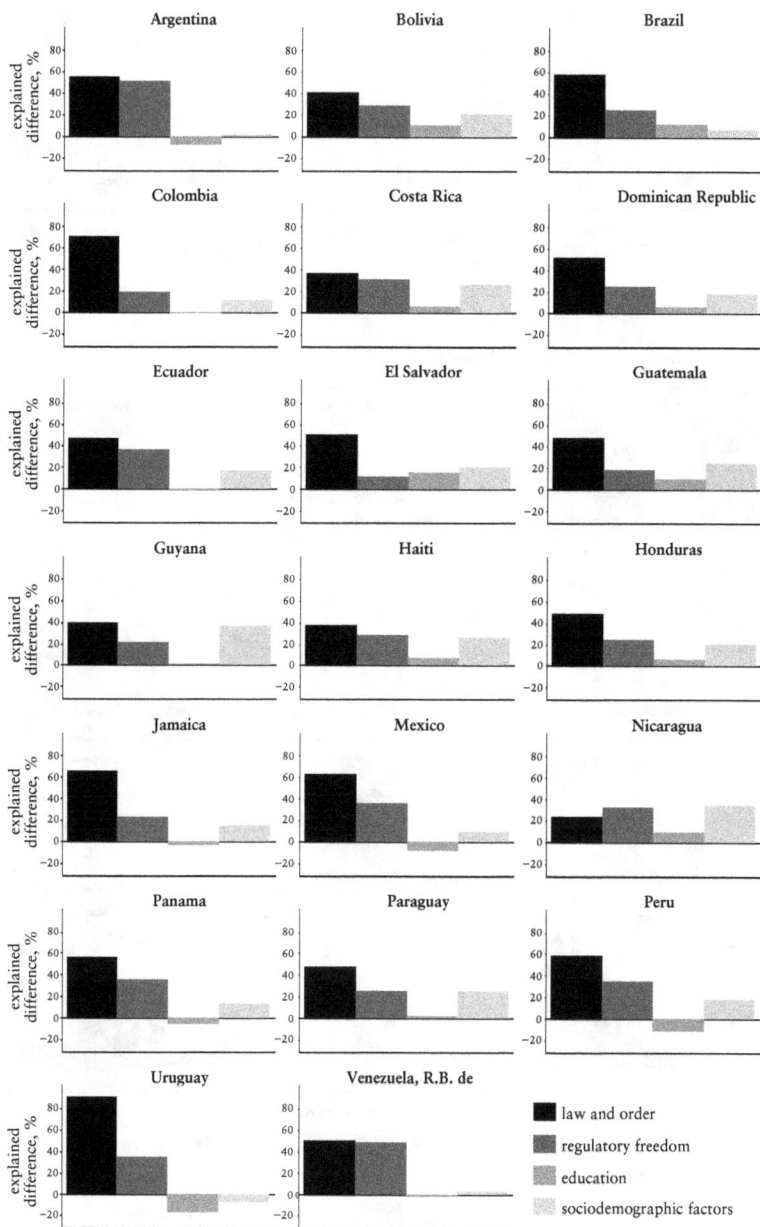

law and order
regulatory freedom
education
sociodemographic factors

Figure 5.5b: Explanation of Differences in Informality
between Latin American Countries and Chile
Heritage Foundation Informal Market Index

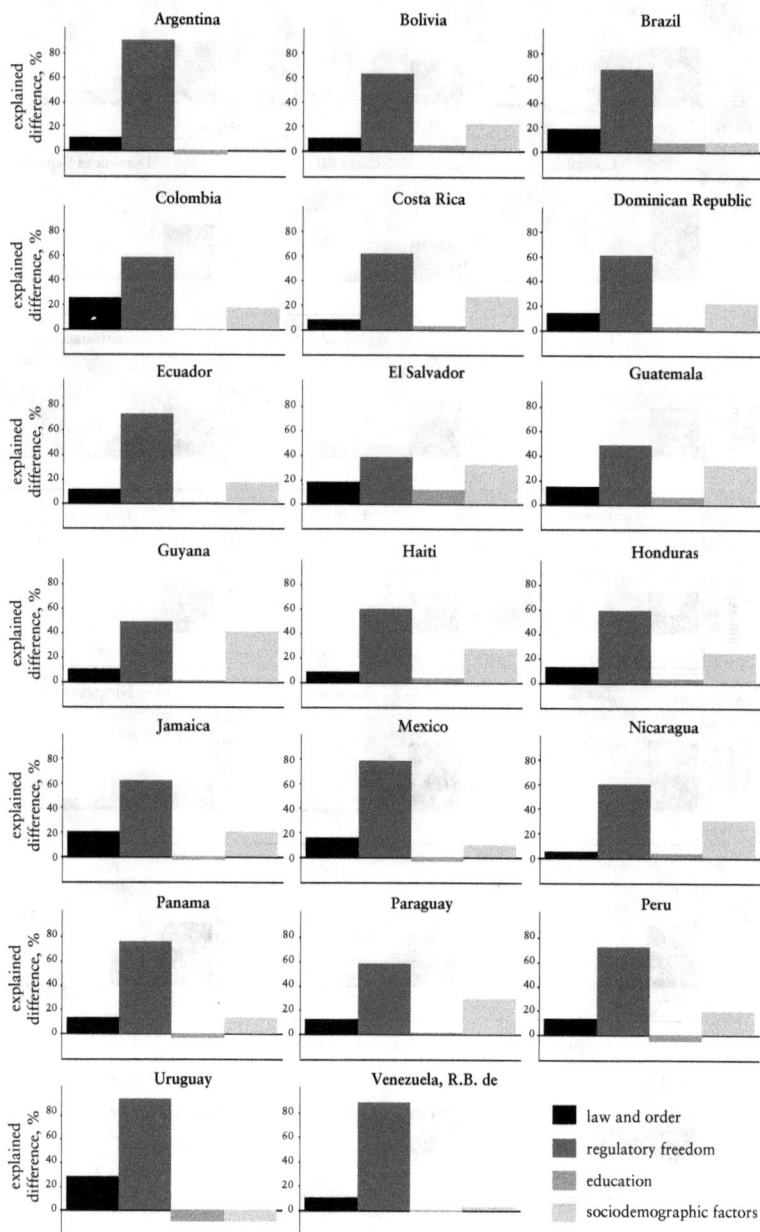

Figure 5.5c: **Explanation of Differences in Informality between Latin American Countries and Chile**

Self-Employment

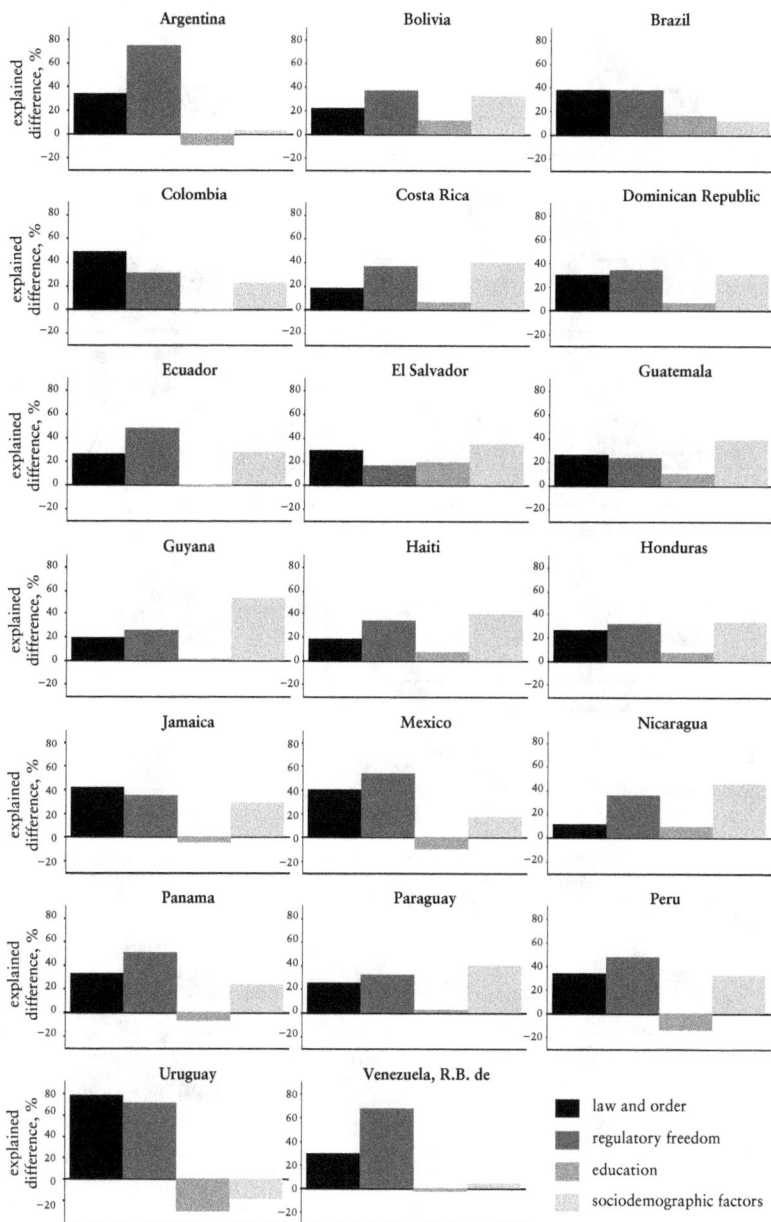

Figure 5.5d: **Explanation of Differences in Informality between Latin American Countries and Chile**

Non-Contributor to Pension Scheme

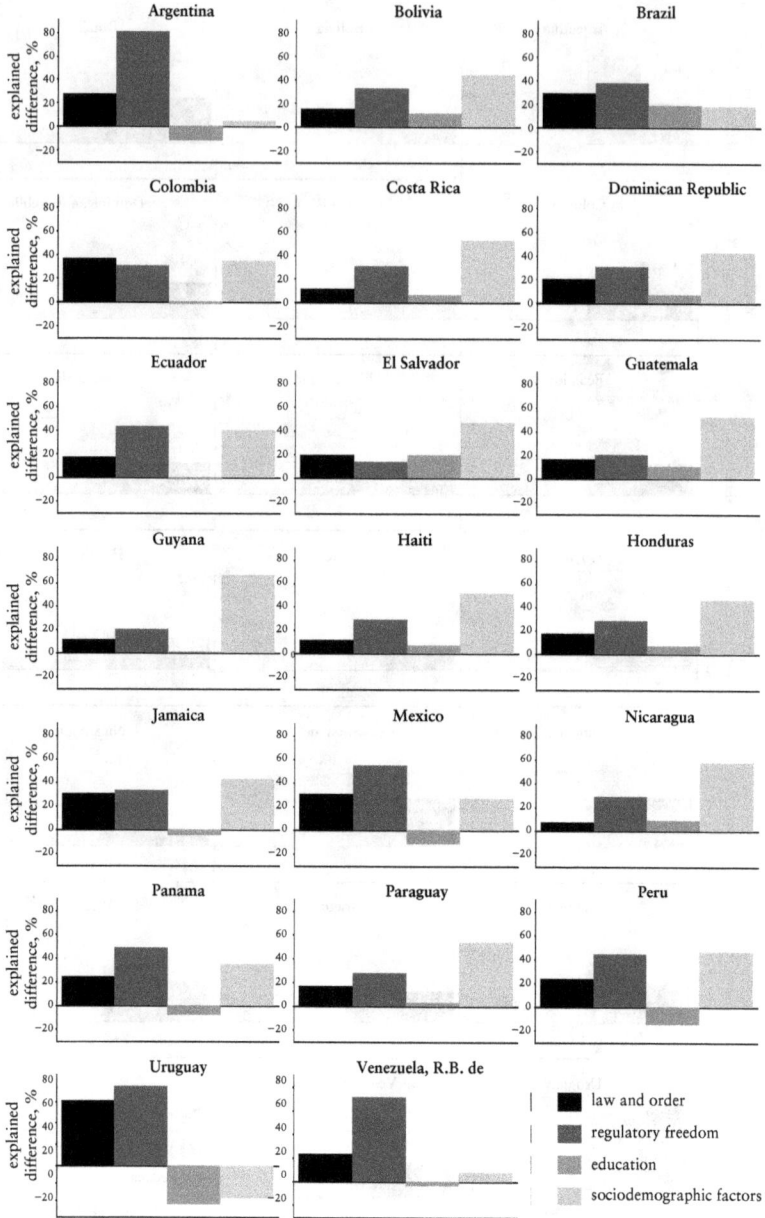

Source: Authors' calculations.

Conclusion

By any measure, informality is quite prevalent in the countries of Latin America and the Caribbean. This is worrisome because it denotes misallocation of resources (labor in particular) and inefficient utilization of government services, which can jeopardize the countries' growth and poverty-alleviation prospects. The evidence presented in this chapter shows that informality has a statistically and economically significant negative impact on growth—and an equally significant positive impact on the incidence of poverty across countries.

Informality arises when the costs of belonging to the economy's legal and regulatory framework exceed the benefits. Thus, informality is more prevalent where the regulatory framework is burdensome, the quality of government services is low, and the state's monitoring and enforcement capacity is weak. However, these cost-benefit calculations are also affected by key structural characteristics of the economy, such as its productive and demographic structure and the availability of skilled labor. This chapter has argued that it is important to take into account all of these factors when trying to ascertain the causes of informality.

In the case of Latin America, this chapter has shown that informality is primarily the outcome of a combination of poor public services and a burdensome regulatory framework. Low levels of education, as measured by secondary schooling, are less important in this respect. In lower income countries, informality (particularly regarding labor markets) is exacerbated when the production structure is heavily based on agriculture and other rural activities and when the labor participation of young people, resulting from recent demographic transition, is large.

Informality is a complex phenomenon that is best understood from several angles, considering different indicators that reflect its various aspects and treating it as both cause and consequence of underdevelopment. This chapter is a modest contribution in this direction.

Annex 5.1: Sample of Countries in the Informality Regressions

Country code	Country	Schneider shadow economy index (84 countries)	Heritage Foundation informal market index (86 countries)	Self-employment (57 countries)	Noncontributor to pension scheme (70 countries)
DZA	Algeria	√	√	√	√
ARG	Argentina	√	√	√	√
AUS	Australia	√	√	√	√
AUT	Austria	√	√	√	√
BGD	Bangladesh	√	√	√	√
BEL	Belgium	√	√	√	√
BOL	Bolivia	√	√	√	√
BWA	Botswana	√	√		
BRA	Brazil	√	√	√	√
CMR	Cameroon	√	√	√	√
CAN	Canada	√	√	√	√
CHL	Chile	√	√	√	√
CHN	China	√	√	√	√
COL	Colombia	√	√	√	
ZAR	Congo, Dem. Rep. of	√			
COG	Congo, Rep. of	√	√		
CRI	Costa Rica	√	√	√	√
DNK	Denmark	√	√	√	√
DOM	Dominican Republic	√	√	√	√
ECU	Ecuador	√	√	√	√
EGY	Egypt, Arab Rep. of	√	√	√	√
SLV	El Salvador	√	√	√	
FIN	Finland	√	√	√	√
FRA	France	√	√	√	√
DEU	Germany	√	√	√	√
GHA	Ghana	√	√	√	√
GRC	Greece	√	√	√	√
GTM	Guatemala	√	√	√	√
GUY	Guyana		√		
HTI	Haiti	√	√		
HND	Honduras	√	√	√	√
HKG	Hong Kong, China	√	√	√	
HUN	Hungary	√	√		√
ISL	Iceland		√	√	
IND	India	√	√		√
IDN	Indonesia	√	√	√	√
IRN	Iran, Islamic Rep. of	√	√	√	√
IRL	Ireland	√	√	√	√

Country code	Country	Schneider shadow economy index (84 countries)	Heritage Foundation informal market index (86 countries)	Self-employment (57 countries)	Non-contributor to pension scheme (70 countries)
ITA	Italy	√	√	√	√
JAM	Jamaica	√	√	√	√
JPN	Japan	√	√	√	
JOR	Jordan	√	√	√	√
KEN	Kenya	√	√		√
KOR	Korea, Rep. of	√	√	√	√
KWT	Kuwait	√	√		
MWI	Malawi	√	√		√
MYS	Malaysia	√	√	√	√
MLI	Mali	√	√		√
MEX	Mexico	√	√	√	√
MAR	Morocco	√	√	√	√
MOZ	Mozambique	√	√		√
NLD	Netherlands	√	√	√	√
NZL	New Zealand	√	√	√	√
NIC	Nicaragua	√	√		√
NER	Niger	√	√		
NOR	Norway	√	√	√	√
PAK	Pakistan	√	√	√	√
PAN	Panama	√	√	√	√
PNG	Papua New Guinea	√			
PRY	Paraguay	√	√		√
PER	Peru	√	√	√	√
PHL	Philippines	√	√	√	√
POL	Poland	√	√	√	√
PRT	Portugal	√	√	√	√
SEN	Senegal	√	√		√
SLE	Sierra Leone	√	√		√
SGP	Singapore	√	√	√	√
ZAF	South Africa	√	√	√	√
ESP	Spain	√	√	√	√
LKA	Sri Lanka	√	√	√	√
SWE	Sweden	√	√		√
CHE	Switzerland	√	√	√	√
SYR	Syrian Arab Rep.	√	√		√
TZA	Tanzania	√	√		√
THA	Thailand	√	√	√	√
TGO	Togo	√	√		√
TTO	Trinidad and Tobago		√	√	
TUN	Tunisia	√	√	√	√
TUR	Turkey	√	√		√

Country code	Country	Schneider shadow economy index (84 countries)	Heritage Foundation informal market index (86 countries)	Self-employment (57 countries)	Non-contributor to pension scheme (70 countries)
UGA	Uganda	√	√		√
ARE	United Arab Emirates	√	√		
GBR	United Kingdom	√	√	√	√
USA	United States	√	√	√	√
URY	Uruguay	√	√	√	√
VEN	Venezuela, R.B. de	√	√	√	√
ZMB	Zambia	√	√	√	√
ZWE	Zimbabwe	√	√		√

Annex 5.2: Definitions and Sources of Variables Used in Regression Analysis

Variable	Definition and Construction	Source
Schneider shadow economy index	Estimated shadow economy as the percentage of official GDP. Average of 2001–02 by country.	Schneider (2004).
Heritage Foundation informal market index	An index ranging 1 to 5 with higher values indicating more informal market activity. The scores and criteria are: (i) Very Low: Country has a free-market economy with informal market in such things as drugs and weapons (score is 1); (ii) Low: Country may have some informal market involvement in labor or pirating of intellectual property (score is 2); (iii) Moderate: Country may have some informal market activities in labor, agriculture, and transportation, and moderate levels of intellectual property piracy (score is 3); (iv) High: Country may have substantial levels of informal market activity in such areas as labor, pirated intellectual property, and smuggled consumer goods, and in such services as transportation, electricity, and telecommunications (score is 4); and (v) Very High: Country's informal market is larger than its formal economy (score is 5). Average of 2000–05 by country.	Miles, Feulner, and O'Grady (2005).
Self-employment	Self employed workers as the percentage of total employment. Country averages but periods to compute the averages vary by country. Average of 1999-2006 by country, but countries in Europe and Central Asia (ECA) are excluded (Loayza and Rigolini 2006).	ILO. Data retrieved from laborsta.ilo.org.
Non-contributor to pension scheme	Labor force not contributing to a pension scheme as the percentage of total labor force. Average of 1993–2005 by country.	World Development Indicators, various years.

Variable	Definition and Construction	Source
Per capita GDP growth	Log difference of real GDP per capita (2000 US$).	World Development Indicators, various years.
Initial GDP per capita	Real GDP per capita (2000 US$) in 1985, in logs.	World Development Indicators, various years.
Initial government expenditure	Ratio of general government final consumption expenditure to GDP in 1985.	World Development Indicators, various years.
Poverty headcount index	The fraction of the population with income below a given poverty line. The poverty line is $1 per person a day, converted into local currency using a PPP-adjusted exchange rate. The latest/final year of each country's poverty spell is used.	Loayza and Raddatz (2006).
Initial Gini index	A measure of income inequality ranging 0 to 100 with higher values indicating more inequal income distribution. The initial year of each country's poverty spell is used.	Loayza and Raddatz (2006).
Law and order	An index ranging 0 to 6 with higher values indicating better governance. Law and order are assessed separately, with each sub-component comprising 0 to 3 points. Assessment of "law" focuses on the legal system, while "order" is rated by popular observance of the law. Average of 2000–05 by country.	ICRG. Data retrieved from www.icrgonline.com.

Business regulatory freedom	An index ranging 0 to 10 with higher values indicating less regulated. It is composed of following indicators: (i) Price controls: extent to which businesses are free to set their own prices; (ii) Burden of regulation/administrative conditions/entry of new business; (iii) Time with government bureaucracy: senior management spends a substantial amount of time dealing with government bureaucracy; (iv) Starting a new business: starting a new business is generally easy; and (v) Irregular payments: irregular, additional payments connected with import and export permits, business licenses, exchange controls, tax assessments, police protection, or loan applications are very rare. Average of 2000–05 by country.	Gwartney, Lawson, Sobel, and Leeson (2007), The Fraser Institute. Data retrieved from www.freetheworld.com.
Average years of secondary schooling	Average years of secondary schooling in the population aged 15 and over. The most recent score in each country is used, while figures are computed for individual country data are not available.	Barro and Lee (1993, 2001); and authors' calculations.
Sociodemographic factors	Simple average of following three variables: (i) Youth (aged 10–24) population as the percentage of total population; (ii) Rural population as the percentage of total population; and (iii) Agriculture as the percentage of GDP. All three variables are standardized before the average is taken. Average of 2000–05 by country.	Authors' calculations with data from World Development Indicators, ILO, and UN.

Annex 5.3: Descriptive Statistics

Data in country averages; periods vary by informality measure

(a) Univariate (regression sample)

Variable	Obs.	Mean	Std. Dev.	Minimum	Maximum
Schneider shadow economy index (% of GDP)	84	32.960	14.735	8.550	68.200
Heritage Foundation informal market index (range 1–5: higher, more informality)	86	3.055	1.251	1.000	5.000
Self-employment (% of total employment)	57	26.204	12.028	7.132	59.335
Non-contributor to pension scheme (% of labor force)	70	53.198	33.482	1.450	98.000

(b) Univariate (full sample)

Schneider shadow economy index (% of GDP)	145	34.838	13.214	8.550	68.200
Heritage Foundation informal market index (range 1–5: higher, more informality)	159	3.409	1.201	1.000	5.000
Self-employment (% of total employment)	86	25.158	12.118	1.119	59.335
Non-contributor to pension scheme (% of labor force)	110	55.999	31.905	1.450	98.500

(c) Bivariate Correlations between Informality Measures

(The upper triangle for regression sample is in italics and the full sample is given in the lower triangle.)

Variable	Schneider shadow economy	Heritage Fndn. informal market	Self-employ-ment	Non-contributor to pension
Schneider shadow economy index (% of GDP)	1.00 145 | 84	*0.68**** 83	*0.71**** 55	*0.72**** 70
Heritage Foundation informal market index (range 1–5: higher, more informality)	0.65*** 132	1.00 159 | 86	*0.88**** 57	*0.90**** 70
Self-employment (% of total employment)	0.65*** 69	0.79*** 76	1.00 86 | 57	*0.89**** 51
Non-contributor to pension scheme (% of labor force)	0.59*** 104	0.77*** 107	0.88*** 57	1.00 110 | 70

Source: Authors' calculations.

Note: Sample sizes are presented below the corresponding coefficients.

*** significant at 1%

Notes

1. This definition, introduced by De Soto (1989) in his classic study of informality, has gained remarkable popularity due to its conceptual strength, which allows it to focus on the root causes of informality rather than merely its symptoms. For an excellent review of the causes and consequences of the informal sector, see Schneider and Enste (2000). Drawing from a public-choice approach, Gerxhani (2004) provides an interesting discussion of the differences of the informal sector in developed and developing countries. The World Bank report by Perry et al. (2007) is the most comprehensive and in-depth study on informality in the Latin America region.

2. Details on definitions, sources, and samples for these and other variables used in this chapter are provided in annex 5.2.

3. The LAC countries under consideration are those included in any of the four regressions where informality is a dependent variable (table 5.3). They are 20 countries plus Chile, which functions as a comparator country, unless otherwise noted. Trinidad and Tobago is also excluded since the World Bank classification (as of July 2007) considers the country as a high-income country. See annex 5.1 for sample of countries in each regression.

4. Self-employment is arguably a lower bound for the measure of informal labor given that tax and regulation evasion occurs massively in all types of firms.

5. See Loayza (1996) for an endogenous-growth model highlighting the negative effect of informality through the congestion of public services.

6. This does not necessarily mean that informal firms are not dynamic or lagging behind their formal counterparts. In fact, in equilibrium the risk-adjusted returns in both sectors should be equalized at the margin. See Maloney (2004) for evidence on the dynamism of Latin American informal firms. The arguments presented in the text apply to the comparison between an excessively regulated economy and one that is not.

7. We also considered as proxy the ratio of tax revenues to GDP. Even though the number of observations drops considerably, the results were similar regarding the negative effect of informality on growth.

8. To be precise, a one-standard-deviation increase of, in turn, the Schneider index, the Heritage Foundation index, the share of self-employment, and the labor force lacking pension coverage leads to a decline of, respectively, 1.1, 0.8, 0.8, and 0.7 percentage points of per capita GDP growth.

9. Again, details on definitions and sources of all variables are presented in annex 5.2.

10. This is constructed by first standardizing each component (to a mean of zero and a standard deviation of 1) and then taking a simple arithmetic average. We use a composite index, rather than the components separately, given the very high correlation among them.

11. Regression results with "LAC country" dummy are not presented but are available upon request. For the Schneider index, the Heritage index, self employment, and pension coverage, t-statistics of the dummy variable are 2.91, 2.46, 1.20, and 2.36, respectively.

References

Barro, Robert, and Jong-Wha Lee. 1993. "International Comparisons of Educational Attainment." *Journal of Monetary Economics* 32(3): 363–94.

———. 2001. "International Data on Educational Attainment: Updates and Implications." *Oxford Economic Papers* 53(3): 541–63.

De Soto, Hernando. 1989. *The Other Path: The Invisible Revolution in the Third World*. New York: HarperCollins.

Fields, Gary. 1990. "Labour Market Modeling and the Urban Informal Sector: Theory and Evidence." In *The Informal Sector Revisited*, ed. David Turnham, Bernard Salomé, and Antoine Schwarz. Paris: OECD, 49–69.

Gerxhani, Klarita. 2004. "The Informal Sector in Developed and Less Developed Countries: A Literature Survey." *Public Choice* 120(3/4): 267–300.

Gwartney, James, Robert Lawson, Russell Sobel, and Peter Leeson. 2007. *Economic Freedom of the World: 2007 Annual Report*. Vancouver, BC: The Fraser Institute. Available at www.freetheworld.com.

ILO (International Labour Organization). 2004. *Global Employment Trends for Youth*. Geneva: ILO.

———. 2007. *Yearbook of Labour Statistics*. Geneva: ILO. Available at LABORSTA Internet, laborsta.ilo.org.

Loayza, Norman. 1996. "The Economics of the Informal Sector: A Simple Model and Some Empirical Evidence from Latin America." *Carnegie-Rochester Conference Series on Public Policy* 45: 129–62.

Loayza, Norman, and Claudio Raddatz. 2006. "The Composition of Growth Matters for Poverty Alleviation." Policy Research Working Paper 4077, World Bank, Washington, DC.

Loayza, Norman, and Jamele Rigolini. 2006. "Informality Trends and Cycles." Policy Research Working Paper 4078, World Bank, Washington, DC.

Maloney, William. 2004. "Informality Revisited." *World Development* 32(7): 1159–78.

Miles, Marc, Edwin Feulner, and Mary O'Grady. 2005. *2005 Index of Economic Freedom*. Washington, DC: Heritage Foundation.

Perry, Guillermo, William Maloney, Omar Arias, Pablo Fajnzylber, Andrew Mason, and Jaime Saavedra-Chanduvi. 2007. *Informality: Exit and Exclusion*. Washington, DC: The World Bank.

PRS Group. 2007. *International Country Risk Guide* (ICRG). Syracuse, NY: PRS Group. Available at www.icrgonline.com.

Schneider, Friedrich. 2004. "The Size of the Shadow Economies of 145 Countries all over the World: First Results over the Period 1999 to 2003." IZA Discussion Paper 1431, Institute for the Study of Labor, Bonn.

Schneider, Friedrich, and Dominik Enste. 2000. "Shadow Economies: Size, Causes, and Consequences." *Journal of Economic Literature* 38(1): 77–114.

United Nations (UN). 2005. *World Population Prospects: The 2004 Revision,* CD-ROM edition. New York: UN.

World Bank. 2006. *World Development Indicators 2006.* Washington, DC: World Bank.

———. 2007. *World Development Indicators 2007.* Washington, DC: World Bank.

6

Slow Recoveries

Raphael Bergoeing, Norman V. Loayza, and Andrea Repetto

Introduction

Why do some countries recover with relative ease from negative shocks while others suffer considerably? Exogenous shocks like a deterioration in terms of trade, a reduction in foreign capital flows, or a rise in international interest rates are common to many developing countries. Although these shocks initially produce a similar fall in economic activity, the recovery paths in their aftermath differ

Reprinted from the *Journal of Development Economics*, 75 (2004): 473–506. It is reprinted with permission from Elsevier B.V. We thank the efficient research assistance provided by Ana María Oviedo and Facundo Piguillem. We acknowledge financial support from the World Bank and Fondecyt # 1030991, and an institutional grant to CEA from the Hewlett Foundation. Useful comments and suggestions have been provided by participants in several seminars and conferences, especially Rodrigo Caputo, Sebastián Claro, Alex Monge, and the participants at the 2003 IASE-NBER conference on Productivity Dynamics. Contact information: raphaelb@dii.uchile.cl, nloayza@worldbank.org, and arepetto@uai.cl.

markedly across countries. This is, for instance, what Bergoeing et al. (2002) find when they compare the experiences of Mexico and Chile in the 1980s. Although those two countries were affected by similar shocks in the onset of the 1980s debt crisis, Chile was able to recover and "find" a decade that turned out to be lost for Mexico and most of Latin America. Bergoeing et al. argue that a key element in Chile's ability to recover was a bankruptcy law that facilitated the retrenchment of weak firms and creation of stronger companies.

Recovery processes are intrinsically costly, as they require significant amounts of resource reallocation. Depending on the type and intensity of shocks, some firms and sectors in the economy contract while others expand. Labor and capital resources are freed by declining firms in order to be used by growing ones, but not without difficulty. Resource reallocation implies adjustment, and this is costly, whether it means the adoption of new technologies and more capital utilization by expanding firms or the shredding of labor and capital, even to the point of disappearance, by weakening firms. Without this costly process, however, economies would be unable to resume full economic activity in the aftermath of shocks.

The main hypothesis of this chapter is that slow and costly recoveries are the result of impediments to the natural process of resource reallocation. Some of these impediments are inherent to the adjustment process and thus can be considered as natural transaction costs (see Caballero and Hammour 1998). However, these impediments can also result from government policy interventions such as excessive labor protection, directed credit to inefficient sectors, entry barriers to the establishment of new plants and firms, and burdensome bankruptcy laws. By reducing the extent of restructuring, these obstacles alter the recovery path that follows aggregate shocks, inducing the stagnation of economic activity during long periods of time.

Recent studies have underscored the connection between rigidities and recovery. Prescott (2002) provides a comprehensive analysis of this link, making clear that this is an important issue not only for developing countries but also for developed economies. The Great Depression in the United States during the1930s had many causes, but it is now clear that policy distortions exacerbated the slowdown. For instance, Cole and Ohanian (1999) argue that labor market regulations stalled the recovery process in the aftermath of the stock market crash.

More recently, Germany and Japan, the second- and third-largest economies in the world, have experienced their worst recessions since the end of World War II. Germany's GDP growth rate was about half of what it was in the rest of Europe during the decade 1995–2005, with the costs of reunification playing only a limited role in the country's stagnation. As Broadbent, Schumacher, and Schels (2004) argue, the subsidized interest rates prevalent in Germany in the 1990s led to overinvestment and low capital returns. After the European Commission dictated in 2001 that public guarantees for state banks should be eliminated, the interest rates paid by German firms started to rise, which prompted the need for massive firm restructuring. However, the process was slow and painful, mostly due to Germany's sclerotic labor markets and, as result, the country's economy was sluggish until the mid 2000s. Japan's experience was even worse. Its economy barely grew during the period 1990–2005, due to a combination of overly conservative monetary policy and mounting debts by Japanese firms. As Hoshi and Kashyap (2004), Hayashi and Prescott (2002), and Caballero, Hoshi, and Kashyap (2008) argue, it is not firms' debt that explains their inability to recover—it is the support that Japanese banks have given to grossly underperforming firms (or "zombies," as they have come to be known). The life support given by mostly insolvent Japanese banks to "zombie" firms can only be explained by a regulatory regime that allows public recapitalization of weak banks and provides overly generous deposit and even creditor and shareholder insurance. Only the shredding of underperforming firms could free the financial and other resources needed by profitable firms to grow and lead the recovery of Japan's economy.

Beyond these country-case examples, in the next section of this chapter we present some cross-country evidence that there is a negative relationship between the burden of the regulatory environment and an economy's ability to recover from shocks. In a sample of 76 countries with average data for the 1990s, we find that countries that impose heavier restrictions on product and factor markets (i.e., firm entry, financial transactions, international trade, bankruptcy procedures, bureaucratic red tape, taxation, and labor markets) suffer from more severe—both deep and prolonged—recessions. This evidence serves mostly as impetus for the theoretical analysis that is the focus of this study.

This chapter analyzes how policy-induced rigidities can impair an economy's ability to absorb and accommodate shocks, producing a more painful and protracted recovery. This is a macroeconomic issue, but it can be properly analyzed only from a microeconomic standpoint. The reason is that policy-induced rigidities affect the dynamics of creation, growth, and destruction of investment projects and firms in a heterogeneous, idiosyncratic manner, even if the shocks are common. Depending on each firm's capital intensity, level of technology, and specific shocks, policy-induced distortions become relevant for some firms and less so for others in the face of common adverse conditions. It is this heterogeneity in firms' responses to shocks that allows us to discern the mechanisms through which rigidities operate.

In order to model the link between slow recoveries and rigidities, we extend the work of Campbell (1998) to allow for policy-induced obstacles to restructuring. Specifically, we develop a dynamic general equilibrium model of heterogeneous plants subject to aggregate and idiosyncratic shocks and rigidities. We model these rigidities as subsidies and taxes that change the relative cost of firm creation, expansion, and survival, thus altering the natural rate of factor reallocation. We then submit the modeled economy to aggregate shocks and compare the recovery path of a distorted economy to that of a fully flexible one.

Ours is a vintage capital model, where different types of capital embody different levels of technology. As the technological frontier expands, capital that represents less advanced technologies will tend to be scrapped. Its salvage value can then be used to produce new capital that embodies the leading-edge technology. In this context, the economy's equilibrium path is characterized by an ongoing process of resource reallocation. When an exogenous rigidity, such as a production subsidy to incumbent firms, is introduced, the natural process of entry and exit is muted, reducing the amount of firm restructuring. In this example, the subsidy allows inefficient plants— which would have otherwise exited—to stay in business longer, and prevents new and more technologically advanced plants to appear. This promotes an inefficient allocation of resources and pushes the economy inside its production possibilities frontier. We believe these explanations for the lack of recovery and growth apply to a wide range of actual economic experiences.

After presenting the model, we simulate two situations representing particular cases of impediments to reallocation with the purpose of showing how they may affect the economy's recovery path. In the first numerical exercise, we compare economies that start off with different levels of a production subsidy to incumbent firms. We expose these economies to the same aggregate shock and then compare their recovery paths. Under our benchmark calibration, we find that an undistorted economy that faces a (one-period) transitory aggregate shock equivalent to 5 percent of steady-state per capita GDP loses about 13 percent of its pre-shock output and completes restructuring in a period of one quarter. However, in the presence of a similar shock, an economy that starts off with a 5 percent (10 percent) subsidy to incumbents loses 14.2 percent (14.3 percent) of initial output with a restructuring period of nine (10) quarters.

In our second exercise, the distortion is a policy response to the aggregate shock. When an exogenous recession hits the economy, jobs are lost and production units are scrapped. To reduce the distress associated with these losses, the government intervenes, subsidizing incumbents one period after the shock hits the economy. This intervention is transitory and phased out gradually, lasting about three quarters in the simulation. In this case, an economy that initially imposes a 3 percent (6 percent) subsidy to incumbents loses about 24 percent (36 percent) of GDP in present value terms with a recovery period that lasts 29 (37) periods. The differences in recovery paths with respect to the fully flexible economy are remarkable, particularly given that we assume that shocks are short-lived and that there is a single distortion present.

Our work builds on the firm heterogeneity models pioneered by Jovanovic (1982) and further extended by Hopenhayn (1992), Ericson and Pakes (1995), and Campbell (1998). This chapter complements the analysis started by Caballero and Hammour (1996). In a series of papers, Caballero and Hammour develop a model of inefficient creative destruction, in which transactional difficulties hamper the process of reallocation. They find that in these economies, the processes of firm creation and destruction are decoupled and their rates are inefficiently low. Our analysis differs from Caballero and Hammour's in that in our model, rigidities are the result of direct policy interventions. Moreover, we focus on the creation and destruction margins, not attempting to explain the "scrambling" of production units according to their level of efficiency. Our work also complements the studies that analyze the *level* effects of policy distortions in the context of firm dynamics. Hopenhayn and Rogerson (1993) build a model of firm heterogeneity to study the effects of a tax on layoffs. They find large employment and welfare effects on the economy's stationary equilibrium. Similarly, Restuccia and Rogerson (2008) develop a model of firm heterogeneity to show that policies that distort the relative prices faced by individual firms can result in large productivity losses. They use the model to help explain the large differences in aggregate output per capita across countries. Our model is complementary to these analyses because, rather than focusing on levels in the steady state, we compare the trajectories of recovery from shocks as represented by transitional dynamics.

Finally, our work is also related to the job reallocation and plant dynamics literature. Davis, Haltiwanger, and Schuh (1996) and others have extensively documented the international evidence on job reallocation. At any given time, and even within the same industry, jobs are created and destroyed, existing plants expand and contract, new plants start up, and old plants shut down. Given that developing countries face larger shocks, thus requiring higher levels of restructuring than industrialized economies, we should then observe higher rates of reallocation in developing economies. However, the facts documented in the literature show surprisingly similar rates of job reallocation across countries. One reading of this evidence is that some developing economies face severe obstacles, whether structural or policy induced, to reshuffling resources across production units. Caballero, Engel, and Micco (2004) reach a similar conclusion after comparing the degree of labor market inflexibility in several Latin American countries, finding, for instance, that Mexico faces more rigidities than Chile.

The chapter is organized as follows. The next section provides some cross-country empirical support for a link between the regulatory environment and the severity of recessions. In the following section, we present a model with heterogeneous plants and policy distortions. We explain the mechanics of the model and describe its equilibrium solution. This is followed by a section in which we calibrate and simulate our model economy to quantify the impact of policy distortions on slow recoveries. The final section concludes our discussion.

Some Empirical Evidence

Our goal is to understand why some countries suffer in recovering from temporary negative shocks. To this macroeconomic question, we postulate a microeconomic answer related to the negative effect that distortionary government-imposed regulations have on firm dynamics. That is, an excessive regulatory environment can weaken the process of destruction of inefficient investment projects and the adoption of improved technologies. Given the crucial role that regulations play in our explanation, a necessary first step is to examine whether the regulatory environment is in practice related to the severity of recessions. Here we illustrate the relevance of this relationship from a cross-country perspective.

The regulatory environment affects the entry, growth, and exit of firms and investment projects. According to this criterion, we can identify and attempt to measure the most relevant aspects of the regulatory regime. Using a variety of cross-country sources, we collected comparable data on the following types of government-imposed regulations in each country for the 1990s: financial restrictions, trade barriers, firm entry costs, inefficient bankruptcy procedures, bureaucratic red tape, tax burden, and labor regulations.[1] Given that our purpose here is to illustrate the regulatory regime's overall, reduced-form effect, we combine these regulation measures into a single index. Specifically, we first standardize the indicators to range between 0 and 1, where a higher number indicates a heavier burden of the corresponding regulation, and then we average them out to obtain a single index. Our sample consists of 76 countries, representing all major regions of the world. To get a sense of the prevalence of regulations across regions, figure 6.1 presents the median of the regulatory index for various groups of countries. We can discern three levels of regulatory burden: Sub-Saharan Africa (AFR), the Middle East and North Africa (MNA), Latin America (LAC), and South Asia (SAS) have the highest level of regulatory burden. East Asia and Pacific (EAP) is in the middle of the range, and industrialized countries (INL) show the lowest level of overall regulations.[2]

The dependent variable in our analysis is the severity of recessions. There is no standard measure in the literature for this concept, but here we propose a simple indicator that captures the extent of downward output deviations from trend for each country during a given period. We first obtain output-gap series by detrending each country's (log) of per capita GDP, using annual data for the period 1960–2000. The detrending procedure is conducted using the bandpass filter of Baxter and King (1999) on a country-by-country basis. We then identify and select only output gaps *below* trend. Finally, the severity-of-recessions indicator for each country results from adding up its recessionary gaps during the period 1990–2000.

The scatter plot in figure 6.2 represents the simple relationship between the regulation index and the severity of recessions. Confirming our priors, stronger regulations are related to more severe recessions, with a correlation coefficient of 0.36. A more formal

Figure 6.1: Regulation Index by Region

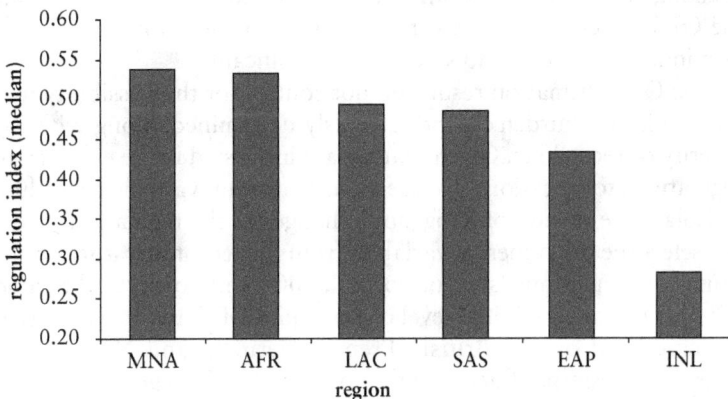

Source: Authors' calculations.

Note: AFR: Africa region; EAP: East Asia and Pacific region; INL: industrial countries; LAC: Latin America and the Caribbean region; MNA: Middle East and North Africa region; SAS: South Asia region. Indices range from 0 to 1.

Figure 6.2: Severity of Recessions and Regulatory Burden

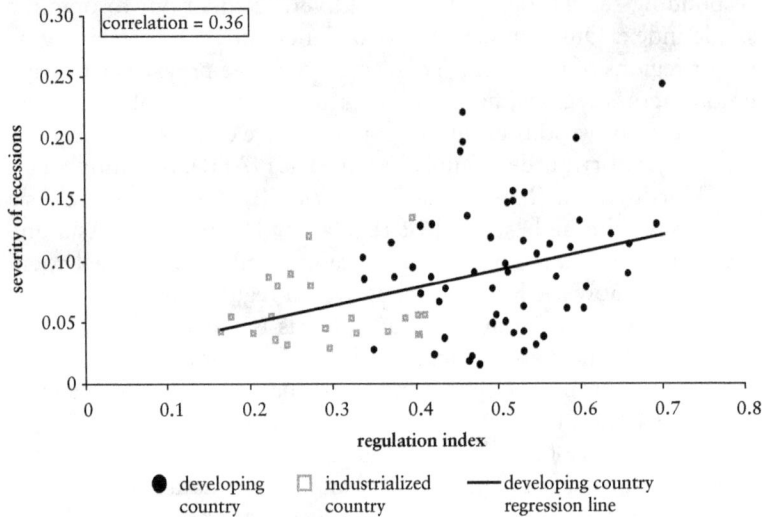

Source: Authors' calculations.

evaluation of the connection between our variables of interest should take into account the additional determinants of the severity of recessions. In particular, it is necessary to control for key shocks that can affect the economy and its downward cycles. Also, we specifically consider the possibility that the severity of recessions is not only related to regulations but also to the volatility of the terms of trade, the volatility of domestic price inflation, and the degree of real exchange rate overvaluation. The first column of table 6.1 presents the OLS regression results. The estimated coefficient on the regulation index is positive and statistically significant.

The OLS estimation results do not control for the possibility that the regulatory burden be endogenously determined, along with the severity of recessions. Given that we are interested in the effect from regulations to recessions, we use an instrumental variable procedure to isolate the impact of exogenous changes in the regulation index. We select the instrumental variables from the recent literature on the causes of regulations (see Botero et al. 2004 and Bolaky and Freund 2004). They are the initial level of per capita GDP and variables that indicate legal origin (British, French, German, and Nordic) and degree of Western influence in the country. The IV regression results are presented in the second column of table 6.1. Hansen's J-test of over-identifying restrictions cannot reject the null hypothesis that the instruments are not correlated with the regression residual. Moreover, the instruments have a large explanatory power over the

Table 6.1: Severity of Recessions and the Burden of
Regulations

*Dependent variable: Severity of recessions: sum of (log) per capita output
gap below trend, 1990–2000*

	OLS	IV
	[1]	[2]
Regulation index	0.09845**	0.10021**
(index ranges from 0 to 1, with		
higher meaning more regulated)	2.54	2.18
Control variables:		
Volatility of terms of trade shocks	0.00089	0.00087
(standard deviation of annual		
terms of trade growth)	0.77	0.74
Volatility of domestic inflation	0.00046	0.00045
(standard deviation of annual		
CPI growth)	1.56	1.59
Real exchange rate overvaluation	0.01203	0.01213
(proportional index, where		
overvaluation if index > 100)	0.85	0.89
R-squared	0.19	0.19
R-squared 1st stage (partial due		
to excluded instruments)		0.74
SPECIFICATION TEST		
Hansen's J-test of overidentifying		
restrictions (p-value):		0.93

Source: Authors' calculations.
Note: The sample is 76 countries. Standard errors are robust to heteroscedasticity
(Newey-West). t-Statistics are presented below the corresponding coefficient. Inter-
cept is included in all estimations but not reported. Instruments: log of per capita GDP
in 1990, binary variables indicating legal origin (British, French, German, Nordic),
variables indicating fraction of population that speaks a major European language.
** significant at 5%

regulatory index ($R^2 = 0.74$). Together, these results indicate that the
instruments are valid and relevant. Interestingly, the IV estimated
coefficient on the regulation index is quite close to its OLS counter-
part in terms of sign, size, and statistical significance.

We can use the IV results to gauge a sense of the economic significance of the effect of regulations on the severity of recessions. A

simple exercise is to measure the impact of reducing the regulation index from the heaviest to the least regulated regions. In particular, consider reducing the regulation index from that of a typical or median country in Africa, the Middle East, Latin America, and South Asia (0.51) to that of the median in developed countries (0.28). Using the IV point estimate for the coefficient on the regulation index (0.1), this reduction in the regulatory burden leads to lessening the severity of recessions by 2.3 percentage points, which represents almost 30 percent of the typical loss due to recessions in developing countries.

A Theory of Plant Selection

We develop a general equilibrium model of heterogeneous production units or "plants," vintage capital, and common and idiosyncratic shocks, based on Hopenhayn (1992) and Campbell (1998). Assume that there exists a distribution of plants characterized by different levels of productivity. In each period, plant managers decide whether to exit or stay in business. If a plant stays in business, the manager must decide how much labor to hire. If the plant exits, it is worth a sell-off value. New technologies are developed every period. Plants face three types of productivity shocks: an aggregate shock common to all plants, an idiosyncratic (plant-specific) shock, and an innovation shock to the leading-edge production technology.

In this context, the economy is characterized by an ongoing process of plant entry and exit, with corresponding job creation and destruction. Plants exit if aggregate economic prospects loom negative. They may also exit if their current technology becomes obsolete and, by selling off their capital, owners gain access to the leading-edge technology—an illustration of Schumpeter's process of creative destruction. However, exiting is costly as capital loses some of its value in the process. These investment irreversibilities, as modeled by Caballero and Engel (1999), combined with idiosyncratic uncertainty, generate an equilibrium solution where plant owners rationally delay their exit decisions.

Our model extends Campbell's (1998) analysis in three dimensions. First, by fully characterizing plant-level dynamics, we consider starting and closing plants, as well as incumbents. This allows us to look not only at plant entry and exit but also at labor creation and destruction resulting from continuing plants.

Second, we consider both aggregate and idiosyncratic productivity shocks. Within this setting, plants can become more productive over time for two reasons: either they are all exposed to better methods of production or some receive a good realization of productivity improvement while others do not. The distinction is relevant since these nonmutually exclusive ways of increasing productivity have different implications. In particular, while aggregate productivity changes are unbounded and do not necessarily entail substantial worker displacement, the increase in efficiency resulting from specific shocks is bounded by the production possibilities frontier and may involve significant reallocation of inputs across firms. Moreover, while the former predicts a negative correlation between entry and exit of plants (and corresponding labor creation and destruction), the latter implies positive co-movement between them.

Finally, we extend Campbell's model to allow for exogenously imposed rigidities. In particular, we study the effect of policies that alter firms' decisions to leave or stay in the market. In our benchmark simulations, markets are fully flexible, so policies that alter the equilibrium reduce welfare. In particular, policies that subsidize incumbents reduce the reallocation of resources that naturally follows a recession, delaying recovery. Governments are willing to impose such policies to reduce the volatility and short-run social and political costs associated with recessions. Our simulation results below are consistent with this fact: as the reallocation process is muted, incumbent protection reduces short-run output losses at the cost of a slow recovery.

In order to better relate our model to the existing micro dynamics literature, we refer to production units as "plants." We should make clear, however, that we do not provide a theory of the firm or the plant. In our model, the size of the firm as a collection of production units is indeterminate, and, therefore, the modeled entry-exit dynamics can occur either within or across *actual* firms or plants. Nevertheless, to the extent that firm or plant activities tend to consist of interrelated production units (or investment projects), we expect that there is considerable correlation between production dynamics in the model and plant dynamics in reality. Moreover, we conjecture that the magnitude of entry and exit implicit in the model is an upper bound of those in reality. We will come back to this point when we discuss the parameterization of the model.

The gap between the definition of production units in the model and in the data implies that our model abstracts from reality in other dimensions that are also relevant for the specification of parameters as well as for the interpretation of our results. On the one hand, only new plants invest. In the data, investment is carried out by both new and old plants. On the other hand, plants may adopt new technologies without actually closing.

In what follows we describe our model in detail.

The model economy: The economy is populated by a continuum of heterogeneous plants. A plant needs labor (n) and capital (k) for production of the unique good, which can be used for consumption or investment. This unique production good is the numeraire.

Each plant's technology is given by

$$y_t = e^{\lambda_t} n_t^\alpha \left(e^{\theta_t} k_t\right)^{1-\alpha}$$

where λ_t is the aggregate productivity shock common to all establishments and θ_t is the idiosyncratic productivity shock. The aggregate productivity shock follows an AR(1) process described by

$$\lambda_{t+1} = \rho_\lambda \lambda_t + \varepsilon_{t+1}^\lambda, \varepsilon_{t+1}^\lambda \sim N\left(0, \sigma_\lambda^2\right)$$

$N(\cdot)$ is the normal distribution, $0 \leq \rho_\lambda \leq 1$, and ε_t^λ is *i.i.d.*

Each type of capital embodies different levels of technology. Since technologies are characterized by constant returns to scale, we can restrict the size of all plants to be equal to one unit of capital. Thus, capital goods are identified with plants so that investing one unit of the aggregate good yields a unit mass of plants.

The aggregate production function of this model economy is:

$$Y_t = e^{\lambda_t} N_t^\alpha \left[\int_{-\infty}^{\infty} e^{\theta_t} k_t(\theta) d\theta\right]^{1-\alpha} = e^{\lambda_t} N_t^\alpha \overline{K}_t^{1-\alpha}$$

where $\overline{K}_t = \int_{-\infty}^{\infty} e^{\theta_t} k_t(\theta) d\theta$ is the aggregate effective capital stock.

Capital embodying relatively low levels of technology is scrapped as its productivity lags behind that of the leading-edge technology. When a plant is retired, a unit of capital that is scrapped has salvage value $s < 1$. The total amount of salvaged capital in period t is then

$$S_t = (1-\delta)s \int_{-\infty}^{\overline{\theta}_t} k_t(\theta_t) d\theta_t$$

where $\overline{\theta}_t$ is the endogenous cut-off level of productivity that determines the exit decision of plants. Units of the production goods not consumed—which are made up of investment and part of last period's scrapped capital—are transformed into new units of capital embodied in the leading-edge technology. That is, the initial productivity level of a plant born in period t is a random variable with a normal distribution

$$\theta_{t+1} \sim N\left(z_t, \sigma^2\right)$$

where z_t is the index of embodied technology that represents the leading-edge production process. This random variable follows a random walk with a positive drift μ_z according to

$$z_{t+1} = \mu_z + z_t + \varepsilon_{t+1}^z, \varepsilon_{t+1}^z \sim N\left(0, \sigma_z^2\right).$$

This drift is the only source of long-run aggregate growth in our economy.

Capital that is not scrapped receives an idiosyncratic shock to its productivity level before the next period production process starts, according to

$$\theta_{t+1} = \theta_t + \varepsilon_{t+1}^\theta, \varepsilon_{t+1}^\theta \sim N\left(0, \sigma_\theta^2\right)$$

This idiosyncratic shock has zero mean and, thus, it does not affect the economy's long-run growth rate. The random walk property of the stochastic process ensures that the differences in average productivity across units of capital persist over time. Thus, at any t, the units of capital with more advanced technology have a lower probability of shutting down.

Summarizing, there are three sources of uncertainty: first, an idiosyncratic productivity shock, ε_t^θ , that determines the plant-level decisions of incumbents. This shock does not alter the aggregate equilibrium allocation. Second, an idiosyncratic productivity shock, ε_t^z , that governs the economy-wide growth. Notice that plants, as they decide to stay or leave, choose between the following distributions:

$$\theta_{t+1} \sim N\left(\theta_t, \sigma_\theta^2\right)$$

$$\theta_{t+1} \sim N\left(z_t, \sigma^2\right)$$

Finally, there is an aggregate shock, ε_t^λ, which introduces aggregate uncertainty, moving transitorily the economy's production possibility frontier.

Plants last one period. At the beginning of the period, firms decide production and hiring. The wage rate in period t is ω_t, and the beginning and end of period prices of a plant with productivity θ_t are $q_t^0\left(\theta_t\right)$ and $q_t^1\left(\theta_t\right)$, respectively. Within this setting, given the number of units of capital with productivity θ_t, k_t (θ_t), the employment assigned to each plant is given by

$$n_t(\theta_t) = N_t^\alpha e^{\theta_t} / \overline{K}_t$$

After production, firms decide which plants should be scrapped and which ones should be maintained in business. Firms sell their production and salvaged capital to the consumer and to a construction firm that produces capital embodying the leading-edge technology.

Capital evolves according to the law of motion

$$k_{t+1}^0(\theta_{t+1}) = \int_{-\infty}^{\infty} \frac{1}{\sigma_\theta} \phi\left(\frac{\theta_{t+1}-\theta_t}{\sigma_\theta}\right) k_t^1(\theta_t) d\theta_t + \phi\left(\frac{\theta_{t+1}-z_t}{\sigma}\right) I_t^c$$

Since asset prices equal discounted expected dividend streams, increases in the level of productivity raise these prices; and since the scrap value of a plant is independent of its productivity, only plants with productivity levels below the threshold $\overline{\theta}_t$ exit the market. The marginal plant, that is, the one with productivity level $\overline{\theta}_t$, has a market value given by the scrap value. The following equation states this condition.

$$s = q_t^1(\overline{\theta}_t)$$

Finally, the purchasing price of a unit of capital is determined not only by its marginal productivity but also by the price at which the capital left after depreciation may be sold at the end of the period. Thus, for each θ_t, the purchase and sale decisions of capital units must be characterized by the zero profit condition:

$$q_t^0(\theta_t) = (1-\alpha)\left(\frac{\overline{K}_t}{N_t}\right)^{-\alpha} e^{\theta_t} + (1-\delta)\left[1\{\theta_t < \overline{\theta}_t\}s + 1\{\theta_t \geq \overline{\theta}_t\}q_t^1(\theta_t)\right]$$

where $1\{\cdot\}$ is an indicator function that equals one if its argument is true and zero otherwise. This condition restricts the beginning of the period price to be the return from using the capital plus the price at which it can be sold at the end of the period.

There is a construction firm whose sole purpose is to incorporate the leading-edge technology into the goods produced by the firm. A construction firm that buys I^c_t units of the aggregate good from the producer incorporates the leading-edge technology at zero cost, and then sells it to consumers at the end of the period at a price per unit

q_t^{1i}. Profit maximization requires the price of the construction project to be equal to the cost of inputs. That is,

$$q_t^{1i} = 1$$

Government subsidies (taxes), τ_t, follow an AR(1) process as the one described for the aggregate productivity shock, λ_t. We consider policies that allow plants to stay in the market longer than they would have without government intervention. We represent them by a subsidy to incumbents that increases the end-of-period price of an old plant. The government's budget constraint is guaranteed to be satisfied by imposing a lump-sum transfer to consumers.

The remainder of the model is standard. There is a continuum of identical infinitely lived consumers who own labor and equity. Their preferences are given by

$$E_0\left[\sum_{t=0}^{\infty} \beta^t \left(\log(c_t) + \gamma(1 - n_t)\right)\right]$$

where c_t and $1 - n_t$ are consumption and leisure respectively, and $\beta \in (0,1)$ is the subjective time discount factor. Every period consumers have a time endowment equal to 1. Following Hansen (1985) and Rogerson (1988), we assume that consumers can work a fixed number of hours or none at all. To avoid non-convexities, consumers are assumed to trade employment lotteries. As a consequence, n_t is interpreted as the fraction of the population that works.

Definition of the equilibrium: A *Competitive Equilibrium* in this economy is a set of contingent plans $\{c_t, I_t, Y_t, \bar{K}_t, N_t, S_t\}_{t=0}^{\infty}$, and contingent prices $\{\omega_t, q_t^1, q_t^0, q_t^{1i}\}_{t=0}^{\infty}$ of labor, plants at the beginning of the period, plants at the end of the period, and construction projects, and a vector $\{\bar{\theta}_t\}_{t=0}^{\infty}$ such that, given contingent prices, the transfer T_t, and production and government stochastic processes $\{z_t, \theta_t, \lambda_t, \tau_t\}$, at each period t:

1) The representative consumer solves

$$E_0\left[\sum_{t=0}^{\infty} \beta^t \left(\log(c_t) + \gamma(1 - n_t)\right)\right]$$

$$c_t + I_t^c q_t^{1i} + (1 - \tau_t)\int_{-\infty}^{\infty} q_t^1(\theta_t) k_t^1(\theta_t) d\theta = \omega_t n_t + \int_{-\infty}^{\infty} q_t^0(\theta_t) k_t^0(\theta_t) d\theta - T_t$$

$$k_{t+1}^0(\theta_{t+1}) = \int_{-\infty}^{\infty} \frac{1}{\sigma_\theta}\phi\left(\frac{\theta_{t+1} - \theta_t}{\sigma_\theta}\right) k_t^1(\theta_t) d\theta_t + \phi\left(\frac{\theta_{t+1} - z_t}{\sigma}\right) I_t^c$$

2) The producer of the consumption good satisfies

$$n_t(\theta) = N_t^\alpha e^{\theta_t} / \overline{K}_t$$

$$\omega_t = \alpha e^{\lambda_t} \left(\frac{\overline{K}_t}{N_t} \right)^{1-\alpha}$$

$$q_t^1(\overline{\theta}_t) = s$$

$$q_t^0(\theta_t) = (1-\alpha)\left(\frac{\overline{K}_t}{N_t} \right)^{-\alpha} e^{\theta_t} + (1-\delta)\left[1\{\theta_t < \overline{\theta}_t\} s + 1\{\theta_t \geq \overline{\theta}_t\} q_t^1(\theta_t) \right]$$

3) The intermediary satisfies

$$I_t^i = q_t^{1i} I_t^c$$

4) The government satisfies

$$\tau_t \int_{-\infty}^{\infty} q_t^1(\theta_t) k_t^1(\theta_t) d\theta = T_t$$

5) The market clearing restriction is satisfied

$$c_t + I_t = Y_t + S_t$$

A Numerical Evaluation

We simulate the transitional path that follows aggregate productivity shocks. We study slow recoveries resulting from distortions that alter plants dynamics. Although these distortions may take various forms, we model a specific policy that subsidizes incumbents. Plants that would have exited after the shock stay longer in the market when the subsidy is positive. To approximate actual experiences, we simulate equilibria for a range of policy values.

Solution method

To solve for the numerical equilibria, we use a three-step strategy. First, we compute the non-stochastic steady state values for the model variables. Second, we linearize the system of equations that characterizes the solution around the long-run values of the variables. Third, we apply the method of undetermined coefficients described in Christiano (2002). To solve the model, we scale the variables by the long-run growth rate such that they converge to a steady state. Then a mapping takes the solution from the scaled objects solved for in the computations to the unscaled objects of interest.

Parameter values

We can separate the parameters into three types, given by the following vectors: aggregate parameters $\{\beta, \delta, \gamma, \mu_z, \alpha, s, \sigma_\lambda, \rho_\lambda\}$; plant-specific parameters $\{\sigma, \sigma_\theta\}$; and policy parameters $\{\tau, \sigma_\tau, \rho_\tau\}$.

The aggregate parameters are calibrated as in a representative firm economy. A period is one quarter. Long-run growth is given by $\mu_z(1-\alpha)/\alpha$, which also represents the growth rate of income per capita since population is stationary. Thus, to have an annual trend growth rate of 2 percent, and given α equal to 0.6—a standard value in the literature—we use μ_z equal to 0.52 percent. The marginal utility of leisure, γ, determines the fraction of available time allocated to labor. We chose γ consistently with N equal to 0.35. The irreversibility s is fixed in 0.9. The remaining aggregate parameters, β, α, and δ, are chosen as in the standard growth literature.

Plant-specific parameters are taken from Campbell (1998). There are two reasons for doing so: first, long series of plant-level data are generally not available for a large sample of countries. Second, we see our economies as equal in all respects but policy. We use the United States as our undistorted long-run benchmark.

Campbell sets parameter values to match the moments of plant dynamics using data from the Annual Survey of Manufactures of the U.S. Census Bureau (Department of Commerce). Although we refer to production units as plants in our model, investment projects provide a better description of them. Thus, an entry or an exit in the model might occur within an actual plant, and thus might not be captured by actual data. In this sense, our model naturally generates much more in the way of dynamics than that observed in the data. Nevertheless, our parameterization underestimates the true variance of investment projects, as we match our model's moments using plant-level data. Had we used the variability of entry and exit of projects across *and within* plants, our results would have assigned a much larger role to reallocation and restructuring as a source of transitional growth.

Policy parameters are also complicated to calibrate since comparable series for plant-level distortions are typically not available across countries. Thus, we approximate different actual experiences by simulating transitional growth using a wide range of policy values.

These distortions are intended to capture different regulations that reduce competition, raise the costs of firm formation, and slow down technological adoption. They may also represent other impediments to the natural process of reallocation across firms such as financial markets imperfections. In general, any policy that affects current and expected productivity, interfering with the natural process of birth, growth, and death of firms, will have a detrimental effect on aggregate growth. For instance, as the cost of entering and exiting the economy changes, the distribution of firms is altered: too many inefficient firms remain in the market and too few efficient firms enter the market. As a result, both the reshuffling of resources from less to more efficient firms and the adoption of the leading-edge technology are impeded. Our choices for the level of the subsidy yield a government size between 18.2 percent and 23.7 percent in steady state. These figures are at ranges within the lower bound of the distribution of actual government shares in GDP (OECD 2003).

Finally, the remaining parameters, σ_λ, ρ_λ, σ_τ and ρ_τ, are picked along with our simulation exercises, i.e., they are used to fix the size and persistence of the shocks imposed on our simulated economies. Table 6.2 summarizes our parameter choices.

Simulating transitional growth

Our benchmark equilibrium is given by an economy without distortions that faces an exogenous 5 percent reduction in its aggregate productivity level (i.e., σ_λ=-0.05). This shock has no persistence (i.e., ρ_λ=0), and thus it lasts only one period. We make the latter assumption to abstract from the intertemporal effects of the shock.

Figure 6.3 shows the impulse responses for four key macroeconomic elements of the benchmark equilibrium: output, consumption, investment, and hours worked. We see that, as expected, a negative aggregate shock to productivity reduces all of them. These impulse responses are consistent with those observed in a representative firm economy. A model with plant heterogeneity introduces an additional margin by allowing entry and exit and the reshuffling of resources across existing plants. These reallocation effects are relevant for aggregate productivity dynamics. Figures 6.4 and 6.5 show impulse responses for the cut-off level of productivity that determines endogenous exit decisions, and job creation and destruction rates, respectively. A one-period reduction in the level of aggregate productivity increases the cut-off level of productivity, since it forces relatively inefficient plants to exit. Moreover, job creation falls and job destruction increases. The aggregate labor response is the net result of these two margins of adjustment.

Table 6.2: Parameterization

Aggregate parameters		
Discount factor	β	0.98
Fraction of hours worked in steady state	N	0.35
Labor share	α	0.6
Technology drift	μ_z	0.0052
Irreversibility	s	0.9
Depreciation rate	δ	0.02
Plant-level parameters		
Standard deviation of shock to incumbents	σ_θ	0.03
Standard deviation of shock to startups	σ	0.25
Simulation parameters		
Aggregate productivity shock	σ_λ	−0.05
Aggregate productivity shock persistence	ρ_λ	0
Policy level	τ	
Exercise 1		−0.05, −0.1
Exercise 2		0
Policy shock	σ_t	
Exercise 1		0
Exercise 2		−0.06, −0.03
Policy shock persistence	ρ_τ	
Exercise 1		n.a.
Exercise 2		0.66

Source: Authors' calculations.

To study differences in recovery paths, we analyze two particular cases of impediments to reallocation that might shed light on actual differences in recovery paths. In the first numerical exercise, we compare economies that start off with different levels of a production subsidy to incumbent firms. We then expose these economies to the same 5 percent aggregate shock, and compare their recovery paths to their own trend. The second exercise simulates an economy with no distortions that imposes a transitory subsidy to incumbents a period after the aggregate shock occurs. When the exogenous recession hits the economy, jobs are lost and production units are scrapped. To reduce the distress associated with these losses, the government intervenes, subsidizing incumbents one period after the shock hits the economy. This policy is short-lived, as it follows an AR(1) with autocorrelation coefficient of 0.66; that is, it lasts about three quarters.[3]

Figure 6.6 shows the recovery path for our first exercise. The trend has been normalized to one in both economies. Initially, the economy that protects the incumbents experiences a smaller fall in output. This is precisely why this type of policy is typically imple-

Figure 6.3: Impulse Response for Macro Variables

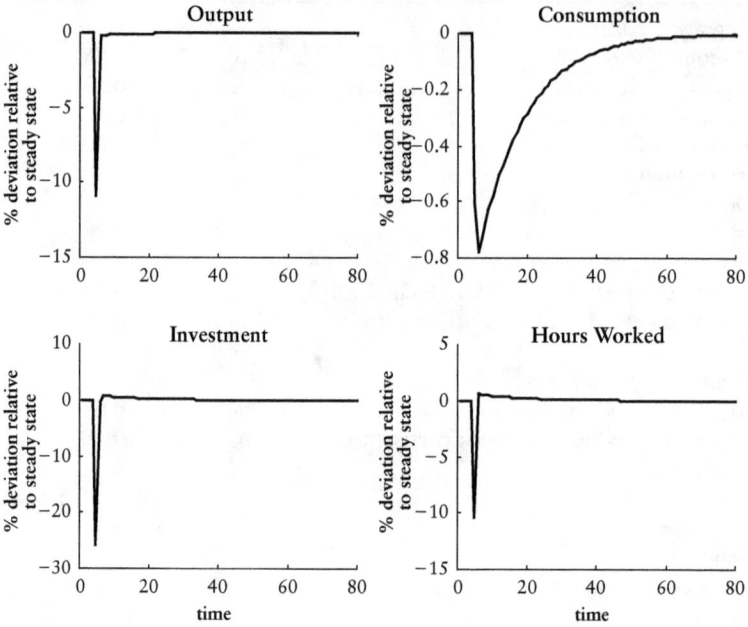

Figure 6.4: Impulse Response for Cut-Off Level

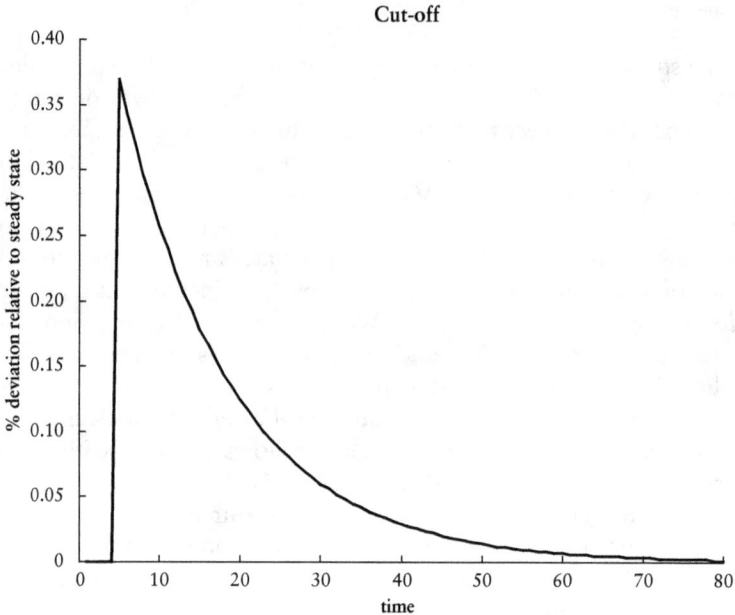

Figure 6.5: Impulse Response for Job Creation and
Destruction Rates

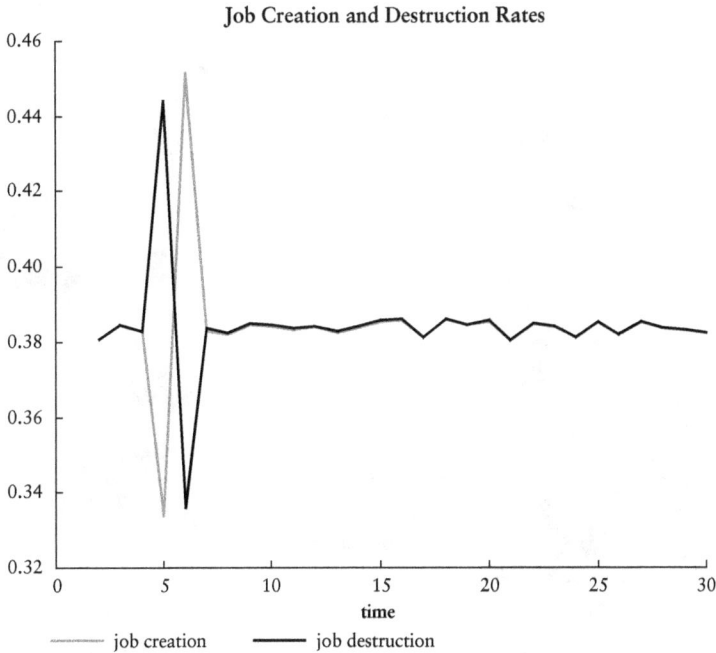

Job Creation and Destruction Rates

Source: Authors' calculations.

mented: to reduce volatility. Over time, however, the protected economy experiences a slow recovery. The results are similar in the second exercise. Figure 6.7 shows the recovery path in this case. As
before, the economy that subsidizes existing plants experiences stag-
nating growth and recovers its pre-crisis output trend level much
later.

To measure the differences in the recovery paths of the undistorted and distorted economies, we provide two types of indicators.
The first type relates to the size of output losses, whereas the second
relates to the time that output takes to recover its long-run trend.

To construct the first indicator (from now on, "the loss"), we start
by normalizing the path of output and its trend in such a way that
all economies start off with the same level of output; that is, GDP
per capita and its trend at time $t = 0$ are all equal to 1. We do this to
account for the fact that distorted economies have lower output in
steady state. Let Y^{τ}_t represent the actual GDP of the economy with
distortion at level τ in period t, and let YT^{τ}_t be its trend. Thus, the
loss is the present value of output deviations from its trend as a fraction of pre-shock output:

Figure 6.6: Slow Recovery—Exercise 1

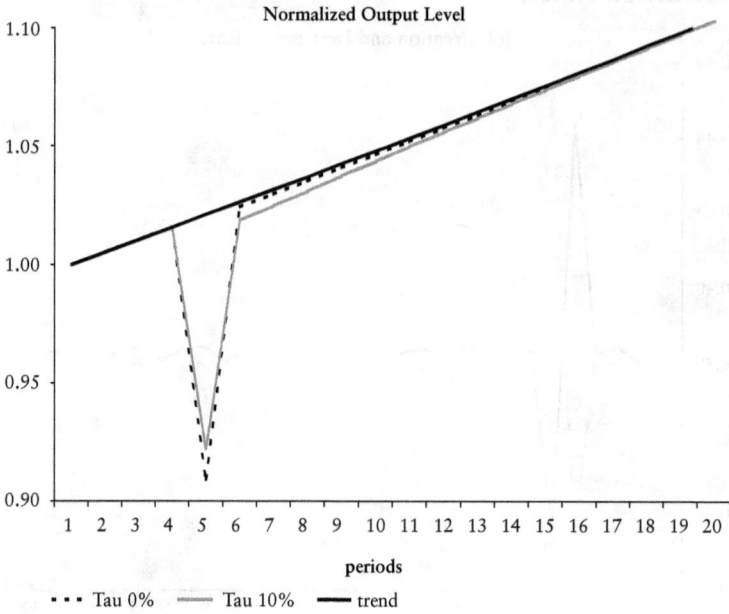

Normalized Output Level

periods

• • • Tau 0%   Tau 10%   trend

Figure 6.7: Slow Recovery—Exercise 2

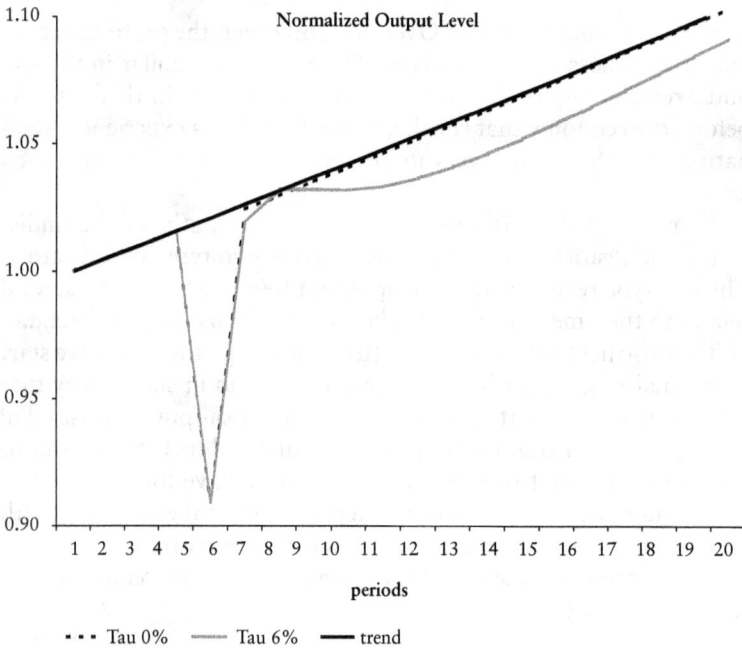

Normalized Output Level

periods

• • • Tau 0%   Tau 6%   trend

$$\frac{\sum\limits_{t=0}^{T} \beta^t (Y_t^\tau - YT_t^\tau)}{Y_0^\tau}$$

We use two sets of recovery length indicators. The first one measures the time it takes the economy to recover its trend after the economy is struck by the exogenous aggregate shock. The second indicator is the fraction of the loss that is realized in a given number of quarters.

Table 6.3 reports these indicators for the simulated economies. The fully flexible economy loses a significant fraction of its pre-crisis GDP over the recovery path: 13.1 percent in present value terms. The economy does not recover instantaneously because there exist technological rigidities—(a scrap value below 1 and) a lag between capital investment and its availability for production. These rigidities imply that the loss of output is larger than the actual shock. If the economy is already distorted when the shock strikes, the loss increases to slightly over 14 percent. This difference, about 1 percent of pre-crisis GDP, is totally due to reduced reallocation, and thus to lower aggregate TFP growth. Recall that we measure the loss after normalizing the path of output, so the loss does not incorporate the fact that the distorted economy is poorer in steady state. This additional loss is large. The measured losses associated with the subsidy that is given right after the crisis starts are much larger (first line of the second panel.) Their larger size is due to the fact that the tax puts the economy below its trend for a long period of time (see figure 6.7).

The second measure shows that the undistorted economy quickly recovers its output trend: it takes only one quarter to reduce the gap to less than one-fifth of 1 percent.[4] The subsidized economies take nine and 10 quarters, respectively. The length of the recovery period increases substantially when the government subsidizes firms right after the crisis starts, with catch-up periods that rise over 30 quarters. Thus, the policy intervention reduces volatility and firm destruction, at the cost of a long period of stagnation.

Our final measure, the fraction of the loss that is realized in 1, 5, 10, 20, and 30 quarters, is reported at the bottom of each panel. Most of the loss is quickly realized in the fully flexible economy, with more than 84 percent of it happening within the first period. Subsidized economies spread these losses over time, with 68 percent to 72 percent realized within the first quarter. Only after 10 quarters did all three simulated economies behave similarly, having realized about 95 percent of the loss. Once again, the differences between this case and the economy that was intervened in during the crisis are striking: only 30 percent to 46 percent of the loss is realized within the first

Table 6.3: Simulated Slow Recovery Indicators

	Subsidy (%)		
Pre-existing distortion	*0*	*5*	*10*
Loss (% of pre-shock GDP)	13.1	14.2	14.3
Catching up with the trend (quarters)			
0.2%	1	9	10
0.5%	1	2	4
% of the loss realized in			
1 quarter	84.2	72.3	68.1
5 quarters	91.1	88.7	90.1
10 quarters	94.5	94.9	96.5
20 quarters	97.8	98.9	99.6
30 quarters	99.1	99.8	100.0
	Subsidy (%)		
Distortion along the way	*0*	*3*	*6*
Loss	13.1	23.7	36.3
Catching up with the trend (quarters)			
0.2%	1	29	37
0.5%	1	17	26
% of the loss realized in			
1 quarter	84.2	46.4	30.3
5 quarters	91.1	57.2	43.6
10 quarters	94.5	71.9	63.5
20 quarters	97.8	88.9	86.0
30 quarters	99.1	95.6	94.6

Source: Authors' calculations.

quarter, spreading the recovery path over a much longer period of time. The economy takes about 30 quarters to realize 95 percent of the loss, i.e., five years more than the undistorted economy.

Our results show that the costs associated with incumbent protection are substantial, in terms of both lost output and recovery length. These costs are much larger whenever the economy is distorted along the recovery path, because within a short period of time, the economy faces two shocks: the exogenous aggregate shock and the policy response to the shock. If the government lets the economy adjust on its own, the initial fall in output is much sharper, but is concentrated over a significantly shorter period of time.

Conclusions

In this chapter we have linked microeconomic rigidities to aggregate transitional growth. By subsidizing incumbents, we have altered the reallocation process, a key source of aggregate efficiency. As plants that would have exited the economy stay longer in the market, aggregate efficiency lowers and growth stagnates. As a result, economies experience slow recoveries and large output losses.

Our findings are consistent with observed recovery paths. The evidence on plant dynamics across countries is also consistent with our findings. Developing and developed economies show surprisingly similar rates of job reallocation, although output volatility is markedly higher in poor countries. This high volatility suggests the need for higher restructuring. Thus, the evidence is consistent with sluggish restructuring in developing countries, perhaps as a result of institutional impediments to resource mobility across production units. Governments are willing to impose these rigidities to reduce the depth of recessions and the associated short-run social and political costs. However, reduced volatility comes at the cost of stagnation and increased output losses in the long run.

Finally, our results suggest further research on other growth-related issues. Market-oriented reforms have been ubiquitously undertaken during the last two decades. However, most reforms are implemented sequentially, so when one reform is undertaken, other obstacles to reallocation stay in place. Our results suggest that the benefits from liberalizing international trade or from privatizing publicly owned firms will be largely reduced if impediments to plant dynamics are not eliminated simultaneously.

Notes

1. We use the database collected and presented in Loayza et al. (2009), also in this volume. See this chapter for specific definitions, sources, and coverage of the data.

2. We should note that this pattern is not homogeneous across types of regulations. For instance, contrary to the overall index, industrialized countries have the highest burden of taxation.

3. Our exercise is highly stylized since the endogenous policy response is more likely to happen in reality when aggregate shocks are persistent.

4. The size of this lag depends crucially on our one quarter time-to-build assumption.

References

Baxter, M., and R. King. 1999. "Measuring Business Cycles: Approximate Band-Pass Filters for Economic Time Series." *Review of Economics and Statistics* 81(4): 575–93.

Bergoeing, R., P. Kehoe, T. Kehoe, and R. Soto. 2002. "A Decade Lost and Found: Mexico and Chile in the 1980s." *Review of Economic Dynamics* 5(1): 166–205.

Bolaky, B., and C. Freund. 2004. "Trade, Regulations, and Growth." Policy Research Working Paper 3255, World Bank, Washington, DC.

Botero, J., S. Djankov, R. La Porta, F. Lopez-de-Silanes, and A. Shleifer. 2004. "The Regulation of Labor." *Quarterly Journal of Economics* 119(4): 1339–1382.

Broadbent, B., D. Schumacher, and S. Schels. 2004. "No Gain Without Pain: Germany's Adjustment to a Higher Cost of Capital." Global Economics Paper 103, Goldman Sachs, New York.

Caballero, R., and E. Engel. 1999. "Explaining Investment Dynamics in U.S. Manufacturing: A Generalized (S, s) Approach." *Econometrica* 67(4): 783–826.

Caballero, R., E. Engel, and A. Micco. 2004. "Microeconomic Flexibility in Latin America." *Economía Chilena* 7(2): 5-26.

Caballero, R., and M. Hammour. 1996. "On the Timing and Efficiency of Creative Destruction." *Quarterly Journal of Economics* 111(3): 805–852.

———. 1998. "The Macroeconomics of Specificity." *The Journal of Political Economy* 106(4): 724–767.

Caballero, R., T. Hoshi, and A.K. Kashyap. 2008. "Zombie Lending and Depressed Restructuring in Japan." *American Economic Review* 98(5): 1943–1977.

Campbell, J. 1998. "Entry, Exit, Embodied Technology, and Business Cycles." *Review of Economic Dynamics* 1(2): 371–408.

Christiano, L. 2002. "Solving Dynamic Equilibrium Models by a Method of Undetermined Coefficients." *Computational Economics* 20(1-2): 21–55.

Cole, H., and L. Ohanian. 1999. "The Great Depression in the United States from a Neoclassical Perspective." *Federal Reserve Bank of Minneapolis Quarterly Review* 23(1): 1–24.

Davis, S., J. Haltiwanger, and S. Schuh. 1996. *Job Creation and Destruction*. Cambridge, MA: The MIT Press.

Ericson, R., and A. Pakes. 1995. "Markov-Perfect Industry Dynamics: A Framework for Empirical Work." *Review of Economic Studies* 62(1): 53–82.

Hansen, G. 1985. "Indivisible Labor and the Business Cycle." *Journal of Monetary Economics* 16(3): 309–27.

Hayashi, F., and E. Prescott. 2002. "The 1990s in Japan: A Lost Decade." *Review of Economic Dynamics* 5(1): 206–235.

Hopenhayn, H. 1992. "Entry, Exit, and Firm Dynamics in Long Run Equilibrium." *Econometrica* 60(5): 1127–1150.

Hopenhayn, H., and R. Rogerson. 1993. "Job Turnover and Policy Evaluation: A General Equilibrium Analysis." *Journal of Political Economy* 101(5): 915–938.

Hoshi, T., and A.K. Kashyap. 2004. "Japan's Financial Crisis and Economic Stagnation." *Journal of Economic Perspectives* 18(1): 3–26.

Jovanovic, B. 1982. "Selection and the Evolution of Industry." *Econometrica* 50(3): 649–670.

Loayza N.V., A.M. Oviedo, and L. Servén. 2009. "Regulation and Macroeconomic Performance." This volume.

OECD. 2003. *Statistiques des Recettes Publiques des Pays Membres de l'OCDE.* Paris.

Prescott, E. 2002. "Prosperity and Depression: 2002 Richard T. Ely Lecture." *American Economic Review Papers and Proceedings* 92(2): 1–15.

Restuccia, D., and R. Rogerson. 2008. "Policy Distortions and Aggregate Productivity with Heterogeneous Establishments." *Review of Economic Dynamics* 11(4): 707–720.

Rogerson, R. 1988. "Indivisible Labor, Lotteries and Equilibrium." *Journal of Monetary Economics* 21(1): 3–16.

7

Market Reforms, Factor Reallocation, and Productivity Growth in Latin America

Marcela Eslava, John Haltiwanger,
Adriana Kugler, and Maurice Kugler

Introduction

The ability of firms to adjust their deployment and use of production factors in the face of shocks is key to promoting both active productivity growth and high levels of aggregate employment. In fact, several studies have confirmed, for different countries and periods of study, the more general finding that changes in the allocation of inputs and outputs across producers are an important source of productivity growth.[1]

We are grateful to Ricardo Caballero, Norman Loayza, Luis Servén and two anonymous referees for valuable comments and suggestions. We thank Rafael Santos for superb research assistance. We acknowledge the World Bank's support for this research. Marcela Eslava also thanks the financial support of CAF for part of this project.

In the policy arena, the debate in terms of factor adjustment and productivity growth has centered on the potential role of institutions and regulations as determinants of adjustment costs. The recognition of the importance of flexibility in factor markets, for instance, has been one of the main reasons behind large-scale reforms around the world. Latin America is no exception: the comprehensive reforms implemented in the region during the 1990s had as a major objective the liberalization of factor markets.[2]

Different types of regulations may impose different types of frictions such as adjustment costs and irreversibilities. For instance, a requirement for firms to obtain government authorization to import machinery essentially imposes a fixed cost on investment (and generates an asymmetry between capital purchases and retirements), while severance payments are mainly per-worker costs. It is thus important to allow for differences in factor adjustment costs when analyzing the impact of reforms on factory flexibility. In fact, it is widely documented that firms face different types of costs of adjusting their use of factors, and that each of these types of costs has different implications for the adjustment process. For example, Cooper and Haltiwanger (2006) have shown that capital adjustment in the United States is best described by a model that incorporates both convex and non-convex costs of adjustment, as well as investment irreversibility. Caballero, Engel, and Haltiwanger (1997), meanwhile, study employment adjustment, and find that it is also lumpy. Non-convex adjustment costs, and the resulting nonlinearities of the adjustment process, are thus key ingredients to analyzing both labor and capital adjustments.[3]

Almost all studies dealing with factor adjustment in the presence of non-convex adjustment costs have focused on only one margin of adjustment—either employment or capital—at a time. Factor demands, however, mutually impact each other. Firms do not analyze different factor adjustment margins separately when considering how much to adjust in each of those margins and, as a consequence, the desired levels of different factors depend on one another. In this sense, adjustment costs in one factor market affect the demand for other factors, and factor adjustment should in principle be studied in a framework that considers the different margins simultaneously. This is particularly important when considering the effects of institutions, as deregulation in one factor market may have effects on the demands of other factors; the study of simultaneous adjustment in different margins may, therefore, provide insights about the desirability of piecemeal, as opposed to comprehensive, reforms.

In Eslava et al. (2006), we develop a framework where simultaneous and interrelated capital and employment adjustments are considered. In that paper, we take advantage of a unique database for

Colombian manufacturing plants to implement our framework, which is highly demanding in terms of data requirements. In this chapter, we try to draw conclusions from that framework for a larger set of Latin American countries. Given the unavailability of the necessary micro data for other Latin American countries, however, we use a simulation environment to generate such data from information on Colombian manufacturing establishments and data on aggregate economic performance and institutions for those other countries.

Moreover, while our framework and approach draw heavily from Eslava et al. (2006), we extend our framework by considering adjustment dynamics separately for skilled (nonproduction) and unskilled (production) workers. Separating the adjustment of production and nonproduction workers is important for two main reasons. First, adjusting employment of highly qualified personnel for a firm may be fundamentally different from adjusting the level of blue-collar workers. Both hiring and dismissal costs are presumably different between these two margins: separating a worker involves not only paying a compensation for job loss, but also losing match-specific capital, usually higher for highly qualified jobs. As a result, firms may also spend more resources screening for the best applicant when trying to fill vacancies that demand high levels of skills. Several studies, in fact, document differences between the adjustment of skilled and less skilled labor (Foster 1999, Nickell 1986), as well as differential effects of labor market regulations on workers of different skills (Kugler 2004, Kugler and Kugler 2009, and Montenegro and Pages 2005).

A second reason why this study emphasizes the difference between production and nonproduction workers is that the policy debate in Latin America has recently focused on the importance of reducing unemployment for less skilled workers, which in many countries is double that of more skilled workers. At the same time, to increase productivity growth, policy discussions have considered the importance of adopting production technologies biased toward more skill-intensive technologies. In a recent study for the World Bank, for instance, De Ferranti and Perry insist on the importance of such shifts: "Trade and FDI have facilitated . . . competitive pressures. . . . Hiring and training more educated workers is one way to respond to this pressure to become more productive" (De Ferranti and Perry 2005, p. 2). Some evidence is already emerging that suggests such a change in the skill mix of labor is occurring in Latin America, and that it is partly driven by the wave of market reforms of the 1990s. For example, Revenga (1995) shows that the Mexican trade liberalization of the late 1980s was followed by a shift in industrial employment toward nonproduction jobs.

Using data for Colombia, we first estimate adjustment functions for capital, skilled, and unskilled workers. Our focus is on the effects of an index of the flexibility of market institutions on adjustment. Even for developed economies, the relationship between factor market institutions and outcomes in those markets is far from settled. For Latin America, the question is particularly interesting, as adjustment in the context of developing economies is an issue that has only recently received attention (Caballero et al. 2005, Eslava et al. 2006, Caballero et al. 2004, and Casacuberta and Gandelman 2006). Based on the adjustment functions estimated for Colombia, we construct counterfactual adjustment functions that would be predicted by our framework for other countries in Latin America, given the level of institutions that characterizes them. Moreover, we use those counterfactual adjustment functions and simulated micro data to project the evolution of employment and the capital stock at the micro level for other countries in Latin America. Finally, we use those projected series to estimate the dynamics of aggregate productivity for those countries both in a hypothetical frictionless environment and under the actual evolution of institutions.

Our findings for basic adjustment functions indicate, first, that for firms the different margins of adjustment are complements. This finding highlights the importance of studying the adjustment processes for different factors in a unified framework. We reported a similar result in Eslava et al. (2006), without considering heterogeneous workers. Second, allowing for a nonlinear adjustment is key for all factors. The nonlinear adjustment of nonproduction workers is much more important on the creation side. The capital adjustment function shows a deep contrast between investment and retirements: while there is active response to shortages in the form of capital formation, firms facing surpluses of capital undertake limited equipment retirements.

In terms of the effects of institutions, we find interesting differential patterns for the two types of workers. While less restrictive institutions make the adjustment of nonproduction workers more dynamic on both the creation and destruction sides, for low-skill jobs they only stimulate robustly the destruction of jobs. This is consistent with the expected pattern of skill-biased change in the composition of the labor force when firms are faced with more competitive and flexible regulations. The effect of institutional changes on the hiring of less skilled workers is highly nonlinear: less regulated environments are associated with greater hiring only for establishments that face large shortages, while the opposite is true for establishments with small desired adjustments. Deregulation also makes the pattern of hiring of high-skill workers more nonlinear, although the effect is much less marked than for blue-collar workers. Interestingly, these nonlinear effects of institutional changes imply that the pattern of employment adjustment functions is more consistent with fixed adjustment costs for less regulated environments. This may suggest that non-convexities in the employment adjustment cost functions are mostly related to technological constraints rather than to regulations.[4] Under more stringent regulations, the convex components of the adjustment cost function appear relatively more salient. In fact, severance payments, which are a large part of adjustment costs on the destruction side, are per-worker costs and, thus, more consistent with convex adjustment costs.

In the capital adjustment margin, investment in response to capital shortages increases as regulations become more flexible. This is consistent with a reduction of adjustment costs generated by more flexible regulations. On the other hand, capital shedding is less responsive to surpluses in less regulated environments. It is possible that this reflects a pattern of substitution away from capital reductions into employment reductions, and thinner secondary markets for capital goods when the demand for such goods can be satisfied with more accessible new equipment.

These findings on the relationship between the structure of adjustment costs and institutions in Colombia serve as the basis for our simulation of adjustment and productivity dynamics for other Latin American countries. We consider a variety of simulations by using the relationship between the driving forces for adjustment (i.e., productivity, demand, and cost shocks), the adjustment functions and institutions, and the actual measured institutions in different countries to simulate the adjustment dynamics in other countries. We find that the market reforms improved factor market flexibility in Latin American especially for those economies with substantial market reforms. In addition, we consider the implications of these simulations for productivity across Latin America. In our earlier work (Eslava et al. 2006), we showed that if Colombia could significantly reduce frictions in labor and capital adjustments, the country could experience considerable productivity gains. In this context, we find that other Latin American countries would also observe very large gains in aggregate productivity if they could remove all frictions affecting factor adjustment.

The chapter proceeds as follows. In the next section, we describe the analytical framework and the process we use for simulating data for Latin American countries other than Colombia. This is followed by a section describing our findings in terms of adjustment functions and their relation to institutions. Next, we describe the implications of those findings for the adjustment in other Latin American countries. Finally, we describe our results regarding the effect of factor adjustment on aggregate productivity for different countries in Latin America, followed by a section that summarizes our main results.

Empirical Strategy

Analytical framework

We briefly describe the theoretical framework used here. A more thorough description for the case of homogeneous workers can be found in Eslava et al. (2006), and for the case of heterogeneous workers in Eslava (2006). The methodology follows the theoretical framework developed by Caballero and Engel (1993), Bertola and Caballero (1994), and Caballero et al. (1995, 1997) to study factor adjustment in the presence of (possibly non-convex) adjustment costs, and frictions due to irreversibility, for a single factor of production. One of the contributions of our work is to extend this framework to simultaneous adjustments of different factors (Eslava et al. 2006). Our previous analysis is based in a two-factor framework with labor and capital. Here we use a similar model based on three factors, where labor is disaggregated between production and nonproduction workers.

The empirical strategy consists of characterizing how the actual adjustment undertaken by a firm relates to its "desired" adjustment; we call this relationship the "adjustment function." The desired adjustment is defined as the adjustment the firm would have undertaken if adjustment costs were *momentarily* removed. We estimate this desired adjustment by approximation to "frictionless" adjustment, which corresponds to the case if adjustment costs were *permanently* removed. We derive the expression for frictionless adjustment by solving the profit maximization problem of the firm, assuming there are no adjustment costs. We obtain in this manner the factor level firms would want to have in the permanent absence of frictions; this is a function of measurable characteristics of the firm, such as its demand for other factors not subject to adjustment costs (e.g., materials, energy, and hours), its total factor productivity, and the demand shocks to which it is subject. Desired and frictionless demands for each factor are proportional with sufficiently persistent shocks, so we also estimate a plant-specific constant to obtain desired demands from frictionless demands, assuming that the two are identical for the year in which the plant displays median adjustment (see details in Eslava et al. 2006).

Having measured desired factors and the resulting desired adjustments with respect to the initial levels, we compare desired and actual adjustments by estimating adjustment functions of the following form:

$$AX_{it}\left(DX_{it}, DY_{it}, DZ_{it}\right) = \lambda_t + \lambda_X DX_{it} + \lambda_Y DY_{it}$$
$$+\lambda_Z DZ_{it} + \lambda_{XX} DX_{it}^2 + \lambda_{YX} DY_{it} DX_{it}$$
$$+\lambda_{ZX} DZ_{it} DX_{it} \tag{1}$$

Here AX_{it} is firm i's hazard rate of adjusting factor X (capital, skilled labor, unskilled labor), defined as the fraction of desired adjustment that is actually undertaken. We are denoting as DX_{it}, DY_{it}, and DZ_{it}, respectively, the desired adjustments of factors X, Y, and Z. The adjustment function (1) characterizes the adjustment hazard for factor X in firm i as a function of i's desired adjustments of factors X, Y, and Z.

In the presence of non-convex adjustment costs, the hazard rate for X should be a function, possibly nonlinear, of the desired adjustment of X, DX. We thus allow AX_{it} to depend on DX in a nonlinear manner. Figure 7.1 presents examples of hypothetical relationships between AX_{it} and DX_{it}. In the absence of adjustment costs, a firm will always undertake its desired adjustment, making the hazard rate equal to one, independent of the value of the desired adjustment (solid grey line). Under convex costs of adjusting, the firm will only undertake a fraction of the desired adjustment, but that fraction will be independent of the level of the desired adjustment (dotted grey line). If, on the other hand, a firm faces fixed costs of adjusting its use of factor X, its response to a given desired adjustment will depend on how large that desired adjustment is. In particular, the firm will show little responsiveness to small shortages of factor X, and will postpone adjustment until its desired adjustment is large enough to justify paying the fixed cost; at this point, it is possible the firm will actually adjust much more than it would in the absence of frictions, adjusting in advance for possible future shocks. We will attempt to capture this adjustment pattern by using a quadratic term in our adjustment cost function (as in the thin solid black line in figure 7.1). It is also possible that there are asymmetries between firms facing shortages of factor X (positive desired adjustments), and those facing surpluses of the same factor (negative desired adjustments). For instance, if investment is irreversible, the hazard rate for capital will likely show less responsiveness to surpluses than shortages. Our framework thus allows for convex and non-convex adjustment

Figure 7.1: Hypothetical Adjustment Functions,
Different Types of Adjustment Costs

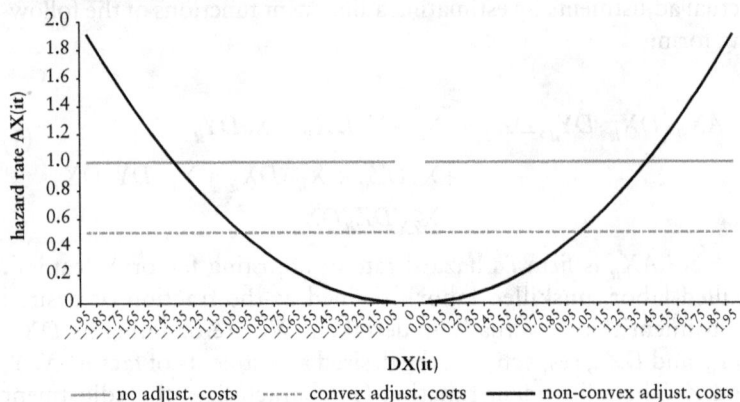

DX(it)

———— no adjust. costs   ------ convex adjust. costs   ———— non-convex adjust. costs

Source: Authors' calculations.

costs, as well as irreversibilities, by making adjustment function (1)
sufficiently flexible to accommodate patterns of adjustment consistent with all of these types of costs.

Note that adjustment function (1) also presents the hazard rate
for factor X as a function of the desired adjustment in the other two
factors. By modeling the adjustment of one factor as a (potential)
function of desired adjustments on the other two margins, we permit
interrelated adjustments of different factors.

Finally, since we are interested in the effect of institutions on
adjustment processes, we extend the adjustment functions to try to
capture these effects. We do this by interacting each term of the
adjustment function (1) with an index of institutions that captures
labor market flexibility, financial liberalization, and trade liberalization. The index is described in detail below.

Empirical implementation

Our analytical framework is highly demanding in terms of data
requirements. In particular, the estimation of desired factor demands
requires information at the establishment level on use of factors not
subject to adjustment costs, and on variables needed to estimate
demand and productivity shocks faced by the establishment (production, factor use, and prices). The availability of all these variables, especially prices, at such a high level of disaggregation is
extremely rare.[5]

We have access to a unique dataset containing all of this information for Colombian manufacturing establishments in the period

1982–98, and we use it here for estimating adjustment functions for the Colombian case. A detailed description of the data available for Colombia can be found in Eslava et al. (2004). Beyond the data used in that paper, we use here information that disaggregates employment into production and nonproduction workers, which we interpret as equivalent to blue- and white-collar workers. We also re-estimate each plant's productivity shock as a residual from a production function that separates employment into these two categories. We estimate that production function using an Instrumental Variables approach and the same instruments used in Eslava et al. (2004). Also following the strategy in that paper, we then use the estimated productivity shocks as instruments for estimating the demand shocks as residuals from a demand function.[6] With all this information, we estimate desired factor demands for the case of Colombia, and use them to then estimate adjustment functions, which we allow to vary with the index of market institutions described below.

However, our interest in this chapter goes beyond a specific country; we are interested in characterizing adjustment and its effect on aggregate productivity for a group of Latin American countries. Given the difficult access to the necessary data for these different countries, we conduct a number of related exercises. First, we use the estimated adjustment functions for Colombia to construct counterfactuals depicting the shape that these adjustment functions would have had if the index of institutions had been at the levels of institutions that characterized other countries during the period of study. Second, we estimate the market fundamentals and factor shortages for other Latin American countries by exploiting the relationship between these fundamentals and shortages with institutions as estimated from the Colombian data. Third, we explore the implications of the relationship between factor adjustments and institutions for productivity with a focus on the effect that removing frictions would have on aggregate productivity for these countries.

Data on institutions

We use the institutional index developed by Lora (2001) as our measure of institutions affecting factor markets. The measure varies from 0 to 1 and is increasing in the degree of liberalization and flexibility. The index displays variation from year to year and also across countries in the Latin American region. Unfortunately, the indicator is only available since 1985, so we restrict our estimations of adjustment functions to the 1985–98 period.[7]

234 ESLAVA, HALTIWANGER, KUGLER, AND KUGLER

Lora's institutions index summarizes the degree of flexibility of labor market institutions, the degree of financial liberalization, and the degree of trade liberalization. Flexible labor market institutions should reduce the costs of adjusting employment. In addition, more developed financial markets open access to credit for firms, potentially reducing an important source of fixed costs of adjustment (especially in terms of capital adjustment). Finally, trade liberalization gives access to more convenient providers of capital goods and introduces incentives to increase productivity due to increased competition (potentially making firms more willing to respond to shortages or surpluses).

The institutions index for different Latin American countries is presented in figure 7.2, which is split into two panels to facilitate its reading. The institutions index takes values between 0.3 and 0.7. There is a sharp increase of the index for almost every country in the sample over the period of study. Exceptions are Chile and Uruguay, where Chile remained at high levels of the institutions index over the whole period, and the opposite is true for Uruguay.[8] For the rest of the countries, the increase in the index is most marked in the late 1980s and early 1990s, but the timing varied substantially across countries. This captures the fact that most Latin American countries went through deep reforms in many policy dimensions in response to the debt crises faced during the 1980s. The index suggests that reforms were more extreme in Peru, Argentina, and Colombia, and more timid in the República Bolivariana de Venezuela. Reforms in Brazil seem to have been much more gradual: the institutions index for this country remained below that of most others over most of the sample, but by the last two years it had caught up with the rest. The data thus display substantial variation both across countries and over time, which is rare when using data on institutions.

Adjustment Functions

We begin by estimating the adjustment functions for Colombia. Using shortages and the observed adjustments in Colombia, we estimate the adjustment functions as described in equation (1).

We also introduce asymmetries between positive and negative adjustments to capture the possibility of differences between the costs of augmenting and the cost of contracting factor demands. This is done by interacting each regressor with a dummy that takes the value of 1 when the shortage of the same variable is positive, and 0 when it is not (that is, when the plant faces a surplus). We therefore allow for the hazard function to be discontinuous. Furthermore,

Figure 7.2: Institutions Index—Latin American Countries, 1985–99

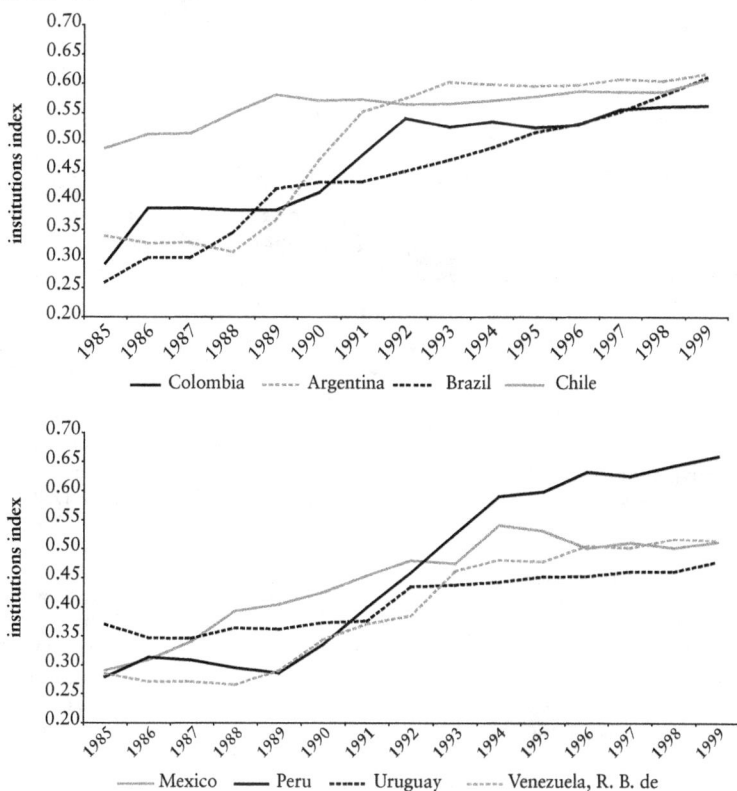

Source: Authors' calculations.

piecewise discontinuity of the hazard functions at zero implies irreversibility.

The estimates for the adjustment functions of capital and of white-collar and blue-collar labor are reported in table 7.1. The basic patterns are also captured in figures 7.3, 7.4, and 7.5, where at this point the reader should focus on the solid black lines, corresponding to average levels of institutions. We observe that the adjustment of white-collar workers is slightly increasing in the corresponding shortage ($ZW > 0$). This pattern indicates the presence of non-convex costs of hiring this type of workers. We observe less response to surpluses. Furthermore, adjustment seems in general more dynamic in the creation side (that is, when faced with shortages), although the differences are not stark. The patterns for blue-collar workers are similar, although in this case there is more responsiveness to surpluses (i.e., $ZB < 0$) than shortages.

Table 7.1: White-Collar Labor, Blue-Collar Labor, and Capital Adjustment Functions

"Shortage" refers to "own shortage"	White-collar labor adjustment	
	(1)	(2)
Constant	0.283	−0.046
	(0.010)	(0.056)
Constant × positive shortage	−0.002	0.156
	(0.017)	(0.072)
Shortage	0.076	0.330
	(0.006)	(0.039)
Shortage × positive shortage	0.030	−0.321
	(0.008)	(0.047)
ZW		
Positive shortage × ZW		
ZB	0.144	0.337
	(0.008)	(0.060)
Positive shortage × ZB	−0.350	−0.325
	(0.011)	(0.072)
X	0.080	0.027
	(0.007)	(0.046)
Positive shortage × X	−0.166	−0.003
	(0.010)	(0.057)
Institutions index		0.665
		(0111)
Institutions index × positive shortage		−0.300
		(0.140)
Shortage × institutions index		−0.508
		(0.077)
Shortage × institutions index Positive shortage		0.242
Institutions index × ZW		(0.014)
Institutions index × ZW × Positive shortage		
Institutions index × ZB		0.017
		(0.014)
Institutions index × ZB × Positive shortage		−0.241
		(0.019)
Institutions index × X		0.023
		(0.013)
Institutions index × X × Positive shortage		−0.093
		(0.017)
R2	0.262	0.265
N		

Source: Authors' calculations.

Note: This table reports adjustment functions for white-collar employment, blue-collar employment, and capital. Functions are estimated using micro-data for Colombia for 1985–98. The sample is a panel of pairwise continuing plants. The positive shortage dummy takes the value of 1 when the desired adjustment of the corresponding factor ("own shortage") is positive (there is a shortage) and the value of 0 when it is negative (there is a surplus). The institutions index takes values between 0 and 1 and it is increasing in the degree of liberalization and flexibility of institutions.

Blue-collar labor adjustment		Capital adjustment	
(3)	(4)	(5)	(6)
0.280	−0.164	0.057	0.387
(0.008)	(0.044)	(0.008)	(0.044)
−0.012	0.971	0.207	−0.268
(0.014)	(0.061)	(0.013)	(0.057)
0.038	0.067	0.053	−0.039
(0.005)	(0.030)	(0.003)	(0.025)
0.022	−0.237	−0.005	0.026
(0.007)	(0.038)	(0.005)	(0.030)
0.062	0.047	0.068	0.009
(0.007)	(0.042)	(0.006)	(0.042)
−0.211	−0.235	−0.173	0.006
(0.009)	(0.056)	(0.008)	(0.052)
	0.079	0.146	
	(0.006)	(0.045)	
	−0.217	−0.104	
	(0.009)	(0.055)	
0.036	0.065		
(0.006)	(0.035)		
−0.089	−0.086		
(0.008)	(0.047)		
0.942		−0.670	
(0.089)		(0.087)	
	−2.078		0.975
	(0.122)		(0.117)
	−0.055		0.190
	(0.060)		(0.048)
	0.549		−0.042
	(0.078)		(0.060)
	0.057		0.107
	(0.084)		(0.083)
	0.014		−0.359
	(0.114)		(0.106)
			−0.123
			(0.088)
			−0.286
			(0.112)
	−0.024		
	(0.071)		
	−0.062		
	(0.095)		
0.269	0.059	0.288	0.291
	51,538		

Figure 7.3: Colombia: Estimated White-Collar Employment
Adjustment Function at Different Levels of Institutions
Index

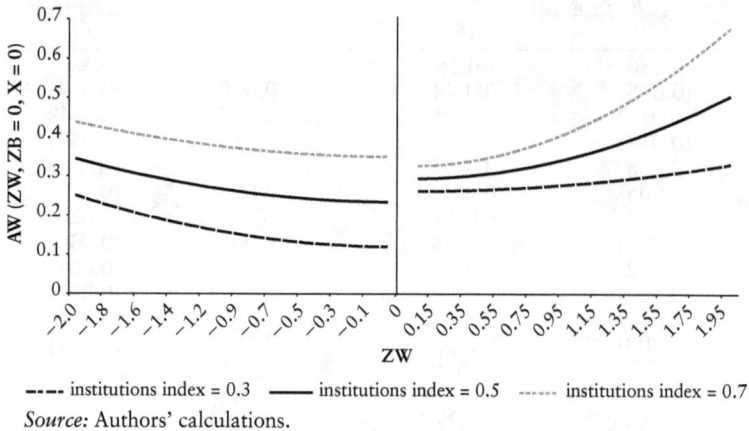

---- institutions index = 0.3 ——— institutions index = 0.5 ------- institutions index = 0.7
Source: Authors' calculations.

There are also important differences with the adjustment function
for capital. Once controlling for changes in the adjustment function
with institutional features in column (6), we see that investment is
clearly increasing in capital shortages while the shedding of capital
is increasing in (the absolute value of) capital surpluses, suggesting
important fixed costs of adjusting capital. Furthermore, notice a
stark difference between capital formation and retirements. Adjustment is much more responsive to shortages than it is to surpluses.

Figure 7.4: Colombia: Estimated Blue-Collar Employment
Adjustment Function at Different Levels of Institutions Index

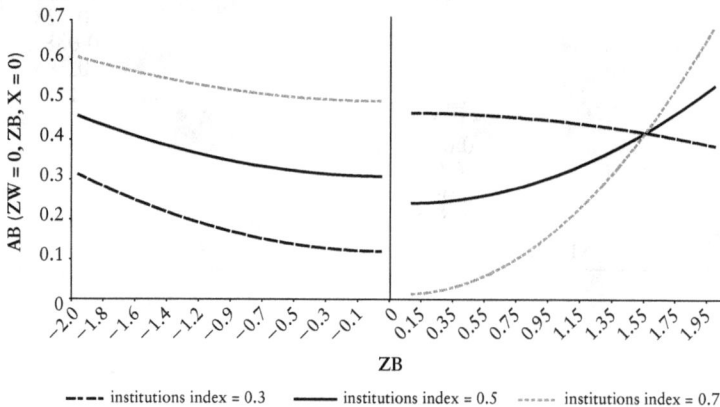

---- institutions index = 0.3 ——— institutions index = 0.5 ------- institutions index = 0.7
Source: Authors' calculations.

Figure 7.5: Colombia: Estimated Capital Adjustment
Function at Different Levels of Institutions Index

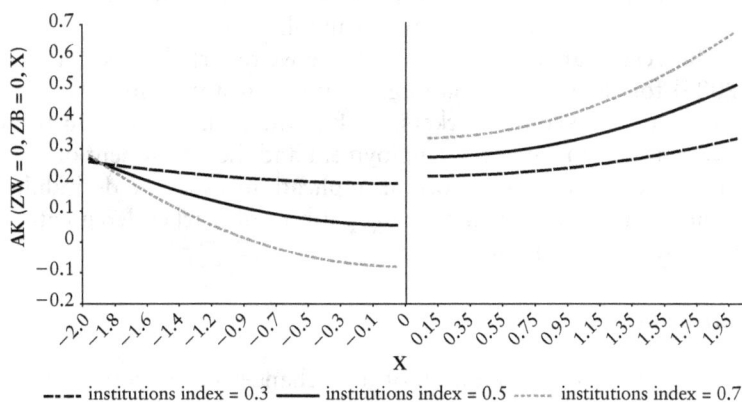

---- institutions index = 0.3 ——— institutions index = 0.5 ······ institutions index = 0.7

Source: Authors' calculations.

This feature indicates investment irreversibility, including a thinner
market for second-hand equipment.

In short, nonlinearities are particularly important to explaining
the patterns of adjustment in all three factors. Moreover, asymmetric
adjustment frictions between increasing and reducing factor usage
are particularly important for explaining capital adjustments,
although they also play a modest role in explaining patterns of
employment adjustment.

Table 7.1 also shows the interactions of the adjustment across
factors. We find, for example, that a shortage in the other factors,
especially blue-collar labor, reduces the response to a shortage of
white-collar employment (a positive coefficient for ZB if ZW is negative, and a negative coefficient for ZB if ZW is positive). Similarly,
a surplus in other factors, especially blue-collar employment, reduces
the shedding of white-collar workers in response to surpluses of this
type of employment. Our results thus suggest complementarities
between the adjustment of white-collar workers and that of other
factors, especially blue-collar employment.

The adjustment of capital and nonproduction workers follows
patterns of interaction with other margins very similar to those
described for production workers above. In both cases, the creation
(destruction) of a given factor is less responsive to shortages (surpluses) in its own margin in the presence of shortages (surpluses) of
some other factor. This suggests dynamic complementarities between
the shortages of different factors. To the extent that a shortage of
capital, for instance, reduces the hiring of production workers, it

reinforces existing shortages of this type of employment. It is also important to highlight that adjustment in any of the two employment margins is much more responsive to desired adjustments in the other employment margin than in capital.

Our results are consistent with those we reported in Eslava et al. (2006) for the case of Colombia. Without distinguishing between blue- and white-collar workers, we find there that plants substitute between the adjustment of employment and the adjustment of capital. This evidence has important implications as to the desirability of different sequencing and timing patterns of market deregulation, which we will flesh out below.[9]

Adjustment and Institutions

We now turn to the question of how changes in institutions affect factor adjustment. Deregulation, if deemed credible by private agents, affects the adjustment choices of firms by reducing adjustment costs.[10] This issue has also been addressed by Eslava et al. (2006). We now add to the discussion by, first, emphasizing the differences in the adjustment of production and nonproduction workers in response to institutional changes. The differential adjustment in these two margins in response to changes in institutions is a key question, as the policy discussion has recently centered around the need for policies that deal with the high unemployment of less skilled workers, but at the same time, the need to encourage firms to upgrade their labor forces in response to increased competition (De Ferranti et al. 2005). In addition, at this point we also exploit the cross-country variation in institutions to address the effect of institutions on adjustments in other Latin American countries.

Next, we explore the link between deregulation and the shape of the adjustment hazards. In particular, we note that the larger the discontinuity at zero, the more acute irreversibilities introduced by institutional frictions (e.g., worker dismissal costs). Also, the more pronounced the slope, the higher the fixed costs introduced by regulation as firms are more keen to adjust only in response to large shocks. While we cannot decompose transitory and permanent effects of reform, we point out that we have more than six years of data after reform implementation, so that the effects we capture, if not permanent, are likely to be at least highly persistent.[11]

Figures 7.3, 7.4, and 7.5 present adjustment functions that vary with the level of the institutional index for the cases of nonproduction workers, production workers, and capital, respectively. Dashed lines are adjustment functions if the institutional index takes a value of 0.3 (the value of the index for most countries in 1985), solid lines show the case where the index is at an intermediate value of 0.5, and dotted faded lines are adjustment functions for an institutions index of 0.7 (a value of the index closer to the values observed by the late 1990s for countries with more decided reform patterns).

Figure 7.3 shows that the adjustment of white-collar workers becomes more dynamic as institutions become more flexible (higher values of the institutional index), both for creation and destruction. It is also the case that the nonlinearity in the creation of white-collar jobs becomes more pronounced when institutions become more flexible. Figure 7.4 shows that the adjustment of production workers responds somewhat differently to changes in institutions. While the destruction of less skilled jobs is also more responsive in more flexible environments, the creation side is in general *less* dynamic in such environments, except for firms faced with very large shortages. As for white-collar workers, the adjustment function in the creation side is increasing only for very high values of the reform index. Interestingly, more flexible institutions are much more effective at increasing job destruction for blue-collar workers than they are in the case of nonproduction workers.

The results thus suggest that factor market regulations play an important role in limiting employment adjustment processes, perhaps more so in the destruction than the creation side. The evidence also seems to imply that non-convexities in the employment adjustment functions are mostly related to technological constraints rather than regulations. This can be seen from the fact that the adjustment functions are increasing only in more flexible environments. In highly regulated countries, the convex components of the adjustment cost function seem to dominate, generating less responsive adjustment rates.

These two effects together suggest the importance of lower firing costs in more flexible labor markets. Firing costs associated with regulation, i.e., severance payments, are primarily per-worker costs and thus convex costs, which explains the relatively flat adjustment function on the destruction side. Lower costs after the reform should induce more firings and shift the adjustment function upward, which is exactly what we observe. Moreover, lowering firing costs also increases the relative importance of hiring costs, which are likely to have more dominant fixed components. This could help explain the importance of nonlinearities in the creation side in more deregulated environments.[12]

In the capital adjustment margin, investment in response to capital shortages increases with the level of the institutional index. This is consistent with a reduction of adjustment costs generated by more flexible financial regulations. On the destruction side, capital shedding is much less responsive to surpluses for high values of the institutional index. Part of the explanation may be related to the greater dynamism of employment reductions when plants are faced with lowering firing costs. In particular, employment cuts (of either production or nonproduction workers) seem to induce less capital shedding after the reforms. The greater responsiveness of employment adjustment to employment surpluses may thus be behind the reduced dynamism of capital shedding.

Analysis for Other Latin American Countries

Using the results for Colombia as a starting point, we extend the analysis to other Latin American economies. We pursue this extension by taking advantage of the relationship between market fundamentals and institutions as well as between adjustment functions and fundamentals. Using these relationships, we can generate counterfactuals that are suggestive of changes in factor adjustment patterns in a country under different institutional reform contexts.[13]

Adjustment functions for other countries

The first step is to generate adjustment functions by country for some additional Latin American countries. This step is accomplished in a relatively straightforward fashion using the estimates from table 7.1 and generating the implied adjustment functions for each country using the respective institutions index for each country. The resulting adjustment functions are reported in figures 7.6a, 7.6b, 7.7a, 7.7b, 7.8a, and 7.8b. Here we characterize those functions for the levels of institutions corresponding to Brazil, Chile, Colombia, and Uruguay, both at the beginning and the end of the sample. We choose these four countries for this exercise because of their different institutional histories. Colombia and Brazil show large changes in the institutions index over the sample period, with institutional changes in Colombia being concentrated at the beginning of the 1990s, and changes in Brazil being much more gradual and spread over the period. On the other hand, Uruguay and Chile show little change in institutions over the period, but the economic environment in Chile was consistently less regulated than that in the rest of the countries as reforms occurred in the 1970s, while the opposite is true for Uruguay.

Figures 7.6a and 7.6b show the estimated white-collar adjustment functions by country for the 1985 and 1998 values of the institutional index, respectively. In terms of cross-sectional variability, it is clear that adjustment for Chile at the beginning of the sample period was more dynamic than adjustment for any of the other countries depicted. Chile was an early reformer in many areas, including labor markets. For example, in 1981 the maximum severance paid to workers was limited to five months of pay, equivalent to compensation for those with five years of tenure (since the law required one month of severance per year worked). In addition, the 1973 coup in Chile also brought a de facto decline in job security and worker dismissal protection, as courts were subsequently less likely to rule

Figure 7.6a: Estimated White-Collar Employment Adjustment Function at 1985 Levels of Institutions for Brazil, Chile, Colombia, and Uruguay

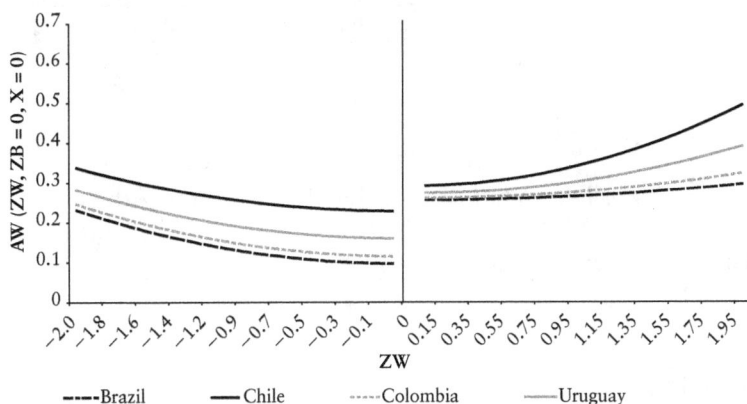

Figure 7.6b: Estimated White-Collar Employment Adjustment Function at 1998 Levels of Institutions for Brazil, Chile, Colombia, and Uruguay

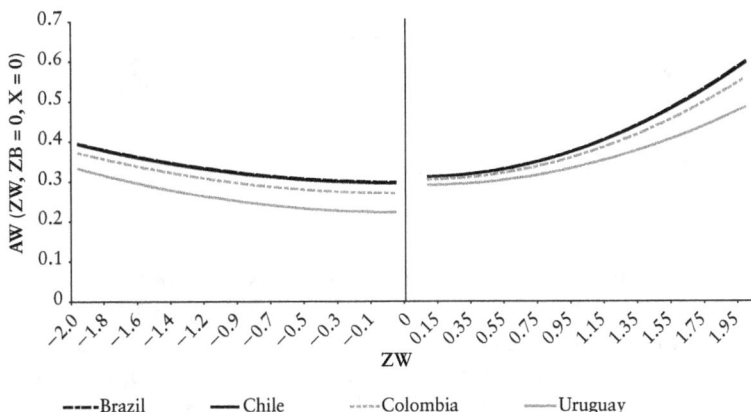

Source: Authors' calculations.

Figure 7.7a: Estimated Blue-Collar Employment Adjustment Function at 1985 Levels of Institutions for Brazil, Chile, Colombia, and Uruguay

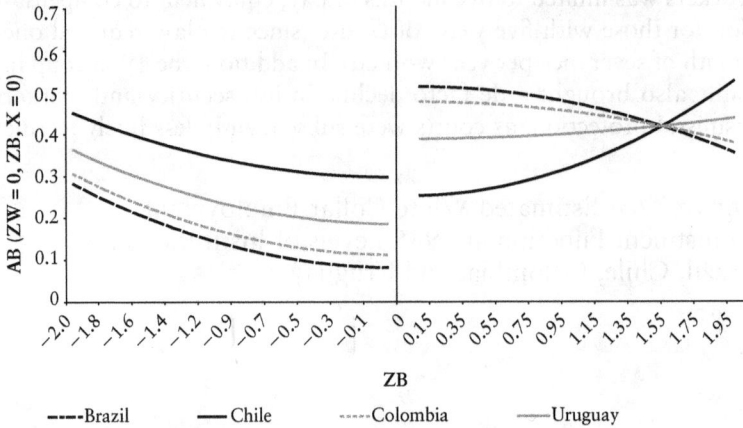

----Brazil — Chile ----Colombia — Uruguay

Figure 7.7b: Estimated Blue-Collar Employment Adjustment Function at 1998 Levels of Institutions for Brazil, Chile, Colombia, and Uruguay

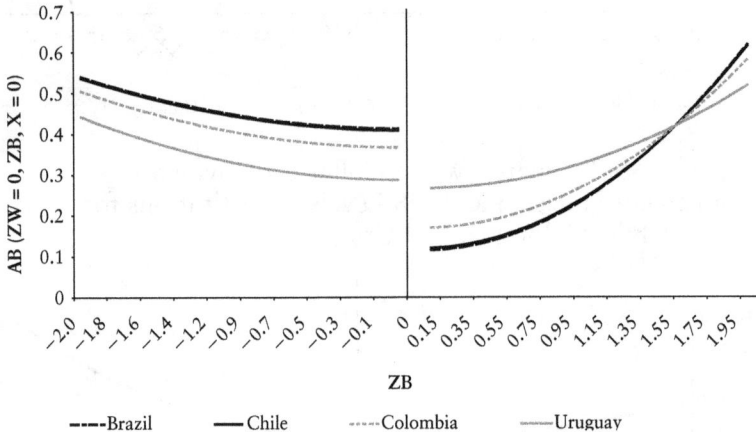

----Brazil — Chile ----Colombia — Uruguay

Source: Authors' calculations.

in favor of workers, thus lowering labor costs (see Montenegro and Pages 2005). Adjustment increased between 1985 and 1998 for the levels of institutions characterizing all countries, both in terms of job creation and job destruction. (Uruguay was an exception, given that the index of institutions changed little over the sample period for this country, resulting in less dynamic change of adjustment.) Remark-

Figure 7.8a: Estimated Capital Adjustment Function at 1985 Levels of Institutions for Brazil, Chile, Colombia, and Uruguay

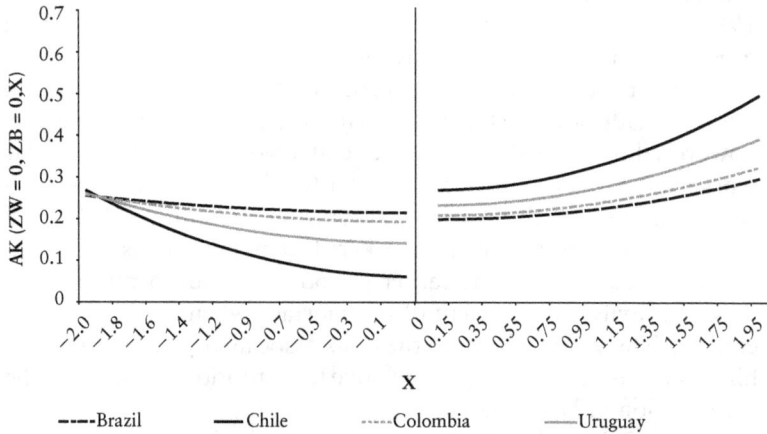

----Brazil ——Chile ·····Colombia ——Uruguay

Figure 7.8b: Estimated Capital Adjustment Function at 1998 Levels of Institutions for Brazil, Chile, Colombia, and Uruguay

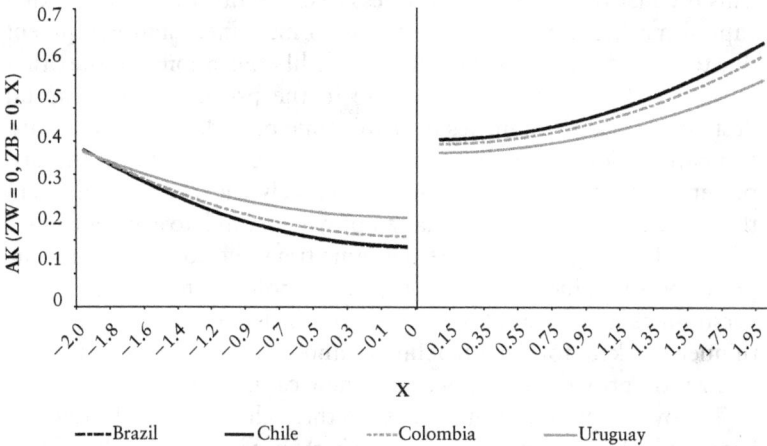

----Brazil ——Chile ·····Colombia ——Uruguay

Source: Authors' calculations.

ably, the adjustment function for Uruguay was closer to that of Chile than were the adjustment functions in Brazil and Colombia at the beginning of the same period. Yet, by 1998, both Brazil and Colombia displayed similar levels of adjustment flexibility as Chile, while Uruguay, in contrast, continued to show less dynamic adjustment than the other three countries.

Figures 7.7a and 7.7b show the blue-collar employment adjustment functions for the 1985 and 1998 values, respectively, of the institutional index. As for white-collar workers, the figures show an increase in adjustments on the destruction side between 1985 and 1998 in all countries. The effect is less marked for Chile, which began the period with an already high level of the institutions index, and for Uruguay, which, according to this index, was a timid reformer. Adjustments for blue-collar workers on the creation side, however, differ from those for white-collar workers. For white-collar workers, we find increased adjustment for the later period, but patterns consistent with non-convex adjustments both for 1985 and 1998. By contrast, blue-collar workers face patterns consistent with convex adjustments in the earlier period, but adjustments come to depend heavily on the extent of the shortage when markets are liberalized. This may be because the costs associated with training and hiring become more important relative to institutional costs after the deregulation of labor markets.

Figures 7.8a and 7.8b show the estimated adjustment functions for capital for the 1985 and 1998 values of the institutional index. Comparing figure 7.8b to figure 7.8a shows an increase in the adjustment function for positive shortages in 1998 compared to 1985. This is consistent with greater access to credit due to better working capital markets and increased access to machinery and equipment due to the lowering of tariffs after trade liberalization. On the other hand, the figures show a decrease in the propensity for capital destruction for all countries over this time period. The shift toward less capital destruction is consistent with a substitution in the displacement toward the factor that is relatively cheaper to displace, in this case, apparently, blue-collar employment (and, to a lesser extent, white-collar employment). At the same time, the adjustment to surpluses becomes increasingly non-convex, pointing to increased irreversibilities after the reforms. This is consistent with increasingly thinner markets for used machinery and equipment after trade liberalization provides easier access to new capital vintages.

The overall pattern from figures 7.6 through 7.8 is that the reforms have made the countries more similar in their white-collar labor, blue-collar labor, and capital adjustment functions. The greater flexibility in adjustment evident in Chile in the 1980s became the norm for many of the Latin American economies over the course of the 1990s.

Market fundamentals and shortages for other countries

The exercise in the previous section provides some interesting and reasonable insights. However, in this section, we take our simulation of adjustment for other countries one step further. In particular, we now simulate market fundamentals for other countries, and then use those fundamentals to simulate the desired factor demands in other countries and, in turn, the shortages in other countries. Using these simulated data, we will later be able to generate counterfactuals to analyze the effect of barriers to adjustment on aggregate productivity.

The first step is to create counterfactual market fundamentals and distributions of shortages by country. The methodological framework described above is based on measuring desired factor demands as functions of some "fundamentals" faced by each establishment: the productivity shock, demand shocks, materials, energy use, and hours worked by white- and blue-collar workers. The simulation we propose in this section generates a distribution of these fundamentals for each of the countries included in the sample as a function of aggregate shocks in the corresponding economy (measures of market institutions and a GDP index). The limited availability of data on those aggregate processes restricts our sample period to 1985–1998. Using these simulated data, we construct desired factor demands, factor use, and shortages for each of the countries we will study.

The simulation process described below amounts to asking what would have been, for example, the productivity shock for plant i in period t if i was not located in Colombia but rather in country C. Our sample of countries, dictated by the availability of institutions and GDP data for the period of study, includes Argentina, Brazil, Chile, Mexico, Peru, Uruguay, and the República Bolivariana de Venezuela.

We start by decomposing any plant-level fundamental, P_{it}, into an aggregate component and an idiosyncratic component. The aggregate component is calculated as the simple average of P_{it} for year t, while the idiosyncratic component is simply the residual of subtracting the aggregate component from P_{it}. Using data for Colombia, we model the aggregate component as a function of the index of institutions II_t for Colombia, GDP_t, and an autoregressive component:

$$P_t = \tau_0 + \tau_1 * P_{t-1} + \tau_2 * II_t + \tau_4 * GDP_t + \varepsilon_t \qquad (2)$$

where $\varepsilon_t - N(0, S)$. We fit this model for the Colombian case, and use the results to obtain $\hat{S}$. We then generate random draws of an $N(0, \hat{S})$ distribution and generate a series of (aggregate, economy-wide) $\hat{P}_t$ for each country in the sample using these random draws and using the institution index and GDP-level realizations for the corresponding country.[14] It is noteworthy that when estimating (2) using the Colombian data, we actually use data at the sector level. That is, the aggregate component is the average of P_{it} for the sector where plant i is located, and the GDP_t variable is sectoral. We do this to exploit as much variation in the data as we can in (2). The maintained assumption underlying this strategy when we later use these results to simulate an aggregate component (country-level) for other countries is that aggregate fundamentals are driven by systemic determinants rather than heterogeneity in sectoral dynamics of fundamentals and sectoral composition changes.[15]

We then represent the idiosyncratic component $p_{it} = P_{it} - P_t$ as a draw from an $N(0, s_t)$ distribution, where s_t varies by country and year as a function of the respective institutional index. To obtain s_t, we rely again on our data for Colombia. For each Colombian plant, we obtain the idiosyncratic component of each fundamental. We then run these components against an autoregressive component, and obtain the residuals:

$$p_{it} = \delta_0 + \delta_1 * p_{it} + v_{it} \tag{3}$$

where $v_{it} \sim N(0, s_t)$. We use the $\hat{v}_{it}$ to calculate $\hat{s}_t$ and then model $\hat{s}_t$ as:

$$\hat{s}_t = \kappa_0 + \kappa_1 * GDP_t + \kappa_2 * II_t + v_{it} \tag{4}$$

which we fit using again data for Colombia. We then use the estimated coefficients $\hat{\kappa}_0, \hat{\kappa}_1, \hat{\kappa}_2$ and the institutions and GDP series for each country to generate a series of $\hat{s}_t$ for each country. Once we have the series of $\hat{s}_t$ for a given country, we generate the idiosyncratic component $\hat{p}_{it}$ for each plant iterating on equation (3), where in each iteration $\hat{v}_{it}$ is a new draw from $\hat{v}_{it} \sim N(0, \hat{s}_t)$.[16] Here again, we use sector-level data when fitting equation (4), even though we later simulate $\hat{s}_t$ for each country at the aggregate level (since for countries other than Colombia we only have II_t and GDP_t at the aggregate level).

Finally, we obtain fundamentals $\hat{P}_{it} = \hat{P}_t + \hat{p}_{it}$ for each of N notional plants. Here, $\hat{P}_t$ is the aggregate component generated for that country, and $\hat{p}_{it}$ is the idiosyncratic component for plant i generated as explained above. Tables 7.2 and 7.3 describe results of different steps of the simulation process. Results from equations (2), (3), and (4) for each of the "fundamentals" are reported in columns (1), (2), and (3), respectively, of table 7.2. Table 7.3 reports summary statistics of the simulated fundamentals for each country, and of the actual fundamentals for the Colombian case, for the 1985–98 period. It is clear that the simulation environment described above generates variability of the simulated fundamentals, both across countries and over time within each country, that is large enough to ensure that we

Table 7.2: Models of Fundamentals

Dependent variable	Regressor	Model for aggregate component (1)	Model for idiosyncratic component (2)	Model for standard deviation of idiosyncratic error (3)
	First lag of TFP	0.931 (0.021)	0.916 (0.002)	
TFP	Reform index	–0.160 (0.081)		0.242 (0.061)
	GDP	–0.0002 (0.0002)		3.6E-6 (0.0001)
	First lag of Dshock	1.003 (0.002)	0.980 (0.001)	
Demand shock	Reform index	0.024 (0.060)		0.157 (0.047)
	GDP	1.4E-6 (0.0001)		–3.5E-5 (0.0001)
	First lag of white collar	0.790 (0.030)	0.327 (0.003)	
White-collar labor hours	Reform index	–67.240 (109.154)		4.8E-13 (1.5E-12)
	GDP	–0.038 (0.250)		2.8E-15 (3.4E-15)
	First lag of blue collar	0.873 (0.023)	0.035 (0.004)	
Blue-collar labor hours	Reform index	146.873 (97.746)		1.2E-12 (2.3E-12)
	GDP	–0.070 (0.223)		3.6E-15 (5.2E-15)
	First lag of materials	0.957 (0.011)	0.974 (0.001)	
Materials	Reform index	0.490 (0.164)		–0.372 (0.079)
	GDP	–0.0003 (0.0004)		0.0005 (0.0002)
	First lag of energy	0.990 (0.008)	0.945 (0.001)	
Energy	Reform index	–0.008 (0.137)		0.317 (0.149)
	GDP	5.8E-5 (0.0003)		0.0001 (0.0003)

Source: Author's calculations.

Note: This table reports results of estimating models for the aggregate and idiosyncratic components of each fundamental, using data for Colombia (1985–98). Standard errors are in parentheses,

Table 7.3: Summary Statistics of Simulated Fundamentals for Latin American Countries

Market fundamental	Colombia	Argentina	Brazil	Chile	Mexico	Peru	Uruguay	Venezuela, R. B. de
TFP	0.887	2.235	2.357	1.981	2.305	2.335	2.238	2.368
	(0.773)	(0.966)	(0.935)	(1.045)	(0.950)	(0.942)	(0.986)	(0.941)
Demand shock	4.912	0.241	0.127	0.462	0.172	0.152	0.274	0.152
	(2.110)	(1.208)	(1.159)	(1.303)	(1.176)	(1.167)	(1.207)	(1.159)
White-collar labor hours	7.264	7.813	7.820	7.799	7.818	7.819	7.817	7.823
	(0.162)	(0.141)	(0.140)	(0.148)	(0.141)	(0.140)	(0.147)	(0.143)
Blue-collar labor hours	7.580	8.024	7.997	8.076	8.007	8.001	8.019	7.993
	(0.111)	(0.202)	(0.208)	(0.178)	(0.204)	(0.207)	(0.186)	(0.200)
Materials	10.020	11.628	10.814	13.213	11.109	10.950	11.709	10.875
	(1.888)	(2.794)	(2.890)	(2.493)	(2.837)	(2.883)	(2.635)	(2.810)
Energy	11.496	8.449	8.452	8.441	8.443	8.443	8.444	8.451
	(1.945)	(2.369)	(2.331)	(2.447)	(2.345)	(2.337)	(2.360)	(2.323)
N				78,355				

Source: Authors' calculations.

Note: This table reports first and second moments of actual fundamentals for Colombia, and of simulated fundamentals for the seven Latin American economies considered, for 1985–98. All figures are in logs. N is the number of plants to which simulated fundamentals were assigned for each country. For Colombia, some plants present missing values of the actual measures.

are not simply mimicking the Colombian data for the other cases. At the same time, the figures are plausible, especially considering that we are not forcing the levels of any of these variables to any mean value. For instance, for the average hours worked by an employee, the mean value fluctuates between 1,300 and 2,200 hours per year across countries, which is a plausible range.

Table 7.4 shows the second moments of the simulated factor shortages by country. We report these statistics for background purposes only, but they indicate that in all countries our simulations suggest a large dispersion in the cross-sectional distribution of shortages. This dispersion in shortages reflects both the dispersion in fundamentals across plants as well as the adjustment frictions in each country. In the next section, we explore the role of such dispersion for the relationship between factor reallocation, institutions, and allocative efficiency.

Factor Reallocation, Institutions, and Aggregate Productivity

In this section, we examine the implications of the role of frictions and institutions in Latin American economies for productivity. In particular, we measure changes in aggregate productivity due to changes in reallocation from the removal of frictions in factor markets. We conduct this exercise by using a cross-sectional decomposition methodology first introduced by Olley and Pakes (1996). We quantify what part of aggregate productivity every year reflects the productivity of the average plant, and what part captures the concentration of activity in the more productive plants, by conducting the following decomposition of aggregate TFP:

$$TFP_t = \overline{TFP_t} + \sum_{j=1}^{J} \left(f_{jt} - \overline{f_t} \right)\left(TFP_{jt} - \overline{TFP_t} \right) \qquad (5)$$

where TFP_t is the aggregate total factor productivity measure for a given sector in year t. These aggregate measures correspond to weighted averages of our plant-level TFP measures, where the weights are market shares (calculated as described below). The first term of the decomposition, $\overline{TFP_t}$, is the average cross-sectional (unweighted) mean of total factor productivity across all plants in that sector in year t. TFP_{jt} is the total factor productivity measure of plant j at time t estimated as described above, f_{jt} is the share or fraction of plant j's output out of sectoral output in year t, and f_t is the cross-sectional unweighted mean of f_{jt} for the sector.[17] The second term in this decomposition allows us to understand whether produc-

Table 7.4: Standard Deviations of White-Collar Labor, Blue-Collar Labor, and Capital Shortages, before and after 1990

Shortage	Period	Argentina	Brazil	Chile	Colombia	Mexico	Peru	Uruguay	Venezuela, R. B. de
White-collar labor	1982–90	0.9773	0.9750	0.9952	0.5627	0.9777	0.9697	0.9733	0.9664
	1991–98	1.0415	1.0338	1.0430	0.6294	1.0348	1.0359	1.0292	1.0291
Blue-collar labor	1982–90	1.0391	1.0361	1.0534	0.5366	1.0383	1.0318	1.0339	1.0285
	1991–98	1.0954	1.0880	1.0960	0.5848	1.0887	1.0910	1.0829	1.0834
Capital	1982–90	1.0705	1.0664	1.0825	0.7079	1.0684	1.0627	1.0638	1.0592
	1991–98	1.1030	1.0941	1.1028	0.7439	1.0947	1.0991	1.0879	1.0892
N	1982–90				24,808				
	1991–98				33,917				

Source: Authors' calculations.

Note: This table reports second moments of desired adjustment, in each of the three margins considered, for the seven Latin American countries under study. For all countries but Colombia, desired factors demands are calculated with simulated fundamentals. For Colombia, some plants present missing values of the actual measures for some of the fundamentals.

tion is disproportionately located at high-productivity plants, and examining this term over time allows us to learn whether the cross-sectional allocation of activity has changed in response to the market reforms.[18] Following the literature, we refer to the latter term as "allocative efficiency." In what follows, we focus on this term.

For each country, we construct two counterfactuals, which allow us to answer (a) what would have been the cross-sectional allocation had frictions in factor markets been removed altogether, and (b) in a related way, what has happened to the cross-sectional allocation of activity given actual changes in institutions within countries. The decompositions used counterfactual output shares, where output is calculated as:

$$\hat{Y}_{jt} = \hat{K}_{jt}^{\hat{a}} \left(\hat{L}_{Ujt} H_{Ujt} \right)^{\hat{\beta}_U} \left(\hat{L}_{Sjt} H_{Sjt} \right)^{\hat{\beta}_S} E_{jt}^{\hat{\gamma}} M_{jt}^{\hat{\phi}} V_{jt} \qquad (6)$$

In each case, the levels of energy E_{jt}, materials M_{jt}, and hours of skilled and unskilled workers, respectively H_{Sjt} and H_{Ujt}, are the ones from the simulated data, and the V_{jt} is the exponential of our TFP measure from the simulated data. The factor elasticities are those estimated using the IV methodology explained above. The levels of capital and employment of skilled and unskilled workers ($\hat{K}_{jt}, \hat{L}_{Sjt},$ and $\hat{L}_{Ujt}$), on the other hand, vary across decompositions.

We start by constructing the counterfactual for each country where $\hat{K}_{jt}, \hat{L}_{Sjt},$ and $\hat{L}_{Ujt}$ are the frictionless levels of capital, nonproduction workers, and production workers. These frictionless demands are constructed using the simulated fundamentals and the first-order conditions of the firm's profit maximization problem in the absence of adjustment costs. These conditions characterize the firm's demand of a factor as a function of the fundamentals the firm faces when no adjustment costs are present. We then construct the counterfactuals for each country using the $\hat{K}_{jt}, \hat{L}_{Sjt},$ and $\hat{L}_{Ujt}$ which are the simulated capital and employment levels using the respective institutions that prevail in the country and the simulated market fundamentals, factor shortages, and adjustment functions associated with those institutions. For each country then we have two time series of allocative efficiency—the allocative efficiency that would emerge in the absence of frictions and the allocative efficiency that is consistent with the actual institutions in the country that year.

The results are presented in table 7.5. For each country, we present two columns. The first column lists the allocative efficiency term for the actual levels of the institutional index for each country, and the second column lists the value of the same term using frictionless shares of output, as described above.[19] In interpreting these results, we focus on comparing the levels of allocative efficiency across countries, since the levels are less likely to be pinned down by our simulation approach.[20]

Our results suggest important improvements associated with reforms enhancing market flexibility. Using the actual institutions for each country, we find that allocative efficiency grows over the period more for countries where the institutions index grew importantly over the period. This is the case, for example, of Colombia, Peru, and Argentina. Countries with a less marked change in institutions, such as Chile, Uruguay, and the República Bolivariana de Venezuela, show more modest growth in our simulation of allocative efficiency over the period.

In column (2) we report the counterfactual productivity in the frictionless case. Comparing column (2) to column (1), we find that the frictionless allocative efficiency is much larger than the actual allocative efficiency for all countries. Moreover, in virtually all countries the growth within the country in column (1) is greater than the growth in column (2) so that reforms are associated with closing the gap between allocative efficiency with actual institutions and allocative efficiency in a frictionless environment. Some caution must be used in interpreting this latter finding, since in some countries we actually observe a decline in the allocative efficiency term in a frictionless environment. This can happen if the simulated fundamentals change yields, for example, less dispersion in TFP shocks over time. With less dispersion in TFP across producers, there is less scope for allocative efficiency to play a role. However, note in such cases that the closing of the gap is in some ways even more impressive as the allocative efficiency with actual institutions would fall from the same changes in fundamentals.

In considering the possible gains in each country from a reduction in frictions implied by the difference between columns (1) and (2), we need to be cautious since even in a well functioning economy not all frictions can be removed. For example, in a deregulated economy with ample market flexibility, such as that of the United States, available evidence implies important frictions due to the nature of the adjustment process itself (e.g., time to install equipment, labor training costs, irreversibilities due to losses associated with capital retirements and worker separations, etc.). Hence, the difference between columns (1) and (2) also reflects the importance of frictions to factor adjustments related to the nature of the production process and technology, in addition to frictions to factor adjustments stemming from regulations and institutions.

Before concluding this section, it is useful to compare and contrast the findings in this section with the recent literature examining the role of allocation distortions in accounting for productivity differences across countries and over time. Restuccia and Rogerson

Table 7.5: Decomposition of Aggregate Productivity under Counterfactual Factor Demands

	Argentina		Brazil		Chile		Colombia	
	Actual institutions (1)	Frictionless institutions (2)	Actual institutions (1)	Frictionless institutions (2)	Actual institutions (1)	Frictionless institutions (2)	Actual institutions (1)	Frictionless institutions (2)
1986	1.168	1.844	1.086	1.713	1.353	2.126	0.464	1.149
1987	1.133	1.970	1.062	1.839	1.315	2.346	0.460	0.745
1988	1.127	2.767	1.075	2.632	1.343	3.334	0.546	0.834
1989	1.171	2.548	1.139	2.437	1.416	3.086	0.538	0.801
1990	1.273	2.541	1.234	2.437	1.505	3.021	0.606	0.878
1991	1.291	2.087	1.236	1.975	1.479	2.364	0.623	0.888
1992	1.356	2.390	1.271	2.225	1.505	2.624	0.745	1.126
1993	1.224	2.760	1.147	2.585	1.354	3.031	0.780	1.040
1994	1.324	2.570	1.213	2.402	1.417	2.851	0.834	1.224
1995	1.272	2.016	1.183	1.889	1.338	2.182	0.942	1.143
1996	1.332	1.973	1.242	1.852	1.384	2.079	1.032	1.272
1997	1.394	1.994	1.309	1.878	1.441	2.085	1.122	1.381
1998	1.394	1.953	1.317	1.848	1.426	2.011	1.149	1.392

(Table continues on the following page.)

Table 7.5: Decomposition of Aggregate Productivity under Counterfactual Factor Demands (*continued*)

	Mexico		Peru		Uruguay		Venezuela, R. B. de	
	Actual institutions (1)	Frictionless institutions (2)	Actual institutions (1)	Frictionless institutions (2)	Actual institutions (1)	Frictionless institutions (2)	Actual institutions (1)	Frictionless institutions (2)
1986	1.119	1.765	1.110	1.749	1.204	1.900	1.106	1.745
1987	1.095	1.901	1.083	1.875	1.165	2.032	1.073	1.853
1988	1.114	2.744	1.083	2.646	1.167	2.869	1.067	2.598
1989	1.168	2.534	1.116	2.434	1.204	2.642	1.104	2.391
1990	1.257	2.518	1.185	2.413	1.275	2.600	1.179	2.379
1991	1.257	2.012	1.189	1.923	1.256	2.038	1.180	1.911
1992	1.296	2.275	1.233	2.198	1.285	2.286	1.211	2.155
1993	1.170	2.648	1.142	2.601	1.159	2.677	1.106	2.526
1994	1.265	2.468	1.242	2.451	1.216	2.497	1.175	2.353
1995	1.210	1.934	1.207	1.924	1.173	1.922	1.146	1.847
1996	1.256	1.875	1.287	1.886	1.214	1.827	1.204	1.796
1997	1.312	1.880	1.356	1.913	1.267	1.828	1.265	1.812
1998	1.304	1.824	1.371	1.899	1.259	1.777	1.268	1.779

Source: Authors' calculations.

(2003), Banerjee and Duflo (2005), Eslava et al. (2004, 2006), Hsieh and Klenow (2009), and Bartelsman, Haltiwanger, and Scarpetta (2006) all explore the idea that distortions to output and factor allocation may underlie productivity differences across countries and within countries over time. The working hypothesis is that allocative distortions prevent resources from being allocated to their highest valued use and this literature develops the underlying theory and related empirical analysis to explore this hypothesis. Our findings here are very much connected to this hypothesis. Our contribution to this burgeoning literature is that, by estimating the relationship between adjustment functions and institutions (and, in turn, fundamentals and institutions), we can provide perspective on how different levels of institutional development, as they prevail in specific Latin American economies, yield changes in the structure of adjustment costs and in turn changes in allocative efficiency.[21]

Conclusions

This chapter studies the effect of a variety of regulations on factor adjustment processes. We do so in a framework that allows for simultaneous and interrelated adjustments of blue-collar labor, white-collar labor, and capital in Latin America.

Our main findings are as follows. First, we found evidence that market reforms in Latin America had substantial and systematic effects on the structure of adjustment. Countries with more substantial reforms exhibited more flexibility in the adjustment of both white-collar and blue-collar labor, especially on the job destruction side. Similarly, countries with more dramatic reforms exhibited greater flexibility in capital adjustment, mainly on the capital formation side. Interestingly, we found that the reforms appeared to move countries toward greater irreversibility of capital. Our interpretation is that this reflects in part substitution toward adjustment in labor on the destruction side. In considering specific countries, we found that Chile had the most flexible factor markets in the 1980s, reflecting the fact that Chile was an early reformer and their institutions were already more flexible by the 1980s. For the countries that reformed their markets during the period of our study, we found that they converged toward Chile in the 1990s in terms of the flexibility of their factor markets.

Our second primary finding is that these market reforms have been consistent with substantial improvements in allocative efficiency in the countries with deeper reforms. By allocative efficiency we mean the extent to which outputs and inputs are allocated to the

258   ESLAVA, HALTIWANGER, KUGLER, AND KUGLER

most productive businesses within a country. In a related fashion, we found that the gap between the allocative efficiency within a country with actual market institutions and the allocative efficiency that would emerge in a frictionless environment declined—and especially for those countries with substantial market reforms. These findings on improvements in allocative efficiency are driven by the improvements in factor market flexibility.

In considering specific countries, we found that early reforms in Chile were consistent with flexible factor markets and high aggregate productivity for this country in the 1980s. For the countries that reformed their markets during the period of our study, convergence toward Chile in the 1990s in terms of the flexibility of their factor markets is shown as a source of convergence also in terms of aggregate productivity.

Our findings suggest that market reforms in Latin American had positive effects on the economies of Latin America on two key dimensions—factor market flexibility and allocative efficiency. However, various caveats are required in interpreting our results. First, our results are most robust for Colombia, the country on which we estimated these relationships using the actual plant-level data. For the other economies, we used the relationships we estimated for Colombia as a function of market institutions to simulate and study other countries. It is obviously of interest to repeat our analysis on a country-by-country basis using the actual plant-level data. Second, our analysis for Colombia and the other countries only covers the manufacturing sector. It neglects nonmanufacturing sectors as well as the informal sector. Third, our simulation approach is well suited to studying the evolution of factor market flexibility as well as allocative efficiency as a function of reforms but is not well suited to studying factors impacting the first moment of (plant-level) productivity in a country. Fourth, our analysis focuses on the impact of market reforms on plant-level adjustment dynamics from the plant perspective—we do not explore the impact on workers of this greater flexibility of factor markets. Our findings point toward greater flexibility on the job destruction margin. An obvious question of interest is what has been the impact on workers from these reforms.

Notes

1. Some of those studies are Baily et al. (1992), Aw et al. (2002), Levinsohn and Petrin (2003), Bartelsman et al. (2004, 2006), Foster et al. (2001, 2006), and Eslava et al. (2004, 2006).

2. The theoretical literature has also paid attention to the impediments on adjustments imposed by regulations. For example, Bertola and Rogerson (1997) and Caballero and Hammour (1994) deal with the impact of regulations on factor adjustment in developed countries, while Kugler (2004) deals with the impact of regulations on labor adjustment in the context of a less developed country with an informal sector.

3. There is a large literature on micro lumpy factor adjustment including the work of Caballero and Engel (1993, 1999), Cooper, Haltiwanger, and Willis (2005), and Doms and Dunne (1998).

4. Factor adjustment costs may arise from regulations or may be related to the technology of adjustment. An example of the latter is the need to stop production to install new machinery.

5. While most datasets are unlikely to have all of the variables at the level of disaggregation we have deployed in the present analyses, the framework that we propose can be used with sectoral prices but the estimation of TFP would have to rely on a method different than the IV approach we use here.

6. A more detailed description of the estimation of shocks for Colombian plants for the case of heterogeneous workers can be found in Eslava (2006).

7. We do use our full set of data for Colombia, covering 1982–1998, to estimate productivity and demand shocks for Colombia. We do this to take maximum advantage of the variability in the data to identify factor and demand elasticities.

8. By construction, Chile acts as the benchmark case of flexible institutions on almost all dimensions included in the index. This is so because each subcomponent of the index is scaled between 0 and 1, where 1 is the "most reformed" case in Latin America, which happens often to be Chile.

9. Note that our characterization of adjustment costs is not based on a social welfare measure of market flexibility but rather on a measure of plant deviations between desired and actual factor demands.

10. Deregulation may also affect the magnitude and variability of the shocks to which firms react. Here we focus on the size of adjustments in response to a given shock.

11. For deregulation to impact adjustment patterns, agents must perceive reforms as being credible and not transitory. Note that this appears to be the case by and large for reforms in Latin America in the 1990s.

12. Similar results are found in Eslava et al. (2006) for the adjustment of employment as a whole.

13. Obviously, if one could collect all the necessary data in a consistent manner for the countries of interest, this would generate much more reliable results. The task is very demanding, though, and the consistency of the data is frequently questionable. In a recent paper, Caballero et al. (2005) are able to

overcome part of these difficulties and collect the data necessary to analyze employment adjustment for a set of countries in Latin America. However, our framework requires much more information. This is due in part to the fact that we are interested in simultaneously studying adjustment on several margins.

14. To initialize the series (that is, to generate P_{1984}), we first generate $P_{1985} = \tau_0 + \varepsilon_{1985}$, where ε_{1985} is a random draw from $N(0,\hat{S})$. We then iterate 50 times using equation 2, obtaining ε_t for each iteration as a new random draw from $N(0,\hat{S})$, and fixing the aggregate level variables at GDP_{1985} and I_{1985} for all iterations (since 1985 is the first year for which we have these two measures).

15. For other countries, we cannot simulate separate sectoral component series, since we only have data on the institutions index and GDP for other countries at the aggregate level.

16. To initialize the p_{it} series, we first generate $P_{1985} = \delta_0 + v_o$, where v_o is a random draw from $N(0,\hat{s}_{1985})$. We then iterate 50 times using equation (3) and a new draw of $N(0,\hat{s}_{1985})$ as v_{it} in each new iteration.

17. The fact that we calculate aggregate measures at the sector level means that our focus is on within-sector reallocation. For measurement and conceptual reasons, comparisons of TFP across sectors (in levels) are more problematic to interpret. Focusing on within-sector allocation permits us to emphasize the degree to which market reforms have led to an improved allocation of activity across businesses due to fewer distortions in factors and goods markets, and the associated intensification of competition.

18. An advantage of this cross-sectional method over methods that decompose changes in productivity over time is that cross-sectional differences in productivity are more persistent and less dominated by measurement error or transitory shocks.

19. Our simulations also yield the first term in the Olley-Pakes decompositions but we think our simulation methods yield more robust patterns on the second term since it is the second term that will reflect the impact of institutions on adjustment frictions.

20. Our simulation of fundamentals is well suited to capture changes in the fundamentals within a country but not well suited to measure the level of fundamentals within a country.

21. Caballero et al. (2004) also consider improvements in allocative efficiency via reductions in adjustment costs.

References

Aw, B., S. Chung, and M. Roberts. 2002. "Productivity, Output, and Failure: A Comparison of Taiwanese and Korean Manufacturers." Working Paper 8766, NBER, Cambridge, MA.

Baily, M., C. Hulten, and D. Campbell. 1992. "Productivity Dynamics in Manufacturing Establishments." *Brooking Papers on Economic Activity: Microeconomics* 187–249.

Barnerjee, Abhijit, and Esther Duflo. 2005. "Growth Theory through the Lens of Economic Development." In *Handbook of Developmental Economics*, Vol. 1a, ed. Dani Rodrik and Mark R. Rosenzweig. Amsterdam: Elsevier, 473–552.

Barnett, Steven, and Plutarchos Sakellaris. 1998. "Non-linear Response of Firm Investment to Q: Testing a Model of Convex and Non-convex Adjustment Costs." *Journal of Monetary Economics* 42(2): 261–288.

Bartelsman, E., J. Haltiwanger, and S. Scarpetta. 2004. *Microeconomic Evidence of Creative Destruction in Industrial and Developing Countries.* Washington, DC: World Bank.

———. 2006. "Cross Country Differences in Productivity: The Role of Allocative Efficiency." Working paper.

Bertola, Giuseppe, and Ricardo Caballero. 1994. "Irreversibility and Aggregate Investment." *Review of Economic Studies* 61(2): 223–246.

Bertola, Giuseppe, and Richard Rogerson. 1997. "Institutions and Labor Reallocation." *European Economic Review* 41(6): 1147–1171.

Caballero, Ricardo, Kevin Cowan, Eduardo Engel, and Alejandro Micco. 2004. "Effective Labor Regulation and Microeconomic Flexibility." Working Paper 10744, NBER, Cambridge, MA.

Caballero, Ricardo, and Eduardo Engel. 1993. "Microeconomic Adjustment Hazards and Aggregate Dynamics." *Quarterly Journal of Economics* 433(2): 359–383.

———. 1999. "Explaining Investment Dynamics in U.S. Manufacturing: A Generalized(S,s) Approach." *Econometrica* 67(4): 783–826.

———. 2004. "Three Strikes and You're Out: Reply to Cooper and Willis." Working Paper 10368, NBER, Cambridge, MA.

Caballero, Ricardo, Eduardo Engel, and John Haltiwanger. 1995. "Plant-level Adjustment and Aggregate Investment Dynamics." *Brookings Papers on Economic Activity* 2: 1–54.

———. 1997. "Aggregate Employment Dynamics: Building from Microeconomic Evidence." *American Economic Review* 87: 115–137.

Caballero, Ricardo, Eduardo Engel, and Alejandro Micco. 2005. "Microeconomic Flexibility in Latin America." In *Labor Markets and Institutions*, ed. J. E. Restrepo and A. Tokman. Santiago: Central Bank of Chile.

Caballero, Ricardo, and Mohamad Hammour. 1994. "The Cleansing Effect of Recessions." *American Economic Review* 84(5): 1350–1368.

Casacuberta, G., and N. Gandelman. 2006. "Protection, Openness, and Factor Adjustment: Evidence from the Manufacturing Sector in Uruguay." Working paper.

Cooper, Russell W., and John C. Haltiwanger. 2006. "On the Nature of Capital Adjustment Costs." *Review of Economic Studies* 73(3): 611–633.

Cooper, Russell W., John C. Haltiwanger, and Jonathan Willis. 2005. "The Dynamics of Labor Demand: Evidence from Plant-level Observations and Aggregate Implications." Working Paper 10297 (revised), NBER, Cambridge, MA.

Cooper, Russell W., and Jonathan Willis. 2003. "The Economics of Labor Adjustment: Mind the Gap." Federal Reserve Bank of Kansas City 03–05, July.

Davis, S., and J. Haltiwanger. 1990. "Gross Job Creation and Destruction: Microeconomic Evidence and Aggregate Implications." *NBER Macroeconomics Annual* 5: 123–168.

———. 1991. "Wage Dispersion between and within U.S. Manufacturing Plants: 1963–1986." *Brookings Papers on Economic Activity: Microeconomics* 1: 115–200.

———. 1992. "Gross Job Creation, Gross Job Destruction, and Employment Reallocation." *Quarterly Journal of Economics* 107: 819–863.

Davis, Steven, John Haltiwanger, and Scott Schuh. 1996. *Job Creation and Destruction*. Cambridge, MA: MIT Press.

De Ferranti, David, and Guillermo Perry. 2005. *Closing the Gap in Education and Technology*. Washington, DC: World Bank.

Doms, Mark, and Tim Dunne. 1998. "Capital Adjustment Patterns in U.S. Manufacturing Plants." *Review of Economic Dynamics* 1: 409–429.

Eslava, Marcela. 2006. "Factor Market Institutions and Factor Market Reallocation in Latin America: The Case of Heterogeneous Workers." Working paper.

Eslava, Marcela, John Haltiwanger, Adriana Kugler, and Maurice Kugler. 2004. "The Effects of Structural Reforms on Productivity and Profitability Enhancing Reallocation: Evidence from Colombia." *Journal of Development Economics* 75(2): 333–371.

———. 2006. "Employment and Capital Adjustments after Factor Market Deregulation: Panel Evidence from Colombian Plants." Revised version of Working Paper 11656 (2005), NBER, Cambridge, MA.

Foster, Lucia. 1999. "On the Sources and Size of Employment Adjustment Costs." Paper CES 99-7, Center for Economic Studies, Bureau of the Census.

Foster, Lucia, John Haltiwanger, and Cornell Krizan. 2001. "Aggregate Productivity Growth: Lessons from Microeconomic Evidence." In *New Developments in Productivity Analysis*, ed. Edward Dean, Michael Harper, and Charles Hulten. Chicago: University of Chicago Press.

———. 2006. "Market Selection, Reallocation and Restructuring in the U.S. Retail Trade Sector in the 1990s." *The Review of Economics and Statistics* 88(4): 748–758.

Foster, Lucia, John Haltiwanger, and Chad Syverson. 2005. "Reallocation, Firm Turnover, and Efficiency: Selection on Productivity or Profitability?" Working Paper 11555, NBER, Cambridge, MA.

Hsieh, Chang-Tai, and Peter Klenow. 2009. "Misallocation and Manufacturing Productivity in China and India." *Quarterly Journal of Economics* 124(4): 1403–1448.

Kugler, Adriana. 1999. "The Impact of Firing Costs on Turnover and Unemployment: Evidence from the Colombian Labor Market Reform." *International Tax and Public Finance Journal* 6(3): 389–410.

———. 2004. "The Effect of Job Security Regulations on Labor Market Flexibility: Evidence from the Colombian Labor Market Reform." In *Law and Employment: Lessons from Latin America and the Caribbean*, ed. J. Heckman and C. Pages. Chicago: University of Chicago Press.

Kugler, Adriana, and Maurice Kugler. 2009. "Labor Market Effects of Payroll Taxes in Developing Countries: Evidence from Colombia." *Economic Development and Cultural Change* 57(2): 335–58.

Levinsohn, J., and A. Petrin. 2003. "Estimating Production Functions Using Inputs to Control for Unobservables." *Review of Economic Studies* 70(2): 317–342.

Lora, Eduardo. 2001. "Structural Reforms in Latin America: What Has Been Reformed and How to Measure It." Working Paper 466, Inter-American Development Bank, Washington, DC.

Montenegro, Claudio, and Carmen Pages. 2005. "Who Benefits from Labor Market Regulations? Chile 1960–1998." In *Labor Markets and Institutions*, ed. J. E. Restrepo and A. Tokman. Santiago: Central Bank of Chile.

Nickell, Stephen. 1986. "Dynamic Models of Labor Demand." In *Handbook of Labor Economics*, ed. O. Ashenfelter and R. Layard. Amsterdam: North Holland Press.

———. 1998. "Job Tenure and Labour Reallocation: A Partial Overview." In *Job Creation: The Role of Labor Market Institutions*, ed. J. Gual. London: Elgar Publishing Co.

Olley, S., and A. Pakes. 1996. "The Dynamics of Productivity in the Telecommunications Equipment Industry." *Econometrica* 64(6): 1263–1297.

Restuccia, Diego, and Richard Rogerson. 2004. "Policy Distortions and Aggregate Productivity with Heterogeneous Plants." Working paper.

Revenga, Ana. 1995. "Employment and Wage Effects of Trade Liberalization: The Case of Mexican Manufacturing." Working Paper 1524, World Bank, Washington, DC.

Rosales, Maria Fernanda. 2005. "La Productividad y sus Determinantes: El Caso de la Industria Manufacturera Bogotana." Working paper, Universidad de Los Andes, Bogota.

Index

Page numbers followed by f or t refer to figures or tables, respectively.]

foreign firm entry, 32
as indicators of regulation,
69–70
in industrialized countries, 125
investment and, 41, 43
labor productivity and, 11*f*, 12,
49, 126, 128–129, 130–131*t*,
131*f*, 145
in measurement of regulation
intensity, 72
as mechanism of regulation
effects on economic performance, 10–11, 70, 119, 121
as mechanism of regulation
effects on labor productivity,
134–135, 145
modeling shock and recovery
dynamics, 200, 206–214
policies impeding efficient reallocation after shocks, 199
regulation effects, 4, 11–12, 25,
38–40, 51, 121–122, 123, 129–
134, 132–133*t*, 214
sectoral differences of regulation
outcomes, 131
taxation effects, 12, 122, 129–
131, 134, 145
firm-level factors
competition effects on productivity mediated by, 29
linkage between innovation and
competition, 31–32
as mechanism of regulation–performance linkage, 11–12
modeling shock and recovery
dynamics, 206–212
production units, 207
fiscal regulation
cross-country comparison, 77,
98
data sources for cross-country
comparison, 105–109*t*
economic outcomes, 82, 87, 91,
96, 98, 99, 120
international comparison, 6*f*
in Latin America, 5
macroeconomic volatility and, 9
measurement, 70, 72, 124

quality of governance as outcome mediator, 91, 96
in typology of regulation, 5
France, 73

G
GDP growth and economic volatility
governance quality mediating
regulation effects in, 87,
88–90*tt*, 92–95*tt*, 96–98
indicators of macroeconomic
performance, 67–68
measurement, 81
regulation effects, 82–87, 83*f*,
84*f*, 85*t*, 86*t*, 88–90*tt*, 91–97,
98–99
regulation research methodology,
80–82, 98
Generalized Method of Moments,
29, 47
Germany, 198–199
governance and policy making
benefits of regulatory and legal
compliance, 169
business climate, 50
causes of informality, 169–170,
179, 185
effects on extent of informal
economy, 15
in factor adjustment processes,
226
government spending relative to
GDP as measure of informality,
163, 165*t*, 168*t*
impediments to efficient reallocation after shocks, 17, 198–200,
201
inability to respond to shocks,
15–17
legal origin and Western influence, 81, 204
measurement of quality, 77, 111*t*
mechanism of market formalization as outcome determinant,
162
modeling shock and recovery
dynamics, 17, 207, 213–214

product market regulation outcomes mediated by, 47–48, 53,
91–96
quality of governance as modifier
of regulation outcomes, 7–9,
10, 19–20, 68–69, 80, 87,
88–90t, 92–95t, 96–99
sequence of implementing regulatory reforms, 20, 221, 240
significance of, in regulation outcomes, 20
subsidies to incumbents, recovery
from shock and, 17, 200–201,
211, 212, 215–217, 219–221
Guatemala, 178, 179

H
Haiti, 13, 73, 179
Heritage Foundation index of
informal markets, 159, 178
Honduras, 178, 179

I
India, 31
industrialized countries
firm entry and turnover patterns,
125
productivity patterns, 48–49
product market regulation, 34, 35
regulation outcomes, 47, 66, 67
regulation patterns, 72–73
see also OECD
inflation, product market regulation and, 53
informal economy
causes of, 12–15, 157–158, 169–
175, 171–174f, 185, 189–191t
costs of evading regulation, 10,
162
cross-country variation, 175,
186–188t
definition and scope, 12, 157
determinants, 16f
economic costs, 13, 162, 163
economic significance, 158, 185
government expenditures relative
to GDP and, 163, 165t

indicators, 159, 163
labor versus production informality, 179
in Latin America, 13, 14f, 158,
159–162, 160–161f, 175–179,
180–184f, 185
measurement methodology, 13,
158–162, 163
mechanism of market formalization as outcome determinant,
13, 162–163
as mechanism of regulation
effects on economic performance, 12–13
per capita GDP and, 163–166,
164t, 167t
positive aspects, 13
poverty and, 166, 167t, 168t,
185
strategies for reducing, 15
structural determinants, 169,
175, 185
innovation
competition and, 28, 31–32,
44–45, 54 n.9
foreign firm entry and, 32
measurement, 44
as mechanism of regulation
effects on economic performance, 121
product market regulation outcomes, 4, 27, 29, 44–45, 52,
66
research needs, 4, 29
investment
firm entry and, 41, 43
privatization outcomes, 41
product market regulation
effects, 4, 40–43, 51–52,
66–67
research and development,
44–45
Iran, Islamic Republic of, 73
Italy, 73

J
Jamaica, 178
Japan, 198, 199

270

INDEX

judicial administration
data sources for cross-country
comparison, 105t
measurement, 72
as regulation indicator, 70
see also law enforcement

L
labor productivity
cross-country and regional comparison, 127, 128f
data sources for regulatory outcomes research, 125, 146t
decomposition modeling, 126–
127
firm turnover and, 11f, 12, 49,
126, 128–129, 130–131t, 131f,
144, 145
mechanism of regulation outcomes, 11
product market regulation and,
49–50, 145
regulation outcomes, 12, 122,
134–135, 136–143tt, 144–145
taxation effects, 122, 135, 145
labor regulation
cross-country and regional comparisons, 73, 77, 124, 124f
economic outcomes, 7, 82, 87,
91, 96, 98–99, 120
employment outcomes, 42, 67
firm turnover and, 12, 120–121,
144
impediments to efficient reallocation after shocks, 198
international comparison, 6f
labor productivity outcomes, 12,
122, 144, 145
in Latin America, 5
macroeconomic volatility and,
7–9
measurement, 70, 72, 124
product market regulation and,
31, 42, 43
quality of governance as outcome mediator, 91, 96
in typology of regulation, 5

Latin American and Caribbean
countries
causes of informality, 15, 175–
179
comparative regulatory burden,
5, 7f, 123–124, 124f
costs of regulation, 10
extent of informal economy, 13,
14f
factor adjustment patterns, 242–
246, 257, 258
factor market reforms, 226
factor shortages, 252t
firm turnover, 125–126, 126f
informal economy, 158, 159–
162, 160–161f, 180–184f,
185
institutions index, 234, 235f
labor productivity growth, 127,
128f
modeling adjustment dynamics,
228
recommendations for factor
adjustment, 19
reforms of 1990s, 19, 257, 258
regulatory outcomes, 10
skill mix in employment trends,
227
susceptibility to financial shocks,
15
see also specific country
law enforcement, causes of informality, 169, 170, 171f, 172f,
173f, 174f, 175, 185

M
markup variation
innovation and, 32
productivity outcomes, 48–49
product market regulation and,
25, 38, 40, 122–123
Mexico
employment trends, 227
recovery from 1980 debt crisis,
198
see also Latin American and
Caribbean countries

N
Netherlands, 73
Nicaragua, 178
Nigeria, 73

O
OECD
comparative regulatory burden, 124, 124f
employment outcomes of regulation, 67
firm turnover, 31, 39, 125–126, 126f
investment outcomes of regulation, 67
labor market regulation, 42
labor productivity growth, 127, 128f
product market regulation, 33–34, 35, 66
regulation effects on technical innovation, 44
regulation patterns, 73

P
Panama, 178
Paraguay, 73
pension coverage, as indicator of informal market activity, 159
Peru, 234
Philippines, 73
political functioning
justification for product market regulation, 33
regulation objectives, 80
regulatory capture, 2, 66
Portugal, 73
poverty, informality and, 166, 167t, 168t, 185
privatization
effects on competition, 26
investment outcomes, 41
productive efficiency and productivity growth
competition effects, 26, 29–30
firm turnover rate and, 38, 207
in industrialized countries, 125

as mechanism of regulation
effects on economic performance, 121
methodology for research on regulation effects, 122
modeling shock and recovery dynamics, 207, 208, 209, 214, 233
monetary incentives for managers, 26–27
product market regulation outcomes, 24–25, 45–51
sectoral outcomes of product market regulation, 49–50
skill-intensive employment and, 227
see also labor productivity; total factor productivity
productivity, aggregate. see total factor productivity
product market regulation
aggregate productivity outcomes, 25–26, 27, 45–47, 48–49, 50–51, 52–53, 66, 67
assessing sectoral differences, 35–36
cross-country and regional comparisons, 5, 6f, 35, 37–53, 77, 124, 124f
data sources for cross-country comparison, 33–35
definition and scope, 3, 33, 73
economic performance outcomes, 4, 82, 98–99, 120
effect of initial economic conditions on outcomes of, 37
employment outcomes, 4, 42–43
firm turnover and, 12, 38–40, 120–121, 123
as impediment to recovery from economic shock, 199
inflation outcomes, 53
innovation and, 4, 27, 44–45, 52, 66
investment behavior and, 4, 40–43, 51–52, 66–67
justifications for, 33

ECO-AUDIT
Environmental Benefits Statement

The World Bank is committed to preserving endangered forests and natural resources. The Office of the Publisher has chosen to print *Business Regulation and Economic Performance* on recycled paper with 30 percent postconsumer waste, in accordance with the recommended standards for paper usage set by the Green Press Initiative, a nonprofit program supporting publishers in using fiber that is not sourced from endangered forests. For more information, visit www.greenpressinitiative.org.

Saved:
- 5 trees
- 1 million BTUs of total energy
- 443 lb. of net green-house gases
- 2,132 gal. of waste water
- 129 lbs. of solid waste

green press
INITIATIVE